C
A Reference Manual

C A Reference Manual

SAMUEL P. HARBISON
GUY L. STEELE JR.

Tartan Laboratories

PRENTICE-HALL, INC., Englewood Cliffs, New Jersey 07632

Library of Congress Cataloging in Publication Data

Harbison, Samuel P.
  C: a reference manual.

  Includes index.
  1. C (Computer program language)   I. Steele, Guy.
II. Title.
QA76.73.C15H38   1984   001.64'24   84-6909
ISBN 0-13-110016-5
ISBN 0-13-110008-4 (pbk.)

Editorial/production supervision by Linda Mihatov
Cover design by Lundgren Graphics
Manufacturing buyer: Gordon Osbourne

Ada is a registered trademark of the United States Government, Ada Joint Program
Office. *DEC, DECSystem-20, PDP, VAX,* and *VMX* are trademarks of Digital
Equipment Corporation. *IBM* is a registered trademark of International Business
Machines Incorporated. *UNIX* is a trademark of Bell Laboratories.

Printed in the United States of America

10   9   8   7   6   5   4   3

ISBN   0-13-110016-5
ISBN   0-13-110008-4 {PBK}   01

Prentice-Hall International, Inc., *London*
Prentice-Hall of Australia Pty. Limited, *Sydney*
Editora Prentice-Hall do Brasil, Ltda., *Rio de Janeiro*
Prentice-Hall Canada Inc., *Toronto*
Prentice-Hall of India Private Limited, *New Delhi*
Prentice-Hall of Japan, Inc., *Tokyo*
Prentice-Hall of Southeast Asia Pte. Ltd., *Singapore*
Whitehall Books Limited, *Wellington, New Zealand*

Contents

Preface

This text is a reference manual for the C programming language. It includes a complete description of the full language, the variations in the language found in some C compilers, and discussions of many of the C programming conventions and styles that have arisen over the years.

Beginning with an overview of the C language and the environment in which C programs are compiled and executed, we present the language in a "bottom-up" order: the lexical structure, the preprocessor, declarations, types, expressions, statements, functions, and programs. Each section includes references to descriptions of other relevant language features, so that the book can be read beginning at any point. We've also included a large chapter on the standard C run-time library routines found on most computers.

We assume that the reader is, or wants to become, a serious C programmer, one capable of engineering large and complex systems in C. In our view, serious programmers are more concerned with correctness and reliability than with programming speed. Their programs are meant to last a generation, not a weekend. Their programming emphasizes clarity, maintainability, and portability rather than clever tricks and the fewest number of source program lines.

We expect that most of our readers are already familiar with one high-level language such as FORTRAN or Pascal, understand basic programming concepts, and may have some experience with C.

This book grew out of our effort to write a family of C compilers for a wide range of computers, from micros to supermainframes. We wanted the compilers to be well documented, to provide precise and helpful error diagnostics, and to generate exceptionally efficient object code. A C program that compiles correctly with one compiler must compile correctly under all the others, and a program that executes correctly on one computer must execute correctly on the other computers, insofar as the hardware differences allow. (This is in keeping with the spirit of C programming.)

In spite of C's popularity, and the increasing number of primers and introductory texts on C, we found that there was no description of C precise enough to guide us in designing the new compilers. Similarly, no existing description was precise enough for our programmer/customers, who would be using compilers that analyzed C programs more thoroughly than was the custom. In this text we have been especially sensitive to language features that affect program clarity, object code efficiency, and the portability of programs among different environments, both UNIX and non-UNIX.

Acknowledgments

We wish to thank our colleagues at Tartan Laboratories and Carnegie-Mellon University, who helped in the writing, editing, and production of this book, especially Sue Broughton and Alex Czajkowski, and also Mady Bauer, Robert Firth, Chris Hanna, Don Lindsay, Joe Newcomer, Kevin Nolish, David Notkin, and Barbara Steele. We also wish to thank our fellow members of the ANSI X3J11 committee on C standardization for their contributions and comments, especially Bill Plauger of Whitesmith's and Larry Rosler of Bell Laboratories.

Some of the example programs in this book were inspired by algorithms appearing in the following works, which we recommend to anyone seriously interested in programming.

- Beeler, Michael; Gosper, R. William; and Schroeppel, Richard. *HAKMEM*. AI Memo 239 (Massachusetts Institute of Technology Artificial Intelligence Laboratory, February 1972).
- Bentley, Jon Louis. *Writing Efficient Programs*. (Prentice-Hall, 1982).
- Bentley, Jon Louis. "Programming Pearls," monthly column appearing in *Communications of the ACM*. (Association for Computing Machinery, first appearance August 1983).
- Kernighan, Brian W., and Ritchie, Dennis M. *The C Programming Language* (Prentice-Hall, 1978).
- Knuth, Donald E. *The Art of Computer Programming* (Addison-Wesley). *Volume 1: Fundamental Algorithms* (1968). *Volume 2: Seminumerical Algorithms* (1969, 1981). *Volume 3: Sorting and Searching* (1973).
- Sedgewick, Robert. *Algorithms* (Addison-Wesley, 1983).

We are indebted to the authors of these works for their good ideas.

Sam Harbison

Guy Steele

C A Reference Manual

1

Introduction to C

C is a member of the "Algol family" of algebraic programming languages, and thus is more similar to languages such as PL/I, Pascal, and Ada, and less similar to BASIC, FORTRAN, or Lisp. A recent collection of papers, *Comparing & Assessing Programming Languages Ada, C, and Pascal* edited by Alan R. Feuer and Narain Gehani (Prentice-Hall, 1984) discusses the similarities and differences found in C, Pascal and Ada.

The C language was designed by Dennis Ritchie at Bell Laboratories in about 1972, and its ancestry dates from Algol 60 (1960), through Cambridge's CPL (1963), Martin Richards's BCPL (1967) and Ken Thompson's B language (1970) at Bell Labs. Although C is a general purpose programming language, it has traditionally been used for systems programming. In particular, the popular UNIX operating system is written in C. Now widely available on both UNIX and non-UNIX systems, C is increasingly popular for applications that must be ported to different computers.

C's popularity is due to several factors. First, C provides a fairly complete set of facilities for dealing with a wide variety of applications. It has all the useful data types, including pointers and strings. There is a rich set of operators and modern control structures. C also has a standard I/O library that is quite flexible for common kinds of input and output to files and terminals.

Second, C programs are efficient. C is a small language, and its data types and operators are closely related to the operations provided directly by most computers. Said another way, there is only a small "semantic gap" between C and the computer hardware.

Finally, there is a growing number of C programs and C programmers. The UNIX operating system provides a large set of tools that improve C programming productivity and can serve as starting points for new applications. Because UNIX has been distributed to universities for several years, many computer science students have UNIX experience.

1

Unfortunately, some of the very characteristics of C that account for its popularity can also pose problems for programmers. For example, C's smallness is due in large part to its lack of "confining rules," but the absence of such rules can lead to error-prone programming habits. To write well-ordered programs, the C programmer often relies on a set of stylistic conventions that are not enforced by the compiler. As another example, to allow C compilers to implement operations efficiently on a variety of computers, the precise meaning of some C operators and types is intentionally unspecified. This can create problems when moving a program to another computer.

In spite of the inelegancies, the bugs, and the confusion that often accompany C, it has withstood the test of time. It remains a language in which the experienced programmer can write quickly and well. Millions of lines of code testify to its usefulness.

1.1 WHO DEFINES C?

Although C tutorials abound, there are no detailed descriptions of the current C language. The information in this book has been compiled from many sources and from personal experience with several C implementations.

The traditional language reference is the book *The C Programming Language*, by Brian Kernighan and Dennis Ritchie (Prentice-Hall, 1978). In fact, it is not uncommon to see references to "Kernighan and Ritchie C" by compiler vendors wanting to emphasize their complete implementations. However, since 1978 the language has evolved; some features have been added and some have been dropped. Usually, a consensus has been reached on these features, although this consensus has not always been documented. Many new implementations of C have added their own variations to the language. When we use the phrase "the original definition of C" in this book, we will mean Kernighan and Ritchie's definition, before the post-1978 changes.

The second source for information on C is the C compilers themselves; you can write a C program and see if it compiles (and, if it does, what code is generated). This approach is almost legitimate for C, because many C compilers are based on the Portable C Compiler (PCC) written at Bell Laboratories. PCC has been retargeted to different computers, and all PCC-derived compilers share a common-language front end. The problem with using PCC as an operational standard is, of course, that PCC has errors like all other compilers, and these errors are often in the gray corners of the language, which is just where clarification would be useful.

In 1982 the American National Standards Institute (ANSI) formed a technical subcommittee on C language standardization, X3J11, to propose a standard for the C language, its run-time libraries, and its compilation and execution environments. We, along with many other people with experience and interest in

C programming, are participating in the ANSI standardization effort. We anticipate that the eventual standard will not deviate too far from current C programming practice, but that is a subject for another book.

This book describes C as it is currently implemented by the major compilers on the larger computers. We do not consider language or implementation subsets found on the smallest microcomputers. Where compilers tend to differ in their implementations, we describe the common variations. Where certain C features tend to lead to bad programming practices, we do not hesitate to suggest a better way to use the language.

1.2 AN OVERVIEW OF C PROGRAMMING

A C *program* is composed of one or more C *source files*. Each source file contains some part of the entire C program, typically some number of external functions. Source files often have associated with them *header* `files` that provide declarations for the external functions used in other files. One source file must contain an external function named `main`; by convention this will be the program's entry point.

Each source file is independently processed by a C *compiler*, which translates the C program text into the instructions understood by the computer. It is the compiler which "understands" the C program and analyzes it for correctness. If the programmer has made an error the compiler can detect, the compiler issues an error message and does not complete the translation. Otherwise, the output of the compiler is usually called *object code* or an *object module*.

When all source files are compiled, the object modules are given to a program called the *linker*, which resolves references between the modules and adds some precompiled *library routines* that handle special functions like input/output. Some programming errors, like the failure to define a needed function, are caught by the linker and cause error messages to be generated. The linker is typically not specific to C; each computer system has a standard linker that is used for programs written in many different languages. The linker produces a single *executable program*, which can then be invoked, or "run."

Although all computer systems go through these steps, they may appear different to the programmer. For instance, suppose that a program to be named `prog` consists of the two C source files `proga.c` and `progb.c`. (The ".c" in the file names is a common convention for C source files.) The file `proga.c` could contain these lines:

```
void hello()
{
    printf("Hello!\n");
}
```

The header file for `proga.c`, named `proga.h`, contains:

```
extern void hello();
```

File `progb.c` contains the main program, which simply calls function `hello`:

```
#include "proga.h"
main()
{
    hello();
}
```

On a UNIX system, compiling, linking, and executing the program takes only two steps:

```
% cc -o prog proga.c progb.c
% prog
```

The first line compiles and links the two source files, adds any standard library functions needed, and writes the executable program to file `prog`. The second line then executes the program, which prints:

```
Hello!
```

The same sequence on a DEC VAX-11 computer running the VMS operating system might be this:

```
$ cc proga,progb
$ link proga,progb/exe=[prog.exe]
$ run prog
Hello!
```

In this book we will largely ignore the details of linking and running C programs; readers are urged to consult their own computer system and C compiler user documentation. We will concentrate instead on how to write the C programs.

1.3 SYNTAX NOTATION

We will use a notation to describe C's syntax that is an outgrowth of the familiar Backus-Naur Form (BNF). The components of the notation are described below.

1.3.1 Nonterminal Symbols

A nonterminal symbol is represented

x

where x can be any sequence of italic alphanumeric characters and hyphens. The occurrence of a nonterminal on the right side of a production stands for all the strings represented by x, as determined by productions in which x appears on the left side.

1.3.2 Terminal Symbols

Terminal symbols are represented in two ways. Language keywords, which are always alphabetic strings, appear as themselves in a special font, as in `register`. Punctuation characters and operators are enclosed in single quotation marks, as in '%'.

In the following production, for example, there are three terminal strings: the keyword `sizeof` and the left and right parentheses.

expression ::= `sizeof` '(' *type-name* ')'

1.3.3 Productions

Productions have the form

$N ::= E$

where N is a nonterminal symbol and E is a metasyntactic expression. The meaning is that N represents all of the terminal strings that can be generated from the expression E. For example:

parameter-declaration ::= *declaration*

1.3.4 Expressions

A metasyntactic expression consists of one or more terms separated by vertical bars:

T1 | *T2* | . . . | *Tn*

An expression represents all terminal strings that can be generated from any one of the *Ti*. For example:

declarator ::= *simple-declarator*
                | ' (' *declarator* ') '
                | *function-declarator*
                | *array-declarator*
                | *pointer-declarator*

1.3.5 Terms and Factors

A term is a sequence of zero or more factors:

F1 F2 . . . Fn

A term represents all terminal strings that can be formed by concatenating strings from the *Fi*. A factor may be:

1. a nonterminal symbol
2. a terminal symbol
3. an iteration form

For example:

switch-statement ::= switch ' (' *expression* ') ' *statement*

1.3.6 Iteration Forms

Iteration forms are used in our notation to express repetitive expressions that require recursive productions in other notations.   All of the forms use the braces ' { ' and ' } ' as delimiters.

{ *A* }?   represents an optional occurrence of the expression *A*.

{ *A* }*   represents zero or more occurrences of the expression *A*.

{ *A* }+   represents one or more occurrences of the expression *A*.

{ *A* # *B* }*   represents zero or more occurrences of the expression *A* separated by strings from the expression *B*.

{ *A* # *B* }+   represents one or more occurrences of the expression *A* separated by strings from the expression *B*.

For example, the `return` statement in C contains an optional expression, which we write as:

return-statement ::= `return` { *expression* }? ';'

A parameter list, consisting of one or more identifiers, has the following syntax notation:

parameter-list ::= { *identifier* # ',' } +

That is, a parameter list can have the form

identifier
identifier , *identifier*
identifier , *identifier* , *identifier*

and so forth.

2

Lexical Elements

This chapter describes the lexical structure of the C language; that is, the characters that may appear in a C source file and how they are collected into lexical units, or *tokens*.

2.1 THE SOURCE CHARACTER SET

A C source file is a sequence of *characters* selected from a *character set*. A C compiler may use any character set as long as it includes at least the following *standard characters*:

1. the fifty-two uppercase and lowercase alphabetic characters:

   A B C D E F G H I J K L M N O P Q R S T U V W X Y Z
   a b c d e f g h i j k l m n o p q r s t u v w x y z

2. the twenty-nine graphic characters:

!	exclamation point	+	plus	"	double quote
#	number sign	=	equal	{	left brace
%	percent	~	tilde	}	right brace
^	circumflex	[	left bracket	,	comma
&	ampersand	]	right bracket	.	period
*	asterisk	\	backslash	<	less than
(	left parenthesis	|	vertical bar	>	greater than
)	right parenthesis	;	semicolon	/	slash
−	hyphen or minus	:	colon	?	question mark
_	underscore	'	apostrophe		

3. the ten decimal digits:

   0   1   2   3   4   5   6   7   8   9

4. the *blank* character
5. the *newline* character, which is the end-of-line marker
6. six formatting characters corresponding to the ASCII characters backspace (BS), horizontal tab (HT), vertical tab (VT), form feed (FF), and carriage return (CR)

The "formatting characters" listed above are not essential to C. Their presence is historical and is legitimized by the existence of special "character escape codes" such as \b that may be used to represent these formatting characters in an implementation-independent way.

All C implementations use character sets that include additional characters not in the standard set. The characters '$' and '@' are common examples. These nonstandard characters may appear only within comments, character constants, or string constants, and even then they may affect the portability of the program.

Finally, C defines the *null* character, a character that is encoded as the value 0. This character is mentioned here for completeness, even though it belongs to the *target* character set rather than the source character set.

References   character constants 2.7.3; comments 2.2; character encodings 2.1.2; character escape codes 2.7.6; string constants 2.7.4; target character set 2.1.3

2.1.1 Whitespace and Line Termination

The blank, newline, and formatting characters are known collectively as *whitespace* characters. These characters are ignored except insofar as they are used to separate adjacent tokens or when they appear in character or string constants. Whitespace characters may be used to lay out the C program in a way that is pleasing to a human reader.

The newline, carriage return, form feed, and vertical tab characters additionally cause *line termination* and are sometimes called *line break* characters. Line termination is important for the recognition of preprocessor control lines. By convention, the character following a line break character is considered to be the first character of the next line. If the first character is itself a line break character then another (empty) line is terminated, and so forth.

C imposes no limit on the maximum length of lines, although many implementations have a fixed limit, typically in the 100-500 character range. We find that keeping line length under 80 characters facilitates reading a program on a display terminal.

References   character constants 2.7.3; preprocessor lexical conventions 3.2; string constants 2.7.4; tokens 2.3

2.1.2 Character Encodings

Each character in a computer's character set will have some conventional *encoding*; that is, some numerical representation on the computer. This encoding is important because C converts characters to integers, and the values of the integers are the conventional encodings of the characters. All of the standard characters listed above must have distinct, nonnegative integer encodings.

A common C programming error is to assume a particular encoding is in use when, in fact, another one holds. For example, the C expression

```
'Z' - 'A' + 1
```

computes one more than the difference between the encodings of 'z' and 'A' and might be expected to yield the number of characters in the alphabet. Indeed, under the ASCII character set encodings the result is 26, but under the EBCDIC encodings, in which the alphabet is not encoded consecutively, the result is 41.

References   source and target character sets 2.1.3

2.1.3 Source and Target Character Sets

There are actually two character sets relevant to any C program. The first is the source computer character set, the one in which the program is written. The second is the target computer character set; that is, the character set available on the computer that will execute the compiled C program. Each character set has its own set of encodings, as discussed above. The only requirement imposed by C is that the source character set include the standard characters, but normally the target character set also includes all the standard characters.

These source and target character sets are the same when a C program is compiled and executed on the same computer and operating system. However, occasionally programs are cross-compiled; that is, compiled on one computer (the *source computer*, or *host*) to generate object code for another computer (the *target*). When a compiler calculates the compile-time value of a constant expression involving characters, it must use the target computer's encodings, not the more natural (to the compiler writer) source encodings.

References   character constants 2.7.3; character encodings 2.1.2; constant expressions 7.10; standard characters 2.1

2.2 COMMENTS

A *comment* in a C program begins with the characters '/*' and ends with the first subsequent occurrence of the characters '*/'. Comments may contain any number of characters and are always treated as whitespace. For example, the following program contains six legal C comments:

```
/**************************************/
/*/ Program to compute the squares of   /*/
/*/   the first 10 integers             /*/
/**************************************/
void Squares()  /* no arguments */
{
    int i;
    /*
      Loop from 1 to 10,
      printing out the squares
    */
    for (i=1;i<=10;i++)
        printf("%d squared is %d\n",i,i*i);
}
```

The preprocessor also treats comments as whitespace. That is, the preprocessor does not look inside comments for commands or for macro invocations, nor do line breaks inside comments terminate preprocessor commands. For example, the following three #define commands all have essentially the same effect.

```
#define   ten    (2*5)

#define   ten /* ten:
                one greater than nine
            */ (2*5)

#define   ten   (2/*/*/*/*/5)
```

(These examples are meant to illustrate comments, not to promote a particular style of programming.)

A minority of C implementations implement "nestable comments," in which each occurrence of '/*' must be balanced by a subsequent '*/'. This implementation has the advantage of allowing a programmer to comment out a large piece of program text without being concerned if the text contains its own comments. However, such a program will not be portable.

The same effect as nested comments can be achieved with the preprocessor's conditional commands. In particular,

```
#if 0
    ...
#endif
```

will effectively "comment out" any section of a program.

Nestable comments are not standard. However, for a program to be acceptable to both implementations of comments, no comment should contain the character sequence '/*' inside it.

References   #if preprocessor command 3.5.1; preprocessor lexical conventions 3.2; whitespace 2.1.1

2.3 TOKENS

The characters making up a C program are collected into lexical *tokens* according to the rules presented in the rest of this chapter. There are five classes of tokens: operators, separators, identifiers, reserved words, and constants.

When collecting characters into tokens, the compiler always forms the longest token possible, so that `external` is interpreted as a single identifier rather than as the reserved word `extern` followed by the identifier `al`. Other examples:

```
b>x        is the same as    b > x
b->x       is the same as    b -> x
b-->x      is the same as    b -- > x
b--->x     is the same as    b -- -> x
```

Adjacent tokens may be separated by whitespace characters or comments. To prevent confusion, an identifier, reserved word, integer constant, or floating-point constant must always be so separated from a following identifier, reserved word, integer constant, or floating-point constant. (In a macro body, separating tokens with comments rather than whitespace characters may have unexpected results in some implementations.)

References   comments 2.2; constants 2.7; identifiers 2.5; macro expansion pitfalls 3.3.6; reserved words 2.6; whitespace characters 2.1.1

2.4 OPERATORS AND SEPARATORS

The simple (one character) operators in C are:

```
!   %   ^   &   *   -   +   =   ~   |   .   <   >   /   ?
```

The compound (multicharacter) operators in C are:

```
->   ++   --   <<   >>   <=   >=   ==   !=   &&   ||
+=   -=   *=   /=   %=   <<=   >>=   &=   ^=   |=
```

The other separator characters are:

```
(  )       [  ]       {  }       ,   ;   :
```

Strictly speaking, each of the compound assignment operators is considered to be two separate tokens that can be separated by whitespace. These operators are:

```
+=     -=     *=     /=     %=     <<=     >>=     &=     ^=     |=
```

For example, one may write

```
total + = subtotal;
```

or even

```
total + /* Addition assignment */ = subtotal;
```

instead of

```
total += subtotal;
```

However, it is better programming style to write the operators as if they were single tokens; that is, without embedded whitespace. As an implementation consideration for C compiler writers, it is more difficult to write an LALR(1) grammar for C that treats the operators as two separate tokens.

References   compound assignment operators 7.8.2

2.5 IDENTIFIERS

An identifier, also called a *name* in C, is a sequence of letters, digits, and underscores. An identifier must not begin with a digit and it must not have the same spelling as a reserved word.

identifier ::= *first-character* { *following-character* }*

first-character ::= *letter* | *underscore*

following-character ::= *letter* | *underscore* | *digit*

letter ::= 'A' | 'B' | 'C' | 'D' | 'E' | 'F' | 'G' | 'H' | 'I'
     | 'J' | 'K' | 'L' | 'M' | 'N' | 'O' | 'P' | 'Q' | 'R'
     | 'S' | 'T' | 'U' | 'V' | 'W' | 'X' | 'Y' | 'Z'
     | 'a' | 'b' | 'c' | 'd' | 'e' | 'f' | 'g' | 'h' | 'i'
     | 'j' | 'k' | 'l' | 'm' | 'n' | 'o' | 'p' | 'q' | 'r'
     | 's' | 't' | 'u' | 'v' | 'w' | 'x' | 'y' | 'z'

underscore ::= '_'

digit ::= '0' | '1' | '2' | '3' | '4' | '5' | '6' | '7' | '8' | '9'

Two identifiers are the same when they are spelled identically, including the case of all letters. That is, the identifiers abc and aBc are distinct.

The original description of C specified that two identifiers spelled identically up to the first eight characters would be considered the same even if they differed in subsequent characters. For example, the identifiers countless and countlessone would be considered the same. Fortunately, many new compilers allow longer identifiers, with all characters treated as significant. This can greatly improve program clarity and reduce errors. Unfortunately, these compilers may not solve all the programmer's problems. First, the programmer concerned with portability should decide whether the program is likely to be compiled by a compiler that adheres to the old rules and then adjust the program accordingly. Second, compilers that allow long names differ in the maximum permitted length of identifiers and in the action taken when this limit is exceeded. Finally, external identifiers may be subject to more stringent length and character set limitations, as discussed below.

Many compilers permit characters other than those specified above to be used in identifiers. For example, the dollar sign ('$') is often allowed in identifiers as either the first or subsequent characters. These extra characters are usually necessary to allow programs to access special non-C library functions provided by some computing systems. Such functions are likely to be nonportable, and the programmer should limit the use of special characters to these cases.

2.5.1 Conventions for Identifiers

Although not part of the C language, there are some conventions in the choice of identifiers which are followed by many C programmers and which may result in programs that are easier to understand and that are more easily ported to different computer systems. Of course, it is more important to be consistent than to follow any one set of conventions slavishly.

It is considered bad style to have distinct identifiers that differ only in the case of their letters, such as `count` and `Count`. In UNIX environments, there has been some tendency to spell preprocessor macro names—especially those that denote numeric constants—with uppercase letters and all other identifiers in lowercase. The following is a typical example.

```
#define TABLESIZE 100
...
int i, squares[TABLESIZE];
for (i=0; i<TABLESIZE; i++)
    squares[i] = i*i;
```

The trend toward longer identifiers may make mixed-case identifiers and the use of underscores more popular, since it is significantly harder to read a name like `averylongidentifer` than `AVeryLongIdentifier` or `a_very_long_identifier`.

An external identifier—any one declared with storage class `extern`—often is subject to additional restrictions on particular computer systems. These identifiers have to be processed by other software, such as debuggers and linkers, which may have their own fixed limits on the lengths of identifiers and which may not distinguish the case of letters. In general, the rule has been to keep external identifiers short (say, six characters) and to not depend on case sensitivity. In UNIX systems, the problem for programmers is slightly worse because the C compilers prefix all of the user's external identifiers with an underscore, '_'.

When a C compiler permits long internal identifiers but the target computer requires short external names, the preprocessor may be used to hide these short names. In the example below, an external error-handling function has the short and somewhat obscure name `eh73`, but the function is referred to by the more readable name `error_handler`. This is done by making `error_handler` a preprocessor macro that expands to the name `eh73`.

```
#define error_handler    eh73
extern void error_handler();
int *p;
...
if (!p) error_handler("nil pointer error");
```

A programmer especially concerned with portability might encapsulate all external names in this way.

References   `#define` (preprocessor macros) 3.3; `extern` storage class 4.3

2.6 RESERVED WORDS

The following identifiers are reserved in the C language and must not be used as program identifiers.

auto	else	long	typedef
break	enum	register	union
case	extern	return	unsigned
char	float	short	void
continue	for	sizeof	while
default	goto	static	
do	if	struct	
double	int	switch	

Experienced C programmers may note that the above list of reserved words differs slightly from that in the original description of C. The names `enum` and `void` are new, reflecting additions to the language. The name `entry` was originally set aside for a use that never appeared; it may or may not actually be reserved in any given C compiler. Finally, some implementations have defined additional reserved words in conjunction with their own language extensions; `asm` and `fortran` are common examples.

A reserved word may be used as a preprocessor macro name, although doing so is usually poor style. As an example of a reasonable use, the following macro definition could be appropriate when a particular C compiler does not implement the `void` type:

```
#define void int
```

References   `#define` (preprocessor macros) 3.3; identifiers 2.5; `void` type specifier 5.10

2.7 CONSTANTS

The lexical class of constants includes four different kinds of constants: integers, floating-point numbers, characters, and strings.

> *constant* ::= *integer-constant*
> | *floating-point-constant*
> | *character-constant*
> | *string-constant*

Such tokens are called *literals* in other languages, to distinguish them from objects whose values are constant (that is, not changing) but which do not belong to lexically distinct classes. An example of these latter objects in C is enumeration constants, which belong to the lexical class of identifiers. In this book, we use the traditional C terminology of "constant" for both cases.

Every constant is characterized by a *value* and a *type*. The formats of the various kinds of constants are described in the following sections.

References   character constant 2.7.3; enumeration constants 5.6; floating-point constant 2.7.2; integer constant 2.7.1; string constant 2.7.4; tokens 2.3; type 5; value 7.3

2.7.1 *Integer Constants*

Integer constants may be specified in decimal, octal, or hexadecimal notation.

1. A decimal integer constant consists of a nonempty sequence of digits, the first of which is not 0.
2. An octal integer constant consists of the digit 0, followed by a possibly empty sequence of the octal digits 0 through 7. Originally, C also allowed the digits 8 and 9 in octal constants, but using them was always considered to be bad style.
3. A hexadecimal integer constant consists of the digit 0, followed by one of the letters 'x' or 'X', followed by a sequence of hexadecimal digits. The hexadecimal digits are the digits 0 through 9, plus the characters 'a' through 'f' (or 'A' through 'F'), which have the values 10 through 15, respectively.

There is a question as to whether "0" is decimal or octal, but it doesn't matter in practice. Any integer constant may be immediately followed by the one of the letters 'l' or 'L' to indicate a constant of type `long`.

> *integer-constant* ::= *decimal-constant*
> | *octal-constant*
> | *hexadecimal-constant*

> *decimal-constant* ::= *nonzero-digit* { *digit* }* { *long-marker* }?

> *octal-constant* ::= '0' { *octal-digit* }* { *long-marker* }?

> *hexadecimal-constant* ::= *hex-marker* { *hex-digit* }+ { *long-marker* }?

> *digit* ::= '0' | '1' | '2' | '3' | '4' | '5' | '6' | '7' | '8' | '9'

> *nonzero-digit* ::= '1' | '2' | '3' | '4' | '5' | '6' | '7' | '8' | '9'

> *octal-digit* ::= '0' | '1' | '2' | '3' | '4' | '5' | '6' | '7'

hex-digit ::= '0' | '1' | '2' | '3' | '4' | '5' | '6' | '7' | '8'| '9'
            | 'a' | 'b' | 'c' | 'd' | 'e' | 'f'
            | 'A' | 'B' | 'C' | 'D' | 'E' | 'F'

long-marker ::= 'l' | 'L'

hex-marker ::= '0x' | '0X'

The value of an integer constant is always nonnegative in the absence of overflow. If there is a preceding minus sign, it is taken to be a unary operator applied to the constant, not part of the constant itself.

The type of integer constants is normally `int`. However, the type will instead be `long` if

1. the value of a decimal constant exceeds the largest positive integer that can be represented in type `int`, or
2. the value of an octal or hexadecimal constant exceeds the largest integer that can be represented in type `unsigned int`, or
3. the constant is terminated by the letter 'l' or 'L'.

If the value of a decimal constant exceeds the largest integer representable in type `long`, or if the value of an octal or hexadecimal constant exceeds the largest integer representable in type `unsigned long`, the result is unpredictable. Most C compilers will not warn the programmer of the problem and will silently substitute another value for the constant. The programmer should take pains to parameterize large constants so that they can be changed when moving to another computer or compiler. For instance:

```
#define MAXPOSINT 0077777
#define MAXNEGINT 0100000
#define MAXPOSLONG 0x37777777
#define MAXNEGLONG 0x80000000
```

To illustrate some of the subtleties in C's integer constants, assume that for some implementation type `int` uses a 16-bit two's-complement representation, and that type `long` uses a 32-bit two's-complement representation. We list in Table 2-1 some interesting integer constants, their true mathematical values, and their types and values under the rules for constants listed above. (Parentheses are used to indicate that the value is undefined under the rules above, but the parenthesized value is likely to be the one used.)

An interesting point to note in this example is that integers greater than $2^{15}-1$ but less than 2^{16} will have positive values when written as decimal constants but negative values when written as octal or hexadecimal constants.

C Constant	True Value	C Type	C Value
0	0	int	0
32767	$2^{15}-1$	int	32767
077777	$2^{15}-1$	int	32767
32768	2^{15}	long	32768
0100000	2^{15}	(int)	(-32768)
65535	$2^{16}-1$	long	65535
0xFFFF	$2^{16}-1$	(int)	(-1)
65536	2^{16}	long	65536
0x10000	2^{16}	long	65536
2147483647	$2^{31}-1$	long	2147483647
0x7FFFFFFF	$2^{31}-1$	long	2147483647
2147483648	2^{31}	(long)	(-2147483648)
0x80000000	2^{31}	long	-2147483648
4294967295	$2^{32}-1$	(long)	(-1)
0xFFFFFFFF	$2^{32}-1$	long	-1
4294967296	2^{32}	(long)	(0)
0x100000000	2^{32}	(long)	(0)

Table 2-1:   Integer constants

In spite of these anomalies, the programmer will rarely be "surprised" by the values of integer constants, at least when the target computer uses the two's-complement representation for integers. (Most computers do.) For the computers that use other integer representations, either the rules for interpreting integer constants or the rules for converting between signed and unsigned integers will have to be adjusted by the implementation.

References   conversions of integer types 6.3; integer types 5.2; overflow 7.2.3; unary minus operator 7.4.3; unsigned integers 5.2.2

2.7.2 *Floating-point Constants*

Floating-point constants may be written with a decimal point, a signed exponent, or both. A floating-point constant is always interpreted to be in decimal radix.

floating-constant ::= *digit-sequence exponent*
$\quad\quad\quad\quad$ | *dotted-digits* { *exponent* }?

exponent ::= ('e' | 'E') { '+' | '−' }? *digit-sequence*
dotted-digits ::= *digit-sequence* '.'
$\quad\quad\quad\quad$ | *digit-sequence* '.' *digit-sequence*
$\quad\quad\quad\quad$ | '.' *digit-sequence*

digit-sequence ::= { *digit* }+

digit ::= '0' | '1' | '2' | '3' | '4' | '5' | '6' | '7' | '8' | '9'

Examples of floating-point constants include:

```
0.              3e1              3.14159
 .0             1.0e-3           1e-3
1.0             .00034           2e+9
```

The value of a floating-point constant is always nonnegative in the absence of overflow. If there is a preceding minus sign, it is taken to be a unary operator applied to the constant, not part of the constant itself.

The type of a floating-point constant is always `double`. Its value will depend on the precision of the representation of type `double`. If the magnitude of the floating-point constant is too great or too small to be represented, the result is unpredictable. Some compilers will warn the programmer of the problem, but most will silently substitute some other value that can be represented.

References   double type 5.3; overflow and underflow 7.2.3; sizes of floating-point types 5.3; unary minus operator 7.4.3

2.7.3 Character Constants

A character constant is written by enclosing a character in apostrophes. A special escape mechanism is provided to write characters that would be inconvenient or impossible to enter directly in the source program.

character-constant ::= ' ' *character* ' '

character ::= *printing-character* | *escape-character*

The printing characters include all the characters in the source character set that have equivalents in the target character set, *except* newline, the apostrophe, and the backslash. These excluded characters may be entered as escape characters, as described in section 2.7.5.

Character constants have type `int`. Their values are the integer encodings of the characters in the target character set. Below are some examples of character constants along with their (decimal) values under the ASCII encodings:

`'a'`	(97)	`'A'`	(65)	`'%'`	(37)
`' '`	(32)	`'?'`	(63)	`'8'`	(56)
`'\r'`	(13)	`'\0'`	(0)	`'\23'`	(19)
`'"'`	(34)	`'\377'`	(255)	`'\\'`	(92)

It is good programming style to restrict the "printing characters" to those characters with a graphic representation, including the blank. The formatting characters, in particular, should always be expressed as escape characters. Some compilers may enforce this restriction.

Although character constants officially have type `int` in the language specification, many C compilers actually treat the constants as having type `char`. This distinction is important when the `char` type is signed (section 5.2.3). For example, if type `char` were implemented as an 8-bit signed type, the character constant `'\377'` would have the value -1 when treated as a value of type `char`. If, under the same implementation, the character were treated as a value of type `int`, it should have the value 255, just like the integer constant `0377`.

An extension to character constants is occasionally seen in C compilers. Because most computers represent integers in a storage area big enough to hold several characters, a few C compilers allow multicharacter constants, such as `'ABC'`. The intent is to create an integer value (not a string) from the characters. The use of this feature, if available, results in very nonportable programs, not only because integers have different sizes on different computers but also because computers differ in the order in which characters are packed into words. Given the constant `'ABC'`, some computers would put `'A'` in the low-order bits and others would put `'A'` in the high-order bits.

References   character encodings 2.1.2; character sets 2.1; character type 5.2.3; escape characters 2.7.5; formatting characters 2.1

2.7.4 String Constants

A string constant is a (possibly empty) sequence of characters enclosed in double quotes. The same escape mechanism provided for character constants can be used to express the characters in the string.

string-constant ::= '"' { *character* }* '"'

character ::= *printing-character* | *escape-character*

In the case of string constants, the printing characters include all the characters in the source character set that have equivalents in the target characters set, except newline, the double quote, and the backslash. These excluded characters may be entered as escape characters, as described in section 2.7.5. A string constant may not contain a newline character unless the newline is immediately preceded by a backslash, in which case the backslash and newline are ignored. This allows string constants to be written on more than one line. (Some implementations also remove leading whitespace characters from the continuation line, although it is incorrect to do so.) A newline character may be inserted into a string value by putting the escape sequence '\n' in the string constant; this should not be confused with line continuation within a string constant. Some examples of string constants include:

```
""
"Total expenditures: "
"\""
"Copyright 1982 Tartan Laboratories Incorporated. \
All rights reserved."
"Comments begin with '/*'.\n"
```

For each string constant of n characters there will be at run time a statically allocated block of $n+1$ characters whose first n characters are initialized with the characters from the string and whose last character is the null character, '\0'. No two string constants are ever represented by the same block of storage, even when they contain the same characters.

The type of a string constant is "array of char," and its value is the $n+1$ characters. For example, the value of sizeof("abcdef") is 7. However, if the string constant appears anywhere except as an argument to sizeof or as an initializer of a character array, the conversions that are usually applied to arrays come into play, and these conversions change the string from an array of characters to a pointer to the first character in the string, of type "pointer to char." Thus we can have

```
char *p = "abcdef";
```

Although not prohibited by the language, it is considered bad programming style to modify the contents of a string constant. Some implementations of C may allocate string constants to read-only memory, preventing such modifications. However, it is known that some UNIX library routines do modify their string arguments. When a pointer to a writable string must be used, it is better to write:

```
char pinit[] = "abcdef";
char *p = pinit;
```

References   array types 5.5; conversions from array types 6.7.3; escape characters 2.7.5; initializers 4.6; pointer types 5.4; preprocessor lexical conventions 3.2; `sizeof` operator 7.4.2; whitespace characters 2.1.1; usual unary conversions 6.12

2.7.5 Escape Characters

Escape characters can be used in character and string constants to represent characters that would be awkward or impossible to enter in the source program directly. The escape characters come in two varieties: "character escapes," which can be used to represent some particular formatting and special characters, and "numeric escapes," which allow a character to be specified by its numeric encoding.

escape-character ::= '\' *escape-code*

escape-code ::= *character-escape-code* | *numeric-escape-code*

character-escape-code ::= 'n' | 't' | 'b' | 'r' | 'f' | 'v' | '\' | ''' | '"'

numeric-escape-code ::= *octal-digit* { *octal-digit* { *octal-digit* }? }?

If the character following the backslash is neither an octal digit nor one of the character escape codes listed above, the result should be considered unpredictable, although traditionally the effect is simply that the backslash is ignored.

2.7.6 Character Escape Codes

Character escape codes are used to represent some common special characters in a fashion that is independent of the target computer character set. The characters that may follow the backslash, and their meanings, are listed below.

n	newline
t	horizontal tabulate
v	vertical tabulate
b	backspace
r	carriage return
f	form feed
\	backslash
'	single quote
"	double quote

To show how the character escapes can be used, here is a small program that counts the number of lines (actually, the number of newline characters) in the input. The function `getchar` returns the next input character until the end of the input is reached, at which point `getchar` returns −1 (the standard name for this conventional value is EOF).

```
/* Count the number of lines in the input. */
main()
{
    int next_char;            /* Next input character */
    int num_lines = 0;        /* Number of newlines seen*/

    while ((next_char = getchar()) != EOF)
                              /* For each character */
        if (next_char == '\n') /*  if it's a newline */
            ++num_lines;       /*    bump the counter.*/

    /* Now print the total. */
    printf("%d lines read.\n",num_lines);
}
```

References   EOF 11.5.1

2.7.7 *Numeric Escape Codes*

Numeric escape codes allow any character to be expressed by writing that character as its octal encoding in the target character set. Up to three octal digits may be used to express the encoding, which is sufficient for characters represented by up to nine bits on the target computer. For instance, under the ASCII encodings, the character 'a' may be written as '\141' and the character '?' as '\77'. The null character, used to terminate strings, is always written as '\0'. The following short segment from a communications protocol program illustrates the use of numeric escape codes.

```
{
    auto char inchar;
    extern char receive();
    extern void reply();
    for (;;) {                /* Repeat "forever" */
        inchar = receive();   /* Receive next character */
        if (inchar == '\0')
            continue;         /* Ignore null characters */
        if (inchar == '\004')
            break;            /* Quit when EOT seen. */
        if (inchar == '\006')
            reply('\006');    /* Reply ACK to ACK. */
        else
            reply('\025');    /* Reply NAK to others. */
    }
}
```

The programmer should be cautious when using numeric escapes for two reasons. First, the syntax for numeric escapes is very delicate; a numeric escape code terminates when three octal digits have been used or when the first character that is not an octal digit is encountered. Therefore, the string "\0111" consists of two characters, '\011' and '1', and the string "\080" consists of three characters, '\0', '8', and '0'.

The second reason is that the use of any numeric escape in a character or string constant—except for the null character—may make the C program non-portable. Character sets are implementation dependent, and if the specified encoding is not present in the target character set, the result is unpredictable. There is an implicit assumption in some C programs that the target computer will use eight bits to represent a character, so that codes '\0' through '\377' will span the target character set. This assumption is not portable, either. It is always much better to hide such escape codes in macro definitions. See how much clearer the previous example becomes:

```
#define NUL '\0'
#define EOT '\004'
#define ACK '\006'
#define NAK '\025'
{
    auto char inchar;
    extern char receive();
    extern void reply();
    for (;;) {                  /* Repeat "forever" */
        inchar = receive();     /* Receive next character */
        if (inchar == NUL)
            continue;           /* Ignore null characters */
        if (inchar == EOT)
            break;              /* Quit when EOT seen. */
        if (inchar == ACK)
            reply(ACK);         /* Reply ACK to ACK. */
        else
            reply(NAK);         /* Reply NAK to others. */
    }
}
```

Some compilers permit numeric escapes expressed in hexadecimal notation, such as '\x1A'. This is a fairly convenient feature, but its use will hinder portability.

References   character constant 2.7.3; #define 3.3; macro definitions 3.3; null character 2.1; string constant 2.7.4; target character set 2.1.3

3

The C Preprocessor

The C preprocessor is a simple macro processor that conceptually processes the source text of a C program before the compiler proper parses the source program. In some implementations of C, the preprocessor is actually a separate program that reads the original source file and writes out a new "preprocessed" source file that can then be used as input to the C compiler. (In such implementations, programs containing no preprocessor commands may typically be compiled directly, bypassing the preprocessing step.) In other implementations, a single program performs the preprocessing and compilation in a single pass over the source file, and no intermediate file is necessarily produced.

3.1 PREPROCESSOR COMMANDS

The preprocessor is controlled by special preprocessor command lines, which are lines of the source file beginning with the character '#'. Note that the character '#' has no other use in the C language. Lines that do not contain preprocessor commands are called lines of source program text. The standard preprocessor commands are:

`#define`	Define a preprocessor macro.
`#undef`	Remove a macro definition.
`#include`	Insert text from another file.
`#if`	Conditionally include some text, based on the value of a constant expression.
`#ifdef`	Conditionally include some text, based on whether a macro name is defined.

`#ifndef`	Conditionally include some text, with the sense of the test opposite that of `#ifdef`.
`#else`	Alternatively include some text, if the previous `#if`, `#ifdef`, or `#ifndef` test failed.
`#endif`	Terminate conditional text.
`#line`	Supply a line number for compiler messages.

There are also two recent additions to the preprocessor commands. They are convenient, but found in only a few C compilers:

`#elif`	Alternatively include text based on the value of another constant expression.
`defined`	Determine if a name is defined as a preprocessor macro. (This operator can be used in `#if` commands and removes the need for `#ifdef` and `#ifndef`.)

The preprocessor effectively removes all preprocessor command lines from the source file and makes additional transformations on the source file as directed by the commands, such as expanding macro calls that occur within the source program text. The resulting preprocessed source text should then be a valid C program and must not contain any occurrences of '#' except for occurrences of the `#line` command and occurrences of '#' in string and character constants.

The syntax of preprocessor commands is completely independent of (though in some ways similar to) the syntax of the rest of the C language. For example, it is possible for a macro definition to expand into a syntactically incomplete fragment, as long as the fragment makes sense (that is, is properly completed) in all contexts in which the macro is called.

References   `#define` 3.3; `defined` 3.5.5; `#elif` 3.5.2; `#else` 3.5.1; `#endif` 3.5.1; `#if` 3.5.1; `#ifdef` 3.5.3; `#ifndef` 3.5.3; `#line` 3.6; `#undef` 3.3.5

3.2 PREPROCESSOR LEXICAL CONVENTIONS

The preprocessor does not parse the source text, but it does break it up into tokens for the purpose of locating macro calls. The lexical conventions of the preprocessor are the same as those for the compiler proper: The preprocessor recognizes identifiers, integer constants, floating-point constants, character constants, string constants, and comments. Preprocessor commands are not recognized within character constants, string constants, or comments. (However, in some implementations names of the formal parameters of macros *are* recognized within character constants and string constants in macro bodies. See section 3.3.2.)

A line whose first character is '#' is treated as a preprocessor command. The name of the command must immediately follow the '#' character. Some implementations of C require the '#' character to be the first character on the line; others allow whitespace to precede it. Some implementations allow whitespace to appear between the '#' character and the name of the command, and others do not. The use of such leading and separating whitespace may make a program more readable but will render it less portable.

The remainder of the line may contain arguments for the command if appropriate. If a preprocessor command takes no arguments, then it is an error if the remainder of the command line is not whitespace.

An identifier may be recognized as the name of a macro defined by a preceding preprocessor command, in which case macro replacement is performed. However, macro replacement is never performed within comments or constants. The preprocessor does not distinguish reserved words from other identifiers, and so it is possible, in principle, to use a C reserved word as the name of a preprocessor macro, but to do so is bad programming practice.

Within a preprocessor command line, if a newline character is immediately preceded by '\', then the newline and the '\' are ignored and the following line is treated as if it were part of the line that ended in '\'. This means that a preprocessor command line can be continued on the following line by ending it with '\'. It also means that if a line ends with '\', the following line will never be treated as a preprocessor command line, even if its first non-whitespace character is '#'. For example,

```
#define err(flag,msg)  if (flag) \
    printf(msg)
```

is the same as

```
#define err(flag,msg)  if (flag) printf(msg)
```

As explained in section 2.2, the preprocessor treats comments as whitespace, and line breaks within comments do not terminate preprocessor commands.

References   comments 2.2; line termination 2.1.1; newline 2.1.1; tokens 2.3

3.3 DEFINITION AND REPLACEMENT

The #define preprocessor command causes a name (identifier) to become defined as a macro to the preprocessor. A sequence of tokens, called the *body* of the macro, is associated with the name. When the name of the macro is recognized in the program source text or in the arguments of certain other preprocessor commands, it is treated as a call to that macro; the name is effectively replaced by a copy of the body. If the macro is defined to accept arguments, then the actual arguments following the macro name are substituted for formal parameters in the macro body. For example, if a macro `sum` with two arguments is defined by

```
#define sum(x,y)   x+y
```

then the preprocessor replaces the source program line

```
result = sum(5,a*b);
```

with

```
result = 5+a*b;
```

3.3.1 Simple Macro Definitions

The `#define` command has two forms, depending on whether or not a left parenthesis '(' immediately follows the name to be defined. The simpler form has no left parenthesis there:

```
#define  name  sequence-of-tokens
```

A macro defined in this manner takes no arguments. It is invoked merely by mentioning its name. When the name is encountered in the source program text or other appropriate context, the name is replaced by the body (the associated *sequence-of-tokens*).

As a point of style, it is customary to put at least one whitespace character after the name of the macro being defined. However, whitespace is not mandatory unless the first character in the *sequence-of-tokens* is a left parenthesis, in which case a whitespace character must separate the left parenthesis from the name. (If a left parenthesis immediately follows the name, the definition is considered to define a macro that takes arguments, as described in section 3.3.2.)

The simple form of macro is particularly useful for introducing named constants into a program, so that a "magic number" such as the length of a table may be written in exactly one place and then referred to elsewhere by name. This makes it easier to change the number later. For example:

```
#define BLOCK_SIZE 0x100
                    /* Size of one disk block. */
#define TRACK_SIZE (16*BLOCK_SIZE)
                    /* Size of one disk track. */
#define HASH_TABLE_SIZE 557
                  /* Initial size of hash table. */
#define ERRMSG "*** Error %d: %s.\n"
                  /* Format for use with printf. */
```

```
/* File protection bits,
     as used in system file directories. */
#define READ_ACCESS      0100000
                   /* May read the file as data. */
#define WRITE_ACCESS     0040000
                   /* May alter existing contents. */
#define APPEND_ACCESS    0020000
                   /* May add new contents. */
#define EXECUTE_ACCESS   0010000
                   /* May execute as code. */
#define DELETE_ACCESS    0004000
                   /* May delete the file. */
#define RENAME_ACCESS    0002000
                   /* May rename the file. */
#define BACKUP_ACCESS    0001000
                   /* May move to backup tape. */
#define ACCESS_ACCESS    0000400
                   /* May modify the access bits. */
```

The syntax of the #define command does *not* require an equal sign or
any other special delimiter token after the name being defined. The body starts
right after the name. (If the body begins with an alphabetic character, digit, or
left parenthesis, then a space is needed to separate the body from the name, of
course.)

A typical programming error is to include an extraneous equal sign:

```
/* Probably wrong:       */
#define NUMBER_OF_TAPE_DRIVES = 5
```

This is a legal definition but causes the name NUMBER_OF_TAPE_DRIVES to
be defined as "= 5" rather than as "5". If one were then to write the source
program line

```
count = NUMBER_OF_TAPE_DRIVES;
```

it would be expanded to

```
count = = 5;                        /* Illegal. */
```

which is syntactically illegal. Worse yet, one might accidentally write

```
result = count + NUMBER_OF_TAPE_DRIVES;
```

which would be expanded to

```
result = count + = 5;    /* Probably wrong. */
```

which is syntactically legal (because '+=' is a valid compound assignment operator even with embedded whitespace) but almost certainly not what was intended! One could write

```
count NUMBER_OF_TAPE_DRIVES;     /* Ugh! */
```

which would be expanded to

```
count = 5;
```

and therefore assign 5 to count, but the best that can be said for this practice is that it is confusing. The lesson is clear: Be careful not to include an extraneous equal sign in a macro definition. For similar reasons, be careful also not to include an extraneous semicolon:

```
#define NUMBER_OF_TAPE_DRIVES 5;
                /* Probably wrong. */
```

An important use of simple macro definitions is to isolate implementation-dependent restrictions on the names of externally defined functions and variables. An example of this appears in Section 2.5.

References   compound assignment operators 7.8.2; operators and separators 2.4

3.3.2 *Defining Macros with Parameters*

The more complex form of macro definition declares the names of formal parameters within parentheses, separated by commas:

```
#define name(name1, name2, ..., namen) sequence-of-tokens
```

The left parenthesis must immediately follow the name of the macro with no intervening whitespace. (If whitespace separates the left parenthesis from the macro name, the definition is considered to define a macro that takes no arguments and has a body beginning with a left parenthesis.)

The names of the formal parameters must be identifiers, no two the same. There is no requirement that any of the parameter names be mentioned in the body (though normally they all will be mentioned).

A macro defined in this manner takes as many actual arguments as there are formal parameters. The macro is invoked by mentioning its name; the name must be immediately followed by a left parenthesis, then one actual argument token sequence for each formal parameter, then a right parenthesis. The actual argument token sequences are separated by commas. For example:

```
#define product(x,y)    ((x)+(y))
...
    return product(a+3,b);
```

(A macro can be defined to have zero formal parameters:

```
#define getchar()    getc(stdin)
```

When such a macro is invoked, an empty actual argument list must be provided:

```
while ((c=getchar()) != EOF) ...
```

This kind of macro is useful to simulate a function that takes no arguments.)

An actual argument token sequence may contain parentheses if they are properly nested and balanced and may contain commas if each comma appears within a set of parentheses (this restriction prevents confusion with the commas that separate the actual arguments). Parentheses and commas may also appear freely within character-constant and string-constant tokens and are not counted in the balancing of parentheses and the delimiting of actual arguments. For example, the arguments to the product macro above could be function calls:

```
int f(), g();
...
    return product( f(a,b), g(a,b) );
```

Braces and subscripting brackets may also appear within macro arguments, but they cannot contain commas and do not have to balance. For example, suppose we define a macro that takes as its argument an arbitrary statement:

```
#define insert(stmt)    stmt
```

The invocation

```
insert(   {a=1; b=1;}    )
```

works properly, but if we change the two assignment statements to a single statement containing two assignment expressions:

```
insert(   {a=1, b=1;}    )
```

then the preprocessor will complain that we have too many macro arguments for insert. To fix the problem we would have to write:

```
insert(   {(a=1, b=1);}    )
```

When possible, a macro invocation should be contained on a single line.

Some preprocessor implementations do not permit the actual argument token list to extend across multiple lines unless the lines to be continued end with a '\' followed by a newline.

When a complex macro call is encountered, the entire macro call is replaced, after parameter processing, by a processed copy of the body. Parameter processing proceeds as follows. Actual argument token strings are associated with the corresponding formal parameter names. A copy of the body is then made in which every occurrence of a formal parameter name is replaced by a copy of the actual argument token sequence associated with it. This copy of the body then replaces the macro call. The entire process of replacing a macro call with the processed copy of its body is called *macro expansion*; the processed copy of the body is called the *expansion* of the macro call.

As an example, consider this macro definition:

```
/* incr: This macro expands into a for statement
    that causes the variable (any lvalue) to take
    on all values from 1 to h, inclusive.  Note
    that v and h may be evaluated more than once.
*/
#define incr(v,1,h)  \
            for ((v) = (1); (v) <= (h); (v)++)
```

This provides a convenient way to make a loop that just counts from a given value up to (and including) some limit. For example, to print a table of the cubes of the integers from 1 to 20, we could write

```
main()
{
    int j;
    printf(" N   N cubed\n");
    incr(j, 1, 20)
        printf("%2d %6d\n", j, j*j*j);
}
```

The call to the macro incr is expanded by the preprocessor to produce this program to be compiled:

```
main()
{
    int j;
    printf(" N   N cubed\n");
    for ((j) = (1); (j) <= (20); (j)++)
        printf("%2d %6d\n", j, j*j*j);
}
```

(The liberal use of parentheses ensures that complicated actual arguments will not confuse the compiler. See Section 3.3.6.)

In many (but not all) implementations of C, macro formal parameter names, unlike macro calls, *are* recognized within string and character constants. Because the actual argument may have been broken down into tokens, possibly with comments and extraneous whitespace discarded, the substitution of an actual argument token sequence into a string may not result in the precise sequence of characters that appeared in the macro call. In recording the body of a macro, the compiler may make certain simplifications. It may eliminate extraneous whitespace. It may reduce constants to a "canonical form," for example reducing 0000400 to 0400 or to 256. Comments may be treated in one of three ways: replaced by whitespace, replaced by an empty comment, or maintained verbatim. Consider this definition:

```
#define MAKESTRING(x) "x"
```

The result of the call

```
MAKESTRING(a += 1    /* Increment counter. */)
```

might be any one of the following representative samples:

```
"a += 1     /* Increment counter. */"
"a += 1 "
"a += 1 /**/"
"a+=1/* Increment counter. */"
"a+=1"
```

Programs are more likely to be portable if actual arguments that are substituted for formal parameters within character constants and string constants are single tokens. Better yet, inasmuch as some implementations don't handle such substitution at all, the programmer can maximize portability simply by avoiding entirely the use of macro formal parameters within character constants and string constants.

3.3.3 Rescanning of Macro Expressions

Once a macro call has been expanded, the scan for macro calls resumes at the *beginning* of the expansion; this is so that names of macros may be recognized within the expansion for the purpose of further macro replacement. Note that macro replacement is not performed on any part of a #define command, not even the body, at the time the command itself is processed and the macro name defined. Macro names are recognized within the body only after the body has been expanded for some particular macro call. Macro replacement is also not performed within the actual argument token strings of a complex macro call at the time the macro call is being scanned. Macro names are recognized within actual argument token strings only during the rescanning of the expansion, assuming that the corresponding formal parameter in fact occurred one or more times within the body (thereby causing the actual argument token string to appear one or more times in the expansion). For example, given the following macro definitions:

```
#define plus(x,y) add(y,x)
#define add(x,y) ((x)+(y))
```

The macro invocation

```
plus( plus(a,b), c )
```

is expanded in the following steps:

```
plus( plus(a,b), c )
add( c, plus(a,b) )
((c)+(plus(a,b)))
((c)+(add(b,a)))
((c)+(((b)+(a))))
```

If a macro expands into something that looks like a preprocessor command, that command will *not* be recognized as a command by the preprocessor. For example, the result of

```
/* This example doesn't work as one might think! */
#define GETMATH #include <math.h>
GETMATH
```

is *not* to include the file `math.h` in the program being compiled. The call to the macro GETMATH expands into the token sequence

```
# include < math . h >
```

but that token sequence is not recognized as a preprocessor #include command; the token sequence is merely passed through and compiled as (erroneous) C code. In general, a line is treated as a preprocessor command line if and only if its first non-whitespace character is '#' *before* any macro replacement has been performed on the line.

Finally, it is possible to write recursive macros whose expansion does not terminate. For example, the macro

```
#define  repeat(x)  x repeat(x)
```

will expand to an infinite sequence of its argument. Most C compilers will not detect this recursion, and will attempt to continue the expansion until they are stopped by some system error.

3.3.4 Predefined Macros

Many implementations of C provide certain predefined macros for use by the programmer. Typically these are used to communicate information about the environment, such as the type of computer for which the program is being compiled. For example, a compiler targeted to the DEC VAX-11 computer might predefine a macro named VAX so that the programmer might write

```
#ifdef VAX
      VAX-specific-code
#endif
```

to cause certain code to be compiled only when the target computer is a VAX. Exactly which macros are predefined is implementation dependent.

References   #ifdef preprocessor command 3.5.3; #if preprocessor command 3.5.1

3.3.5 Undefining and Redefining Macros

Implementations of C differ in how they handle an attempt to define a name that has already been defined, and is still defined, as a macro. Some implementations will discard the old definition, replace it with the new one, and perhaps issue a warning message. Others consider the situation an error unless the presence, number, and names of formal parameters match identically and the old and new bodies, considered as sequences of tokens, also match identically. (This rule effectively says that redundant definitions are permissible, but not conflicting definitions.) It is best for the programmer to avoid the problem by "undefining" a macro before attempting to redefine it.

The #undef command can be used to make a name be no longer defined:

```
#undef name
```

This command causes the preprocessor to forget any macro definition of the specified name. It is not an error to undefine a name that is currently not defined. Once a name has been undefined, it may then be given a completely new definition (using #define) without error. Macro replacement is not performed within #undef commands.

Unfortunately, implementations also differ in their handling of #undef. Some preprocessor implementations handle #define and #undef so as to maintain a stack of definitions. When a name is redefined with #define, its old definition is pushed onto a stack and then the new definition replaces the old one. When a name is "undefined" with #undef, the current definition is discarded and the most recent previous definition (if any) is popped from the stack to replace it. Thus, after the sequence of commands

```
#define X 10
#define X 12
#undef X
```

X would be defined as 10.

The programmer should consult the implementation documentation to determine the precise behavior of #define and #undef when transporting a C program to a new implementation. The preprocessor commands #ifdef and #ifndef may be used to determine whether or not a name is currently defined as a preprocessor macro.

References   #define command 3.3; #ifdef command 3.5.3; #ifndef command 3.5.3

3.3.6 Some Pitfalls to Avoid

Macros operate purely by textual substitution of tokens. Parsing of the body into declarations, expressions, or statements occurs only after the macro expansion process. This can lead to surprising results if care is not taken. Consider this macro definition:

```
#define SQUARE(x) x*x
```

The idea is that SQUARE takes an argument expression and produces a new expression to compute the square of that argument. For example, SQUARE(5) expands to 5*5. However, the expression

```
SQUARE(z+1)
```

expands to

```
z+1*z+1
```

When this expression is parsed, it is interpreted as

```
z+(1*z)+1
```

which will not produce the same result as (z+1)*(z+1) unless z happens to be zero. It would be somewhat safer to put parentheses around occurrences of the formal parameter in the definition of SQUARE:

```
#define SQUARE(x) (x)*(x)
```

Even this definition does not provide complete protection against precedence problems. Consider casting the squared value to a new type:

```
(short) SQUARE(z+1)
```

This would expand to:

```
(short) (z+1)*(z+1)
```

which would then be parsed as

```
((short) (z+1))*(z+1)
```

because a cast has higher precedence than multiplication. The definition can be improved further to avoid this difficulty:

```
#define SQUARE(x) ((x)*(x))
```

As a rule, it is safest always to parenthesize each parameter appearing in the macro body. The entire body, if it is syntactically an expression, should also be parenthesized.

Macros can also produce problems with side effects. Consider the macro SQUARE shown above and also a function square that does (almost) the same thing:

```
int square(x)
  int x;
{
    return x*x;
}
```

The function, unlike the macro, can square only integers, not floating-point numbers. Also, calling the function is likely to be somewhat slower at run time than using the macro. But these differences are less important than the question of side effects. In the program fragment

```
a = 3;
b = square(a++);
```

the variable b gets the value 9 and the variable a ends up with the value 4. However, in the superficially similar program fragment

```
a = 3;
b = SQUARE(a++);
```

the variable b will get the value 12 and the variable a will end up with the value 5, because the expansion of the last fragment is

```
a = 3;
b = ((a++)*(a++));
```

When a function, such as square, is used, the argument expression is evaluated exactly once, so any side effects of the expression occur exactly once. When a macro, such as SQUARE, is used, an actual argument may be textually replicated and therefore executed more than once, and side effects may occur more than once. Macros must be used with care to avoid such problems.

Although the original definition of C explicitly described macro bodies as being sequences of tokens, not sequences of characters, nevertheless some C compilers expand and rescan macro bodies as if they were character sequences. This becomes apparent primarily in the case where the compiler also handles comments by eliminating them entirely (rather than by replacing them with a space), a situation exploited by some cleverly written programs:

```
#define INC ++
#define TAB internal_table
#define INCTAB table_of_increments
#define CONC(x,y) x/**/y
CONC(INC,TAB)
```

The proper interpretation of the body of CONC is as a sequence of the tokens x and y, separated by a comment or a space. The comment does, in all implementations, serve to separate x and y so that they are recognized as formal parameters of the macro CONC. The call

```
CONC(INC,TAB)
```

ought to expand to the sequence of tokens

```
INC TAB
```

which will in turn expand to

```
++ internal_table
```

However, those implementations that simply eliminate comments and that rescan macro bodies as character sequences rather than token sequences will expand the call

```
CONC(INC,TAB)
```

into the character sequence

```
INCTAB
```

and then, in rescanning it, interpret it as the single token INCTAB, which will then expand into

```
table_of_increments
```

which is a very different thing altogether. Because not all implementations treat this the same way, depending on such implicit concatenation of tokens through rescanning may render a program nonportable.

Some implementations of C do not perform stringent error checking on macro definitions and calls. For example, some implementations permit newlines not preceded by '\' to appear within actual argument token sequences. Some implementations permit an incomplete token in the definition to be completed by text appearing after the macro call; for example, the following definition and call

```
#define FIRSTPART "This is a split
...
    printf(FIRSTPART string.");          /* Yuk! */
```

will, after preprocessing, result in compiling the source text

```
    printf("This is a split string.");
```

The lack of error checking by certain implementations does not make clever exploitation of that lack legitimate.

   References   casts 7.4.1; comments 2.2; defined 3.5.3; identifiers 2.5 precedence of operators 7.2.2

3.4 FILE INCLUSION

The #include preprocessor command causes the entire contents of a specified source text file to be processed as if those contents had appeared in place of the #include command. The #include command has two forms. If the first non-whitespace character following the command name #include is a double quote '"', then the last non-whitespace character on the command line must also be a double quote. If the first non-whitespace character following the command name #include is '<', then the last non-whitespace character on the command line must be '>'. In either case, all the characters between the two delimiters constitute a file name (whose format is implementation dependent).

If the first non-whitespace character following the command name is neither '"' nor '<', then macro replacement is performed on the part of the command line following #include; this allows a macro call to expand into a file name (including the appropriate delimiters).

The two forms differ in how the specified file is to be located if the location is not completely specified in the command. The form

```
#include  "filename"
```

typically searches for the file first in the same "directory" in which the file containing the `#include` command was found, and then perhaps in other places according to implementation dependent search rules. However, the form

    #include <*filename*>

typically does *not* search for the file in the same "directory" in which the file containing the `#include` command was found, but only in certain "standard" places according to implementation dependent search rules. The general intent is that the `"..."` form is used to refer to other files written by the user, whereas the `<...>` form is used to refer to standard "library" files.

In principle an included file may itself contain `#include` commands. The permitted depth of such `#include` nesting is implementation dependent, but most implementations will allow nesting to at least five or six levels.

3.5 CONDITIONAL COMPILATION

The preprocessor conditional commands allow lines of source text to be passed through or eliminated by the preprocessor on the basis of a computed condition.

3.5.1 The #if, #else, and #endif Commands

The following preprocessor commands are used together to allow lines of source text to be conditionally included in or excluded from the compilation: `#if`, `#else`, and `#endif`. They are used in the following way:

    #if *constant-expression*
        group-of-lines-1
    #else
        group-of-lines-2
    #endif

A "group of lines" may contain any number of lines of text of any kind, even other preprocessor command lines, or no lines at all. The `#else` command may be omitted, along with the group of lines following it; this is equivalent to including the `#else` command with an empty group of lines following it. Either group of lines may also contain one or more sets of `#if`-`#else`-`#endif` commands; that is, conditional compilation commands nest properly.

A set of commands such as shown above is processed in such a way that one group of lines will be passed on for compilation and the other group of lines will be discarded. First the *constant-expression* in the `#if` command is evaluated. If its value is not 0, then *group-of-lines-1* is passed through for compilation and *group-of-lines-2* (if present) is discarded. Otherwise, *group-of-lines-1* is discarded; and if there is an `#else` command, then *group-of-lines-2* is passed through; but if there is no `#else` command, then no group of lines is passed through. The constant expressions that may be used in a `#if` command are described in detail in sections 3.5.4 and 7.10.

A group of lines that is discarded is not processed by the preprocessor. Macro replacement is not performed and preprocessor commands are ignored. The one exception is that, within a group of discarded lines, the commands `#if`, `#else`, and `#endif` are recognized for the sole purpose of counting them; this is necessary to maintain the proper nesting of the conditional compilation commands. (This recognition in turn implies that discarded lines are scanned and broken into tokens and that string constants and comments are properly recognized, for example.)

Macro replacement is performed within the part of a command line that follows an `#if` command, so macro calls may be used in the *constant-expression*.

3.5.2 The #elif Commands

The `#elif` command is a fairly recent addition to C and is present in only a few compilers. It is convenient because it simplifies nested preprocessor conditionals.

The `#elif` command is like a combination of `#else` and `#if`. It is used between `#if` and `#endif` in the same way as `#else` but has a constant expression to evaluate in the same way as `#if`. It is used in the following way:

```
#if  constant-expression-1
    group-of-lines-1
#elif  constant-expression-2
    group-of-lines-2
#elif  constant-expression-3
    group-of-lines-3
    . . .
#elif  constant-expression-n
    group-of-lines-n
#else
    last-group-of-lines
#endif
```

A set of commands such as shown above are processed in such a way that at most one group of lines will be passed on for compilation and all other groups of lines will be discarded. First the *constant-expression-1* in the `#if` command is evaluated. If its value is not 0, then *group-of-lines-1* is passed through for compilation and all other groups of lines up to the matching `#endif` are discarded. If the value of the *constant-expression-1* in the `#if` command is 0, then the *constant-expression-2* in the first `#elif` command is evaluated; if that value is not 0, then *group-of-lines-2* is passed through for compilation. In the general case, each *constant-expression-i* is evaluated until one produces a nonzero value; the preprocessor then passes through the group of lines following the command containing the nonzero constant expression, ignores any other constant expressions in the command set, and discards all other groups of lines.   If no *constant-expression-i* produces a nonzero value, but there is an #else command, then the group of lines following the #else command is passed through; but if there is no #else command, then no group of lines is passed through. The constant expressions that may be used in a #elif command are the same as those used in a #if command (see Sections 3.5.4 and 7.10).

Within a group of discarded lines, #elif commands are recognized in the same way as #if, #else, and #endif commands, for the sole purpose of counting them; this is necessary to maintain the proper nesting of the conditional compilation commands.

Macro replacement is performed within the part of a command line that follows an #elif command, so macro calls may be used in the *constant-expression*.

While the #elif command is very convenient when it is appropriate, it is not necessary, because anything it accomplishes can be done using only #if, #else, and #endif. For example, this set of commands:

```
#if  constant-expression-1
    group-of-lines-1
#elif  constant-expression-2
    group-of-lines-2
#elif  constant-expression-3
    group-of-lines-3
#else
    last-group-of-lines
#endif
```

can be rewritten in this way:

```
#if  constant-expression-1
    group-of-lines-1
#else
#if  constant-expression-2
    group-of-lines-2
#else
#if  constant-expression-3
    group-of-lines-3
#else
    last-group-of-lines
#endif
#endif
#endif
```

Unfortunately, the #elif command is not supported by all compilers, and so we regretfully recommend that it not be used in portable code.

3.5.3 The #ifdef and #ifndef Commands

The `#ifdef` and `#ifndef` commands can be used to test whether a name is defined as a preprocessor macro. A command line of the form

```
#ifdef name
```

is equivalent in meaning to

```
#if 1
```

when *name* has been defined and is equivalent to

```
#if 0
```

when `name` has not been defined or has been undefined with the `#undef` command. The `#ifndef` command has the opposite sense; it is true when the name is not defined and false when it is.

Note that `#ifdef` and `#ifndef` test names only with respect to whether they have been defined by `#define` (or undefined by `#undef`); they take no notice of names appearing in declarations in the C program text to be compiled.

These commands have come to be used in several stylized ways in C programs. First, it is a common practice to implement a preprocessor-time enumeration type by having a set of symbols of which only one is defined. For example, suppose that we wish to use the set of names VAX, PDP11, IBM360, and IBM1401 to indicate the computer for which the program is being compiled. One might insist that all these names be defined, with one being defined to be 1 and the rest 0:

```
#define VAX      0
#define PDP11    0
#define IBM360   0
#define IBM1401  1
```

One could then select machine-dependent code to be compiled in this way:

```
#if VAX
    VAX-dependent code
#endif
#if PDP11
    PDP11-dependent code
#endif
#if IBM360
    IBM360-dependent code
#endif
#if IBM1401
    IBM1401-dependent code
#endif
```

However, the customary method defines only one symbol:

```
#define IBM1401 1
/* All the other symbols are not defined. */
```

Then the conditional commands test whether each symbol is defined:

```
#ifdef VAX
    VAX-dependent code
#endif
#ifdef PDP11
    PDP11-dependent code
#endif
#ifdef IBM360
    IBM360-dependent code
#endif
#ifdef IBM1401
    IBM1401-dependent code
#endif
```

Another use for the `#ifdef` and `#ifndef` commands is in providing default definitions for macros. For example, a library file might provide a definition for a name only if no other definition has been provided:

```
/* Library file <table.h>.
   Maintains an internal table.
 */

#if !defined(TABLE_SIZE)
#define TABLE_SIZE 100
#endif
...
static int internal_table[TABLE_SIZE];
...
```

A program might simply include this file:

```
#include <table.h>
```

in which case the definition of TABLE_SIZE would be 100, both within the library file itself and after the #include; or the program might provide an explicit definition first:

```
#define TABLE_SIZE 500
#include <table.h>
```

in which case the definition of TABLE_SIZE would be 500 throughout.

References   #define 3.3; #include 3.4; preprocessor lexical conventions 3.2; #undef 3.3.5

3.5.4 Constant Expressions in Conditional Commands

The constant expressions that may be used in #if and #elif commands are described in detail in section 7.10. The value of the constant expression must be determined in exactly the same way as for any other constant expression in the program: The result of evaluating a constant expression must be identical to the result of evaluating the same expression at run time.

If the entire rest of the command line following #if or #elif is not, after macro replacement, a syntactically legal constant expression, or if any error occurs while determining its value (for example, division by 0), then some implementation dependent action is taken. Some compilers issue an error message and assume the entire expression has the value 0; that is, the conditional test fails and the following group of lines is discarded. This assumption is made purely for the purpose of continuing the compilation process in order to search for additional errors.

3.5.5 *The* `defined` *Operator*

There is one operator, `defined`, that can be used in `#if` and `#elif` expressions but nowhere else in the C language. An expression of the form

    defined *name*

or

    defined(*name*)

evaluates to 1 if *name* is defined in the preprocessor, and 0 if it is not. This allows one to write

    #if defined(VAX)

instead of

    #ifdef VAX

The `defined` operator is more convenient to use because it is possible to build up complex expressions, such as

    #if defined(VAX) && !defined(UNIX) && debugging
    ...

Unfortunately, the `defined` operator is a new addition to C and is implemented by only a few compilers.

3.6 EXPLICIT LINE NUMBERING

The `#line` preprocessor command advises the C compiler that the source program was generated by another tool and indicates the correspondence of places in the source program to lines of the original user-written file from which the C source program was produced. The `#line` commands may have one of two forms. The form

    #line *integer-constant* "*filename*"

indicates that the next source line was derived from line *n* of the original user-written file named by *filename*. The form

    #line *integer-constant*

indicates that the next source line was derived from line *n* of the original user-written file last mentioned explicitly in a `#line` command.

Macro replacement is performed on the part of the command line following the name #line before the command line is interpreted. This allows a macro call to expand into the *integer-constant*, the *filename*, or both.

The information provided by the #line command is used purely for the sake of giving more informative error messages. Some tools that generate C source text as output will use #line so that error messages can be related to the tool's input file instead of the actual C source file. Some compilers do not implement #line, ignoring it when present.

Some implementations of C allow the preprocessor to be used independently of the rest of the compiler. Indeed, sometimes the preprocessor is a separate program that is executed to produce an intermediate file that is then processed by the "real" compiler. In such cases the preprocessor may generate new #line commands in the intermediate file; the compiler proper is then expected to recognize these even though it does not recognize any other preprocessor commands. Whether the preprocessor generates #line commands is implementation dependent. Similarly, whether the preprocessor passes through, modifies, or eliminates #line commands in the input is also implementation dependent.

Older versions of C allow simply "#" as a synonym for the #line command:

    # *integer-constant filename*

This syntax is considered obsolete, but many implementations of C continue to support it for the sake of compatibility.

Many implementations allow a '#' on a line by itself to mean a "do nothing" command; the preprocessor eliminates the line and takes no other action.

4

Declarations

To *declare* an identifier in the C language is to associate the identifier with some C object, such as a variable, function, or type. The identifiers that can be declared in C are:

- variables
- functions
- types
- type tags
- structure and union components
- enumeration constants
- statement labels
- preprocessor macros

Except for statement labels and preprocessor macros, all identifiers are declared by their appearance in C *declarations*. Variables, functions, and types appear in *declarators* within declarations, and type tags, structure and union components, and enumeration constants are declared in certain kinds of *type specifiers* in declarations. Statement labels are declared by their appearance in a C function, and preprocessor macros are declared by the #define preprocessor command.

Declarations in C are difficult to describe for several reasons. First, they involve some unusual syntax that may be confusing to the novice. For example, the declaration

```
int (*f)();
```

does not declare f to be some kind of integer but rather a pointer to a function returning an integer.

Second, many of the abstract properties of declarations, such as *scope* and *extent*, are not clearly evident in C's realization. Before jumping into the actual declaration syntax, we will discuss these properties in section 4.2.

Finally, some aspects of C's declarations are difficult to understand without a knowledge of C's type system, which is described in Chapter 5. In particular, discussions of type tags, structure and union component names, and enumeration constants is left to that chapter, although some properties of those declarations will be discussed here for completeness.

References   enumeration type 5.6; #define preprocessor command 3.3; statement labels 8.3; structure types 5.7; type specifiers 4.4; type tags 5.12.2; union types 5.8

4.1 ORGANIZATION OF DECLARATIONS

Declarations may appear in several places in a C program, and where they appear affects the properties of the declarations. To give an overview, a *program* consists of a sequence of *top-level declarations* (of functions, variables, and other things). Each function has *parameter declarations* and a body; the body in turn may contain *blocks* (compound statements). A block may contain a sequence of *inner declarations*.

The syntax below shows the location of declarations in a C program. (Some of the syntactic alternatives are not relevant to this discussion and have been elided, as indicated by ". . .".)

program ::= { *top-level-declaration* }*

top-level-declaration ::= *function-definition*
                          | *declaration*

function-definition ::= { *storage-class-specifier* }?
                          { *type-specifier* }?
                          declarator
                          { *parameter-declaration* }*
                          compound-statement

compound-statement ::=
        '{' { *inner-declaration* }* { *statement* }* '}'

statement ::= *compound-statement* | . . .

parameter-declaration ::= *declaration*

> *inner-declaration* ::= *declaration*
>
> *declaration* ::= { *storage class-specifier* }?
>   *type-specifier*
>   { *possibly-initialized-declarator* # ',' }* ';'
>
> *possibly-initialized-declarator* ::=
>   *declarator* { '=' *initializer* }?
>
> *declarator* ::= *identifier* | . . .
>
> *initializer* ::= *expression* | . . .

As you can see, all declarations except function definitions share the same syntax. In fact, semantic rules will prohibit certain syntactically valid declarations, depending on the location and form of the declaration. These rules will be considered later.

References   declarators 4.5; expressions 7; function definitions 9; initializers 4.6; statements 8; storage class specifiers 4.3; type specifiers 4.4

4.2 TERMINOLOGY

In order to describe the meaning of declarations in a C program, we must establish some terminology

4.2.1 Scope

The *scope* of a declaration is the region of the C program text over which that declaration is active. A declaration might have as its scope a single compound statement, a function body, or a larger section of the source program.

In C, identifiers may have one of five scopes.

- An identifier declared in a top-level declaration has a scope that extends from its declaration point (section 4.2.3) to the end of the source program file.
- An identifier declared in a formal parameter declaration has a scope that extends from its declaration point to the end of the function body.
- An identifier declared at the beginning of a block has a scope that extends from its declaration point to the end of the block.
- A statement label has a scope that encompasses the entire function body in which it appears.
- A preprocessor macro name has a scope that extends from the #define

command that declares it through the end of the source program file, or until the first `#undef` command that cancels its definition.

Nonpreprocessor identifiers declared within a function or block are often said to have *local scope.*

The scope of every identifier is limited to the C source file in which it occurs. However, some identifiers can be declared to be *external*, in which case the declarations of the same identifier in two or more files can be linked in a fashion described in section 4.8.

> **References**   #define preprocessor command 3.3; external names 4.8; #undef preprocessor command 3.3.5

4.2.2 Visibility

A declaration of an identifier is *visible* in some context if a use of the identifier in that context will be bound to the declaration; that is, the identifier will have an association made with that declaration. A declaration might be visible throughout its scope, but it may also be *hidden* by other declarations whose scope and visibility overlap that of the first declaration. For example, in the following program, the declaration of `foo` as an integer variable is hidden by the inner declaration of `foo` as a floating-point variable. The outer `foo` is hidden only within the body of function `main`.

```
int foo = 10;   /* foo defined at the top level */

main()
{
    float foo;  /* this foo hides the outer foo */
    ... sin(foo) ...
}
```

In C, formal parameter declarations can hide top-level declarations, and declarations at the beginning of a block can hide declarations outside the block. For one declaration to hide another, the declared identifiers must be the same, must belong to the same overloading class (See section 4.2.4), and must be declared in two distinct scopes, one of which contains the other.

> **References**   block 8.4; overloading class 4.2.4; parameter declarations 9.3; top-level declarations 4.1

4.2.3 Forward References

Except in a few selected situations, an identifier may not be used before it is declared. To be precise, we define the *declaration point* of an identifier to be the position of the identifier's lexical token in the declaration. Any use of the identifier after the declaration point is permitted. In the example below, an integer, intsize, can be initialized to its own size because the use of intsize in the initializer comes after the declaration point.

```
static int intsize = sizeof(intsize);
```

When an identifier is used before its declaration point, a *forward reference* to the declaration is said to occur. C permits forward references in two situations. First, a statement label may appear in a goto statement before it is defined:

```
    if (error) goto recover;
    ...
recover:
    CloseFiles();
    ...
```

Second, a structure, union, or enumeration tag may be used before it is declared. That situation is discussed in section 5.7.

Illegal forward references are illustrated in the following example of an attempt to define a self-referential structure with a typedef declaration. In this case, the last occurrence of cell on the line is the declaration point, and therefore the use of cell within the structure is illegal.

```
typedef struct { int Value; cell *Next; } cell;
```

Closely related to the idea of forward references are *implicit declarations* and *duplicate declarations*.

References   duplicate declarations 4.2.5; goto statement 8.10; implicit declarations 4.7; pointer types 5.4; structure types 5.7

4.2.4 Overloading of Names

In C and other programming languages, the same identifier may be associated with more than one program entity at a time. When this happens, we say that the name is *overloaded*, and the context in which the name is used determines the association that is in effect. For instance, an identifier might be both the name of a variable and a structure tag. When used in an expression, the variable association is used; when used in a type specifier, the tag association is used.

When a name is overloaded with several associations, each association has its own scope and may be hidden by other declarations independent of other associations. For instance, if an identifier is being used both as a variable and a structure tag, an inner block may redefine the variable association without altering the tag association.

There are five *overloading classes* for names in C. (We sometimes refer to them as *name spaces*.)

1. *Preprocessor macro names.* Because preprocessing logically occurs before compilation, names used by the preprocessor are independent of any other names in a C program.

2. *Statement labels.* Named statement labels are part of statements. Definitions of statement labels are always followed by ':' (and are not part of `case` labels). Uses of statement labels always immediately follow the reserved word `goto`.

3. *Structure, union, and enumeration tags.* These tags are part of structure, union, and enumeration type specifiers and, if present, always immediately follow the reserved words `struct`, `union`, or `enum`.

4. *Component names* Component names are allocated in name spaces associated with each structure and union type. That is, the same identifier can be a component name in any number of structures or unions at the same time. Definitions of component names always occur within structure or union type specifiers. Uses of component names always immediately follow the selection operators '.' and '->'.

5. *Other names.*
   All other names fall into an overloading class that includes variables, functions, typedef names, and enumeration constants.

These rules differ slightly from those in the original definition of C. First, the original definition of C put statement labels in the same name space as ordinary identifiers, and enough compilers still follow this rule that the programmer should be aware of it. The problem is that using a single name space can be a source of great confusion, since labels do not obey normal block structure. For instance, in the following example, does the integer declaration of L hide the label, or is it an illegal duplicate definition of L?

```
{    ...
    goto L;
    ...
    {   int L;
        ...
        {   ...
            L = 10;
            ...
          L:
            ...
        }
    }
}
```

Compilers placing labels in the same name space as variables consider it an illegal duplicate definition.

Secondly, the original definition of C allocated all structure and union component names from a single name space instead of separate name spaces for each type. Thus, if x was a component of one structure type, it couldn't be the member of another structure type. (Actually, there were complicated rules that allowed identifiers to be in more than one structure if their offsets in the structure were identical.) Fortunately, this is now rarely seen in C compilers and has been corrected in the current language definitions.

Finally, the inclusion of structure, union, and enumeration type tags in the same overloading class is according to the current language definition, although the syntax of C is such that they could be in separate name spaces (and some compilers do define them that way).

References   component names 5.7.2; duplicate definition 4.2.5; enumeration tags 5.6; goto statement 8.10; selection operators 7.3.5; statement labels 8.10; structure tags 5.7; structure type specifiers 5.7; typedef names 5.11; union tags 5.8; union type specifiers 5.8

4.2.5 Duplicate Declarations

It is illegal to make two declarations of the same name (in the same overloading class) in the same block or at the top level. Such declarations are said to *conflict*. In the following example, the two declarations of howmany are conflicting but the two declarations of str are not (because they are in different name spaces).

```
extern  int     howmany;
extern  char    str[10];
typedef double  howmany();
extern  struct str {int a, b; } x;
```

There are two exceptions to the prohibition against duplicate declarations. First, any number of external (*referencing*) declarations for the same name may exist, as long as the declarations assign the same type to the name in each instance. This exception reflects the belief that declaring the same external library function twice should not be illegal.

Second, if an identifier is declared as being external, that declaration may be followed with a *definition* (section 4.8) of the name later in the program, assuming that the definition assigns the same type to the name as the external declaration(s). This exception allows the user to generate legal forward references to variables and functions. For instance, in the following example we define two functions, f and g, that reference each other. Normally, the use of f within g would be an illegal forward reference. However, by preceding the definition of g with an external declaration of f, we give the compiler enough information about f to compile g. (Without the initial declaration of f, a one-pass compiler could not know when compiling g that f returns a value of type `double` rather than `int`.)

```
extern double f ();

double g (x, y)
  double x, y;
{
    ... f (x-y) ...
}

double f (z)
  double z;
{
    ... g (z, z/2.0) ...
}
```

There is a deficiency in this mechanism. Variables that are the subject of forward references from within the same file must be declared `extern`, when they could otherwise have storage class `static`. Some compilers, when they see an external declaration followed by a static definition of the same name, will guess (correctly or not) what is going on and not generate an external reference at link time.

References   defining and referencing declarations 4.8; `extern` storage class 4.3; forward references 4.2.3; overloading class 4.2.4; `static` storage class 4.3

4.2.6 Duplicate Visibility

Because C's scoping rules specify that a name's scope begins at its declaration point rather than at the head of the block in which it is defined, a situation can arise in which two nonconflicting declarations can be referenced in different parts of the same block.

In the example below there are two variables named `i` referenced in the block labeled `B`—the integer `i` declared in the outer block is used to initialize the variable `j`, and then a floating-point variable `i` is declared, hiding the first `i`.

```
    {
        int  i = 0;
        ...
    B:{
            int  j = i;
            float  i = 10.0;
            ...
        }
    }
```

The reference to i in the initialization of j is ambiguous.   Which i was
wanted? Most compilers will do what was (apparently) intended; the first use of
i in block B is bound to the outer definition and the redefinition of i then
hides the outer definition for the remainder of the block.

We consider this usage to be bad programming style; it should be avoided.

4.2.7 Extent

Variables and functions, unlike types, have an existence at run time; that is,
they have storage allocated to them. The *extent* of these objects is the period of
time that the storage is allocated.

An object is said to have *static extent* when it is allocated storage at or before the beginning of program execution and the storage remains allocated until
program termination. In C, all functions have static extent, as do all variables
declared in top-level declarations. Variables declared at the beginning of blocks
may have static extent, depending on the declaration.

An object is said to have *local extent* when (in the case of C) it is created
upon entry to a block or function and is destroyed upon exit from the block or
function. If a variable with local extent has an initializer, the variable is initialized each time it is created. Formal parameters have local extent, and variables
declared at the beginning of blocks may have local extent, depending on the
declaration. A variable with local extent is often called *automatic* in C.

Finally, it is possible in C to have data objects with *dynamic extent*; that is,
objects that are created and destroyed explicitly at the programmer's whim.
However, dynamic objects must be created through the use of special library
routines such as malloc and are not viewed as part of the C language itself.

References   auto storage class 4.3; initializers 4.6; malloc function 11.4.5; static
storage class 4.3; storage allocation functions 11.4

4.2.8 Initial Values

Allocating storage for a variable does not necessarily establish the initial contents of that storage. Most variable declarations in C may have *initializers*, expressions used to set the initial value of a variable at the time that storage is
allocated for it. If an initializer is not specified for a variable, its value after

allocation is unpredictable.

It is important to remember that a static variable is initialized only once and that it retains its value even when the program is executing outside its scope. In the following example, two variables, L and S, are declared at the head of a block and both are initialized to 0. Both variables have local scope, but S has static extent while L has local (automatic) extent. Each time the block is entered, both variables are incremented by one and the new values printed.

```
{
    static int S = 0;
    auto   int L = 0;
    L = L + 1;
    S = S + 1;
    printf("L = %d, S = %d\n", L, S);
}
```

What values will be printed? If the block is executed many times, the output will be this:

```
L = 1, S = 1
L = 1, S = 2
L = 1, S = 3
L = 1, S = 4
. . .
```

There is one dangerous feature of C's initialization of automatic variables declared at the beginning of blocks. The initialization is guaranteed to occur *only* if the block is entered normally; that is, if control flows into the beginning of the block. Through the use of statement labels and the goto statement, it is possible to jump into the middle of a block; if this is done, there is no guarantee that automatic variables will be initialized. The same is true when case or default labels are used in conjunction with the switch statement to cause control to be transferred into a block. In the following example, for instance, the initialization of variable sum will not occur when the goto statement transfers control to label L, causing erroneous behavior.

```
goto L;
...
{
    static int vector[10] = {1,2,3,4,5,6,7,8,9,10};
    int sum = 0;
  L:
    /* Add up elements of "vector". */
    for ( i=1; i<10; i++ ) sum += vector[i];
    printf("sum is %d", sum);
}
```

References   goto statement 8.10; initialization of variables 4.6; storage classes 4.3; switch statement 8.7

4.2.9 External Names

A special case of scope and visibility is the *external* variable or function. An external object is treated just like a static object in the file containing its declaration. However, an identifier declared to be external is *exported* to the linker, and if the same identifier is similarly declared in another program file, the linker will ensure that the two files reference the same object (variable or function).

We have discovered that many C compilers violate normal scope and visibility rules when processing external declarations. In this program fragment, for instance, the occurrence of E in the second assignment statement should be illegal (undefined), since the scope of the external declaration should not extend beyond the inner block:

```
{
    {
        extern E;
        E = 0;
    }
    E = 1;
}
```

In practice, however, it seems that many C compilers treat the declaration of E as if it had occurred at the top level, thus extending over the second assignment.

References   external name conventions 2.5.1; external name definition and reference 4.8; scope 4.2.1; visibility 4.2.2

4.2.10 Compile-time Objects

So far the discussion has focused mainly on variables and functions, which have an existence at run time. However, the scope and visibility rules apply equally to identifiers associated with objects that do not (necessarily) exist at run time:

typedef names, type tags, structure and union component names, and enumeration constants. When any of these identifiers are declared, their scope is the
same as that of a variable defined at the same location.

References   enumeration constants 5.6; scope 4.2.1; structure type 5.7; type tags 5.12.2;
typedef name 5.11; visibility 4.2.2

4.3 STORAGE CLASS SPECIFIERS

We now proceed to examine the pieces of declarations: storage class specifiers,
type specifiers, declarators, and initializers.

The storage class specifier in a declaration mainly determines the extent of
the object declared. At most one storage class specifier may appear in a declaration. (Although the syntax in section 4.1 indicates that storage class specifiers
must precede type specifiers, and we think that is good style, the original definition of C allows them to occur in any order.)

> *storage-class-specifier* ::= `auto`
> | `extern`
> | `register`
> | `static`
> | `typedef`

The meanings of the storage classes are given below. Note that not all
storage classes are permitted in every declaration context.

`auto`   This storage class specifier is permitted only in declarations of
variables at the heads of blocks. It indicates that the variable
has local (automatic) extent.

`extern`   This storage class specifier may appear in declarations of external functions and variables, either at the top level or at the
heads of blocks. It indicates that the object declared has static
extent and its name is known to the linker. Section
4.8 discusses how to distinguish defining external declarations
from referencing external declarations.

`register`   This storage class specifier may be used for local variables or
parameter declarations. It has the same meaning as `auto`,
except that it additionally provides the compiler a hint that
the local variable (or parameter) will be heavily used and
should be allocated in a way that minimizes access time. (For
instance, it might be allocated to a machine register.)

`static`   This storage class specifier may appear on declarations of
functions or variables. On function definitions, it is used only
to specify that the function name is *not* to be exported to the

linker. On data declarations, it always signifies a defining declaration that is not exported to the linker. Variables declared with this storage class have static extent (as opposed to local extent, signified by `auto`).

typedef

When this "storage class" appears, it indicates that the declaration is defining a new data type rather than a variable or function. The name of the new data type appears where a variable name would appear in a variable declaration, and the new data type is the type that would have been assigned to the variable name. (See section 5.11.)

The `register` storage class has some additional restrictions. Only variables of certain types may have this storage class, and the set of permitted types may vary among different computers and C compilers, with type `int` always permitted. The compiler is permitted to limit the number of `register` variables in a function. When this limit is reached, further `register` variables are treated as `auto` variables. The programmer is advised to stick to one or two such variables. Finally, variables declared `register` may not have the address operator, '`&`', applied to them. An attempt to do so may elicit an error or may simply cause `register` to be ignored.

References   address operator 7.4.6; formal parameter declarations 9.3; function definition 9; initializers 4.6; top-level declarations 4.1; typedef names 5.11

4.3.1 Default Storage Class Specifiers

If no storage class specifier is supplied on a declaration, one will be assumed on the basis of the declaration context:

1. Top-level declarations (and function definitions) are assumed to have storage class `extern`. (However, `extern` that is *assumed* and `extern` that is *stated* can mean different things. See section 4.8.)
2. Parameter declarations do not take any storage class except `register`. Omitting the storage class means only "not `register`."
3. For declarations at the head of blocks, `extern` is assumed for functions and `auto` is assumed for everything else.

In spite of these rules, it is a good programming practice to supply the storage class `extern` explicitly when it applies and not allow it to default. On the other hand, omitting `auto` in variable declarations is a common practice and is considered good style.

References   blocks 8.4; parameter declarations 9.3; top-level declarations 4.1;

4.3.2 Examples of Storage Class Specifiers

The following code implements the heap sort algorithm for sorting the contents of an array. It is beyond the scope of this book to explain how it works. We remark only that the algorithm regards the array as a binary tree such that the two subnodes of element b[k] are elements b[2*k] and b[2*k+1], and that a *heap* is a tree such that every node contains a number that is no smaller than any of the numbers contained by that node's descendants. We exhibit the code here as a practical example of the use of storage class specifiers.

```
/* Heap sort. */

#define SWAP(x, y) (temp = (x), (x) = (y), (y) = temp)

/* If v[m+1] through v[n] is already in heap form,
   this puts v[m] through v[n] into heap form. */
static void adjust(v, m, n)
    int v[], m;
    register int n;
{
    register int *b, j, k, temp;
    /* Array in C are 0-origin, but heapsort is
       more easily coded and understood in terms
       of 1-origin arrays. The variable "b"
       effectively remaps the array "v" to be
       1-origin: v[j] is the same as b[j-1]. */
    b = v - 1;
    j = m;
    k = m * 2;
    while (k <= n) {
        if ((k < n) && (b[k] < b[k+1])) ++k;
        if (b[j] < b[k]) SWAP(b[j], b[k]);
        j = k;
        k *= 2;
    }
}
```

```
/* Sort v[0]...v[n-1] into increasing order. */
void heapsort(v, n)
    int v[], n;
{
    int *b, j, temp;
    b = v - 1;
    /* Put the array into the form of a heap. */
    for (j = n/2; j > 0; j--)
        adjust(v, j, n);
    /* Repeatedly extract the largest element and
        put it at the end of the unsorted region. */
    for (j = n-1; j > 0; j--) {
        SWAP(b[1], b[j+1]);
        adjust(v, 1, j);
    }
}
```

The main function is `heapsort`; it must be visible to users of the sort package, and so it has the default storage class, namely `extern`. The auxiliary function `adjust` does not need to be externally visible, and so it is declared to be `static`. The speed of the `adjust` function is crucial to the performance of the sort, and so its local variables have been given storage class `register` as a hint to the compiler. The formal parameter n is also referred to repeatedly within `adjust`, and so is also specified with storage class `register`. The other two formal parameters for `adjust` are referred to only once, and are defaulted to "not `register`." The local variables of function `heapsort` are not so important to performance as those in `adjust`; they have been given the default storage class, namely `auto`.

4.4 TYPE SPECIFIERS

A type specifier provides some of the information about the data type of the program entity being declared. (We say "some" because the declarators in a declaration provide additional type information.) The type specifier may also declare (as a side effect) type tags, structure and union component names, and enumeration constants. (Although the syntax in section 4.1 indicates that type specifiers must follow storage class specifiers, and we think that is good style, the original definition of C allowed them to occur in any order.)

type-specifier ::= *enumeration-type-specifier*
            | *floating-point-type-specifier*
            | *integer-type-specifier*
            | *structure-type-specifier*
            | *typedef-name*
            | *union-type-specifier*
            | *void-type-specifier*

Examples of type specifiers include:

```
void                        union { int a; char b; }
int                         enum {red, blue, green}
unsigned long int           char
my_struct_type              float
```

The type specifiers are described in detail in chapter 5, and we will defer
further discussion of particular type specifiers until then. However, there are a
few general issues surrounding type specifiers that will be dealt with here.

References   enumeration type specifier 5.6; floating-point type specifier 5.3; integer type
specifier 5.2; structure type specifier 5.7; typedef name 5.11; union type specifier 5.8; void type
specifier 5.10

4.4.1 Default Type Specifiers

C allows the type specifier in a variable declaration or function definition to be
omitted, in which case it defaults to int. One often sees this in function
definitions:

```
/* Sort v[0]...v[n-1] into increasing order. */
sort(v, n)
  int v[], n;
{
    ...
}
```

This is bad programming style in modern C. Older compilers did not implement
the void type, so a rationale behind omitting the type specifier on function
definitions was to indicate to human readers that the function didn't really
return a value (although the compiler had to assume that it did). The modern
style is to declare those functions with the void type:

```
/* Sort v[0]...v[n-1] into increasing order. */
void sort(v, n)
  int v[], n;
{
    ...
}
```

When using a compiler that doesn't implement void, it is much nicer to define void yourself and then use it explicitly than to omit the type specifier entirely.

```
/* Make "void" be a synonym for "int". */
typedef int void;
```

At least one compiler we know actually reserves the identifier void but doesn't implement it. For that compiler, the preprocessor definition

```
#define void int
```

is one of the few cases in which using a reserved word as a macro name is justified.

The C syntax requires declarations to contain either a storage class specifier, a type specifier, or both. This requirement avoids a syntactic ambiguity in the language. If all specifiers were defaulted, the declaration

```
extern int f();
```

would become simply

```
f();
```

which is syntactically equivalent to a statement consisting of a function call. We think that the best style is to always include the type specifier and to allow the storage class specifier to default, at least when it is auto.

A final note for LALR(1) grammar aficionados. Both the storage class specifier and the type specifier can be omitted on a function definition, and this is very common in C programs, as in

```
main()
{
    ...
}
```

There is no syntactic ambiguity in this case, because the declarator in a function declaration must be followed by a comma or semicolon, whereas the declarator in a function definition must be followed by a left brace.

References   declarations 4.1; function definitions 9.1; void type specifier 5.10

4.4.2 Missing Declarators

The following discussion deals with a subtle point of declarations and type specifiers. Type specifiers that are structure, union, or enumeration type definitions have a side effect of defining new types. For example, the type specifier

```
struct S { int a, b; }
```

defines a new structure type S with components a and b. The type can be referenced later by using just the specifier

```
struct S
```

When using these specifiers, it makes sense to omit all the declarators from the declaration, so that the whole declaration consists of just a type definition:

```
struct S { int a, b; };
```

The C grammar permits this, and so do all C compilers. However, the grammar also permits some nonsensical variations on this declaration. Most C compilers will not notice these variations, although they are clearly programming errors.

The first variation is omitting the type tag, as in

```
struct { int a, b; };
```

This is clearly nonsensical because without a tag it is impossible to refer to the type later in the program.

The second variation is including a storage class specifier, which will be ignored:

```
static struct S { int a, b; };
```

This may mislead the programmer into thinking that a later declaration of the form

```
struct S x,y;
```

will cause x and y to have the storage class static. It won't.

The final variation is using a type specifier that has no side effects:

```
int ;
```

References   enumeration types 5.6; declarators 4.5; structure types 5.7; type specifiers 4.4; union types 5.8

4.5 DECLARATORS

Declarators introduce the name being declared and also supply additional type information. No other programming language has anything quite like C's declarators.

> *declarator* ::= *simple-declarator*
> | ' (' *declarator* ') '
> | *function-declarator*
> | *array-declarator*
> | *pointer-declarator*

The different kinds of declarators are described below.

4.5.1 Simple Declarators

Simple declarators are used to define variables of arithmetic, enumeration, structure, and union types.

> *simple-declarator* ::= *identifier*

Suppose that S is a type specifier and that *id* is any identifier. Then the declaration

> *S id* ;

indicates that *id* is of type S. The *id* is called a *simple declarator*. For example:

```
int i;                  /* i is an integer variable */
float velocity;
        /* velocity is a floating-point variable */
struct S { int a; float b; } a_and_b;
    /* a_and_b is a structure of two components */
```

Simple declarators may be used in a declaration when the type specifier supplies all the typing information. This happens for arithmetic, structure, union, enumeration, and void types, and for types represented by typedef names. Pointer, array, and function types require the use of more complicated declarators. However, every declarator has in its "middle" an identifier, and we thus say that a declarator "encloses" an identifier.

References   type specifiers 4.4; typedef names 5.11

4.5.2 Pointer Declarators

Pointer declarators are used to declare variables of pointer types.

> *pointer-declarator* ::= '*' *declarator*

Suppose that *D* is any declarator enclosing the identifier *id*, and that the declaration "*S D*;" indicates that *id* has type ". . . *S*." Then the declaration

> *S* *D ;

indicates that *id* has type ". . . pointer to *S*." For example, in the following three declarations of x, *id* is x, *S* is int, and ". . ." is, respectively, "", "array of," and "function returning."

```
int *x;          /* x is a pointer to an integer */
int *x[];        /* x is an array of pointers
                    to integers */
int *x();        /* x is a function returning a
                    pointer to an integer */
```

It's harder to explain than it is to learn.

References   array declarators 4.5.3; function declarators 4.5.4; pointer types 5.4

4.5.3 Array declarators

Array declarators are used to declare objects of array types.

> *array-declarator* ::= *declarator* '[' { *constant-expression* }? ']'

> *constant-expression* ::= *expression*

If *D* is any declarator enclosing the identifier *id*, and if the declaration "*S D*;" indicates that *id* has type ". . . *S*," then the declaration

> *S* (*D*)[*e*] ;

indicates that *id* has type ". . . array of *S*." For example, in the following two declarations, *id* is x, *S* is int, and ". . ." is, respectively, "", "pointer to," and "array of."

```
int (x)[];       /* x is an array of integers */
int (*x)[];      /* x is a pointer to an array of
                    integers */
int (x[])[];     /* x is an array of arrays of
                    integers */
```

(The parentheses may often be elided according to the precedence rules in constructing declarators; see section 4.5.5.)

The integer constant expression e, if present, specifies the number of elements in the array. C's arrays are always "0-origin"; that is, the array

```
int A[3];
```

consists of the elements `A[0]`, `A[1]`, and `A[2]`. The number of elements in an array must be greater than 0, although some popular C compilers do not check this.

As in the example above, higher-dimensioned arrays are declared as "arrays of arrays." For example:

```
int judges_scores[10][2];
int checker_board[8][8];
```

The length of the array, a constant expression, may be omitted as long as it is not needed to allocate storage. It is not needed when:

1. The object being declared is a formal parameter of a function.
2. The declarator is accompanied by an initializer from which the length of the array can be deduced.
3. The declaration is not a defining occurrence; that is, it is an external declaration that refers to an object defined elsewhere.

An exception to these cases is that the declaration of any n-dimensional array must include the sizes of the last $n-1$ dimensions so that the accessing algorithm can be determined. For example:

```
static int vector[5];     /* defining occurrence */
char prompt[]="Yes or No?";
                          /* can deduce size */
extern matrix[][10];

                          /* external, but last
                             dimension must be
                             supplied */
```

For more information, see section 5.5.

References   array types 5.5; constant expressions 7.10; formal parameters 9.3; initializers 4.6; referencing and defining declarations 4.8

4.5.4 Function Declarators

Function declarators are used to declare objects of function types.

function-declarator ::= *declarator* ' (' { *parameter-list* }? ') '

parameter-list ::= { *identifier* # ' , ' } +

If *D* is any declarator enclosing the identifier *id*, and if the declaration "*S D*;" indicates that *id* has type ". . . *S*," then the declaration

```
S (D) () ;
```

indicates that *id* has type ". . . function returning *S*." For example, in the following declarations of x, *id* is x, *S* is int, and ". . ." is, respectively, "", "pointer to," and "array of pointers to."

```
int (x)();      /* x is a function returning
                   an integer */
int (*x)();     /* x is a pointer to a function
                   returning an integer */
int (*x[])();   /* x is an array of pointers to
                   functions returning integers */
```

The parentheses around x in the first declaration may be elided according to the precedence rules in constructing declarators; see section 4.5.5.

The syntax for a function declarator includes an optional parameter list that may be supplied between the open and close parentheses of the declarator. This parameter list is supplied only when defining a function:

```
void f(x, y)
  int x, y;
{
    ...
}
```

The parameter list is omitted in all other cases:

```
extern void f();      /* f is an external function
                         reference */
static void (*f)();   /* f is a pointer, not
                         a function */
```

References   array declarators 4.5.3; defining and referencing declarations 4.8; function types and declarations 5.9; function definitions 9.1; pointer declarators 4.5.2

4.5.5 *Composition of Declarators*

Declarators can be composed to form more complicated types, such as "5-element array of pointers to functions returning int," which is the type of ary in this declaration:

```
int (*ary[5])();
```

The only restriction on declarators is that the resulting type must be a legal one in C. The only types that are *not* legal in C are:

1. Any type involving `void` except ". . . function returning `void`." (`void` is discussed in section 5.10.)
2. "Array of function of . . . ." Arrays may contain pointers to functions, but not functions themselves.
3. "Function returning array of . . . ." Functions may return pointers to arrays, but not arrays themselves.
4. "Function returning function of . . . ." Functions may return pointers to other functions, but not the functions themselves.

When composing declarators, the precedence of the declarator expressions is important. Function and array declarators have higher precedence than pointer declarators, so that "`*x()`" is equivalent to "`*(x())`" ("function returning pointer . . .") instead of "`(*x)()`" ("pointer to function returning . . ."). Parentheses may be used to group declarators properly.

Here are some sample declarations with the associated types of the enclosed identifiers.

```
int *Sum1();      /* Sum1 is a function returning a
                     pointer to an integer. */

int (*Sum2)();    /* Sum2 is a pointer to a function
                     returning an integer. */

void (*F)();      /* F is a pointer to a function
                     returning no result. */

void *F();        /* ILLEGAL! Can't have a pointer
                     to void. */
```

Although declarators can be arbitrarily complex, it is better programming style to factor them into several simpler definitions. That is, rather than writing

```
int *(*(*(*x)())[10])();
```

write instead

```
typedef int *(*print_function_ptr)();
typedef print_function_ptr (*digit_routines)[10];
digit_routines (*x)();
```

(x is a pointer to a function returning a pointer to a 10-element array of pointers to functions returning pointers to integers, in case you wondered.)

By the way, the rationale behind the syntax of declarators is that they mimic the syntax of a use of the enclosed identifier. For instance, if you see the declaration

```
int *(*x)[4];
```

then the type of the expression

```
*(*x)[i]
```

is `int`.

4.6 INITIALIZERS

The declaration of a variable may be accompanied by an initializer that specifies the initial value the variable should have at the beginning of its lifetime. The full syntax for initializers is

> *initializer* ::= *expression*
> | '{' { *initializer* # ',' }+ { ',' }? '}'

The optional trailing comma inside the braces does not affect the meaning of the initializer.

The initializers permitted on a particular declaration depend on the type and storage class of the variable to be initialized and on whether the declaration appears at the top level or at the head of a block. In general, the initializer for any variable with static extent must be a constant expression; such initialization happens prior to execution of the C program. This applies to all top-level variable declarations (static and external) and to variable declarations at the heads of blocks that have storage class `static`. Any static variable that does not have an explicit initializer will be initialized to zero.

Initializers for automatic variables may be arbitrary expressions. These variables will always be declared at the heads of blocks, and the compiler will emit code to evaluate the initializer expression and assign the result to the variable upon block entry.

Declarations of formal parameters may not have initializers.

The "shape" of an initializer—the brace-enclosed lists of initializers—should match the structure of the variable being initialized.

However, there are special rules for abbreviating initializers.

The following sections explain the special requirements for each type of variable.

References   automatic and static lifetime 4.2.7; declarations 4.1; `static` 4.3;

4.6.1 Integers

The form of an initializer for an integer variable is

declarator = expression

Any constant expression of integral type may be used to initialize an external or static integer variable.   Any expression of arithmetic type (not necessarily constant) may be used to initialize an integer variable with storage class `auto` or `register`. In all cases the usual assignment conversions are applied. For example,

```
static int Count = 4*200;
extern int getchar();

main()
{
    int ch = getchar();
    ...
}
```

The original definition of C specified that the initializer for an integer variable may optionally be surrounded by braces, although such braces are logically unnecessary. We recommend that braces not be used in this situation, but be reserved to indicate aggregate initialization.

References   constant expression 7.10; integer types 5.2; static and automatic extent 4.2.7; usual assignment conversions 6.11

4.6.2 Floating-point

The form of an initializer for a floating-point variable is

declarator = expression

All C compilers allow the initialization of static or external floating-point variables; the type of the initializer should be floating-point, but some compilers will permit expressions of any arithmetic type. Automatic variables of floating-point types can be initialized with any expression of arithmetic type. The usual assignment conversions are applied in initializing the variable. For example:

```
static void process_data(K)
  double K;
{
    static double epsilon = 1.0e-6;
    auto float fudge_factor = K*epsilon;
    ...
}
```

The original definition of C specified that the initializer for a floating-point variable may optionally be surrounded by braces, although such braces are logically
unnecessary. We recommend that braces not be used in this situation, but be
reserved to indicate aggregate initialization.

C compilers generally shy away from performing compile-time floating-
point arithmetic, so initializers for static and external floating-point variables
should be restricted to floating-point constants, perhaps with a preceding unary
minus operator.

References   arithmetic types 5; floating-point constant 2.7.2; floating-point types 5.3; static
and automatic extent 4.2.7; unary minus 7.4.3; usual assignment conversions 6.11

4.6.3 Pointers

The form of an initialization of a pointer variable is

declarator = expression

Any constant expression of type *PT* ("pointer to *T*") may be used to initialize an external or static variable of type *PT*. Any expression of type *PT* may
be used to initialize a local variable of type *PT*.

Constant expressions used as initializers of pointer type *PT* may be formed
from the following elements.

1. The integer constant 0 yields a null pointer of any type; it is usually
   refered to by the name NULL.

   ```
   #define NULL 0
   double *dp = NULL;
   ```

2. The name of a static or external function of type "function returning *T*" is
   converted to a constant of type "pointer to function returning *T*."

   ```
   extern int f();
   static int (*fp)() = f;
   ```

3. The name of a static or external array of type "array of *T*" is converted to
   a constant of type "pointer to *T*."

```
char ary[100];
char *cp = ary;
```

4. The '&' operator applied to the name of a static or external variable of type *T* yields a constant of type "pointer to *T*."

```
static short s;
auto short *sp = &s;
```

5. The '&' operator applied to an external or static array of type "array of *T*," subscripted by a constant expression, yields a constant of type "pointer to *T*."

```
float PowersOfPi[10];
float *PiSquared = &PowersOfPi[2];
```

6. An integer constant cast to a pointer type yields a constant of that pointer type, although this is not portable.

```
long *PSW = (long *) 0xFFFFFFF0;
```

Not all compilers accept casts in constant expressions.

7. A string literal yields a constant of type "pointer to `char`" when it appears as the initializer of a variable of pointer type.

```
char *greeting = "Type <cr> to begin ";
```

8. The sum or difference of any expression shown for cases 3 through 7 above and an integer constant expression.

```
static short s;
auto short *sp = &s + 3, *msp = &s - 3;
```

In general, the initializer for a pointer type must evaluate to an integer or to an address plus (or minus) an integer constant. This limitation reflects the capabilities of most linkers.

The original definition of C specified that the initializer for a pointer variable may optionally be surrounded by braces, although such braces are logically unnecessary. We recommend that braces not be used in this situation, but be reserved to indicate aggregate initialization.

References   & address operator 7.4.6; array types 5.5; conversions involving pointers 6.7; function types 5.9; integer constants 2.7.1; pointer declarator 4.5.2; pointer types 5.4; string constants 2.7.4; usual assignment conversions 6.11

4.6.4 Arrays

If I_j (for $j = 0, 1, \ldots, n-1$) are each initializers for type T, then

$$\{ \ I_0, \ I_1, \ \ldots, \ I_{n-1} \ \}$$

is an initializer for type "n-element array of T." The initializer I_j is used to initialize element j the array (zero origin). For example:

```
int ary[4] = { 0, 1, 2, 3 };
```

Multidimensional arrays follow the same pattern, with initializers listed by row. (The last subscript varies most rapidly in C.)

```
int ary[4][2][3] =
      { { { 0,   1,   2}, { 3,   4,   5} },
        { { 6,   7,   8}, { 9,  10,  11} },
        { {12,  13,  14}, {15,  16,  17} },
        { {18,  19,  20}, {21,  22,  23} } };
```

Arrays of structures may be initialized analogously:

```
struct {int a; float b;} a[3] = { {1,   2.5},
                                  {2,   3.9},
                                  {0,  -4.0} };
```

Static and external arrays may always be initialized in this way. The original definition of C stated that automatic arrays could not be initialized, but some newer compilers are relaxing this restriction. (The compiler generates a sequence of assignments to initialize the elements of the automatic array at run time.)

Array initialization has a number of special rules. First, the number of initializers may be less than the number of array elements, in which case the remaining elements are initialized to zero. That is, the initializations

```
int ary[5] = { 1, 2, 3 };
int mat[3][3] = { {1, 2}, {3} };
```

are equivalent to

```
int ary[5] = { 1, 2, 3, 0, 0 };
int mat[3][3] = { {1, 2, 0},
                  {3, 0, 0},
                  {0, 0, 0} };
```

If the number of initializers is greater than the number of elements, the initializer is in error.

Second, the bounds of the array need not be specified, in which case the bounds are derived from the shape of the initializer. For example,

```
int squares[] = { 0, 1, 4, 9 };
```

is the same as

```
int squares[4] = { 0, 1, 4, 9 };
```

Finally, string literals may be also be used to initialize variables of type "array of char." In this case, the first element of the array is initialized by the first character in the string, and so forth. Space must be left for the terminating '\0'. Thus, the initializations

```
static char x[5]  = "ABCD";
static char str[] = "ABCDEF";
```

are the same as

```
static char x[5] = { 'A', 'B', 'C', 'D', '\0' };
static char str[7] = { 'A','B','C','D','E','F','\0' };
```

Finally, a list of strings can be used to initialize an array of character pointers:

```
char *astr[] = { "John", "Bill", "Susan", "Mary" };
```

References   array types 5.5; character constants 2.7.3; character type 5.2.3; pointer types 5.4; string constants 2.7.4

4.6.5 Enumerations

The form of initializers for variables of enumeration type *E* is

declarator = expression

where the expression is of the same enumeration type *E*. Some compilers will tolerate braces around the initialization expression, just as for integer initializers, but they are not necessary. We recommend that braces not be used in this situation, but be reserved to indicate aggregate initialization.

An initializer for a static or external variable of type *E* must be a constant expression of type *E*; that is, it must be an enumeration constant of type *E*. An initializer for an automatic or register variable of type *E* can be any expression of type *E*, which in practice means that it can be either an enumeration constant or an enumeration variable of the same type. For example:

```
static enum E { a, b, c } x = a;
auto enum E y = x;
```

Section 5.6 mentions that some compilers treat enumeration types as integer types. Those compilers will allow initializers for enumeration variables to be integer expressions as well as expressions of enumeration types. (More generally, an initializer should be legitimate in a given implementation if an equivalent assignment statement would be; the same conversions are performed.) However, we recommend adhering to the stricter rules as a matter of good style, and using explicit casts where conversions are needed.

References   cast expressions 7.4.1; constant expressions 7.10; enumeration types 5.6; usual assignment conversions 6.11

4.6.6 Structures

If a structure type T has n components of types T_j (for $j = 1, \ldots, n$) and if I_j is an initializer for type T_j then

$$\{ \; I_1, \; I_2, \; \ldots, \; I_n \; \}$$

is an initializer for type T.

Static and external variables of structure types can be initialized, and the component initializers must be legal initializers for static or external variables of the component types. (In principle bit fields may be initialized, too. However, a few implementations do not support this, or have otherwise peculiar and nonstandard rules for handling structure initializers.) Automatic and register variables of structure types cannot be initialized.

```
struct S {int a; char b[5]; double c; };
struct S x = { 1, "abcd", 45.0 };
```

As with array initializers, structure initializers have some special rules. In particular, if there are fewer initializers than there are structure components, the remaining components are initialized to zero. Thus, given the structure declaration

```
struct S1 {int a;
           struct S2 {double b;
                      char c; } b;
           int c[4]; };
```

the initialization

```
struct S1 x = { 1, {4.5} };
```

is the same as

```
struct S1 x = { 1,
                { 4.5, '\0' },
                { 0, 0, 0, 0 }
              };
```

If there are too many initializers for the structure, it is an error.

References   bit fields 5.7.4; constant expressions 7.10; structure types 5.7

4.6.7 Unions

The C language does not permit initialization of any variables of union type, on the grounds that there is no obvious way in the language to specify which union component is being initialized.

However, some compilers allow the initialization of union variables, treating them as if they were variables of the type of the first component. For instance,

```
enum Greek { alpha, beta, gamma };
union U {
    struct { enum Greek tag; int Size; } I;
    struct { enum Greek tag; float Size; } F;
    };
static union U x = { alpha, 42 };
```

The compilers that permit such initializations may restrict them to static and external variables.

References   static extent 4.2.7; union types 5.8

4.6.8 Other Types

The only other types are function types and `void`, neither of which can have initializers.

4.6.9 Eliding Braces

C permits braces to be dropped from initializer lists under certain circumstances, although it is usually clearer to retain them. The general rules are these:

1. If a variable of array or structure type is being initialized, the outermost pair of braces may not be dropped.
2. Otherwise, if an initializer list contains the correct number of elements for the object being initialized, the braces may be dropped.

The most common use of these rules is in dropping inner braces when initializing a multidimensional array:

```
int matrix[2][3] = { 1, 2, 3, 4, 5, 6 };
        /* same as { {1, 2, 3}, {4, 5, 6} } */
```

Many C compilers treat initializer lists very casually, permitting too many or too few braces. We advise keeping initializers simple and using braces to make their structure explicit.

4.7 IMPLICIT DECLARATIONS

In C it is permitted to call an external function that has not been declared previously. If the compiler sees an identifier *id* followed by a left parenthesis, and if *id* has not been previously declared, then a declaration is implicitly entered at the top level. For example, consider this program fragment:

```
void process()
{
    ... f(i, j) ...
}
```

If f has not been declared, the compiler implicitly inserts a declaration

```
extern int f();
```

immediately before the process function definition.

Allowing functions to be declared in this way is hazardous to program portability. In particular, we've been bitten by the following sequence of events. A pointer-returning function, such as malloc (section 11.4.5), is allowed to be implicitly declared as

```
extern int malloc();
```

rather than the correct

```
extern char *malloc();
```

The program works fine because the compiler and computer being used happen to allocate the same size storage to the int type as to pointer types, and the compiler automatically converts between integer and pointer types. (This is normal in older C compilers.) One day the program is moved to another computer and compiler, under which pointers occupy four bytes and type int only two bytes. When the compiler sees

```
char *p;
...
p = malloc();
```

it generates code to zero-extend the (presumably two-byte) value returned by `malloc` to the four bytes required by the pointer. The compiler issues no warning, and only the low half of the address returned by `malloc` is assigned to p. All of a sudden the program doesn't work.

4.8 EXTERNAL NAMES

An important issue with external names is ensuring consistency among the declarations of the same external name in several files. For instance, what if two declarations of the same external variable specified different initializations? For this and other reasons, it is useful to distinguish a single *defining declaration* of an external name within a group of files. The other declarations of the same name are then considered *referencing declarations*; that is, they reference the defining declaration.

It is a well-known deficiency in C that defining and referencing occurrences of external variable declarations are difficult to distinguish. In general, compilers use one of three complicated schemes to determine when a top level declaration is a defining occurrence.

4.8.1 The Omitted-extern Solution

In this scheme, the storage class `extern` must be explicitly included on all referencing declarations and the storage class must be omitted from the (one) defining declaration for each external variable. The defining declaration can include an initializer but it is not required to do so.

This solution is probably the most common one.

4.8.2 The FORTRAN "named COMMON" Solution

This scheme is so named because it is related to the way multiple references to a FORTRAN COMMON block are merged into a single defining occurrence in some FORTRAN implementations.

Both defining and referencing external declarations have storage class `extern`, whether explicitly or by default. Among all the declarations for each external name in all the object files linked together to make the program, only one may have an initializer. At link time, all external declarations for the same identifier (in all C object files) are combined and a single defining occurrence is conjured, not necessarily associated with any particular file. If any declaration specified an initializer, that initializer is used to initialize the data object. (If several declarations did, the results are unpredictable.)

This solution is the most painless for the programmer, the most demanding on system software, and the most likely to lead to confusion on the part of people reading a program. It is hypothesized that the presence of a linker on the PDP-11 that handled these COMMON declarations lured the early C implementors into depending on this capability.

4.8.3 The Initializer Solution

In this scheme, it is the presence of an initializer on an external declaration that signals a defining occurrence, not the presence or absence of the `extern` storage class.   Programmers seem to like this solution least of all because it forces them to write useless initializations.

4.8.4 Mixed Strategies

The Berkeley 4.2BSD UNIX C compiler for the VAX has a mixed strategy:

1. If `extern` is omitted, and an initializer is present, a definition for the symbol is emitted. Having two or more such definitions among all the files comprising a program results in an error at link time or before.
2. If `extern` is omitted, and no initializer is present, a "common" definition (a la FORTRAN) is emitted. Any number of "common" definitions of the same identifier may coexist.
3. If `extern` is present, the declaration is taken to be a reference to a name defined elsewhere. It is illegal for such a declaration to have an initializer. If the identifier so declared is never actually used, the compiler will not issue an external reference to the linker.

4.8.5 Advice

To remain compatible with the largest number of compilers, we recommend following these rules:

1. Have a single definition point (source file) for each external variable; in the defining declaration, omit the `extern` storage class and include an explicit initializer:

   ```
   int errcnt = 0;
   ```

2. In each source file referencing an external variable defined in another module, use the storage class `extern` and do not supply an explicit initializer:

   ```
   extern int errcnt;
   ```

Independent of the defining/referencing distinction, an external name should always be declared with the same type in all files making up a program. The C compiler cannot verify that declarations in different files are consistent in this fashion, and the punishment for inconsistency is erroneous behavior at run time. The lint program, part of UNIX, can check multiple files for consistent declarations.

5

Types

A *type* is a set of *values* and a set of *operations* on those values. For example, the values of an integer type consist of integers in some specified range, and the operations on those values consist of addition, subtraction, inequality tests, and so forth. The values of a floating-point type include numbers represented differently from integers, and a set of different operations: floating-point addition, subtraction, inequality tests, and so forth.

We say a variable or expression "has type *T*" when its values are constrained to the domain of *T*. The types of variables are established by the variable's declaration; the types of expressions are given by the definitions of the expression operators.

The C language provides a large selection of built-in types, including integers of several kinds, floating-point numbers, pointers, enumerations, arrays, structures, unions, and functions. There is also a special "type," `void`, which has no values; it is used to specify functions that return nothing.

It is useful to organize C's types into the categories pictured below.

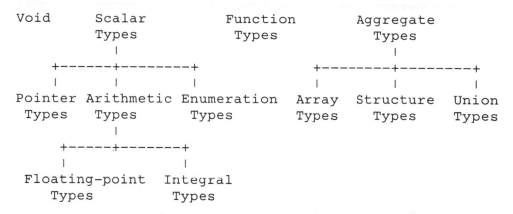

The *void* type has no values and no operations. The term *integral types* includes all forms of integers and characters. The term *arithmetic types* includes the integral and floating-point types. The term *scalar types* includes the arithmetic types, pointer types, and enumeration types. The *function types* are the types "function returning . . . ." *Aggregate types* include arrays, structures, and unions.

All of C's types are discussed in this chapter. For each type, we indicate how objects of the type are declared, the range of values of the type, any restrictions on the size of the type, and what operations are defined on values of the type.

References   array types 5.5; character types 5.2.3; declarations 4.1; enumeration types 5.6; floating types 5.3; function types 5.9; integer types 5.2; pointer types 5.4; structure types 5.7; union types 5.8; void type 5.10

5.1 STORAGE UNITS

In the C language, data types and their representations are closely connected. Most C programmers have an intuitive feel for how types are actually laid out in memory.

All data objects in C are represented at run time in the computer's memory as an integral number of abstract *storage units*. By definition, the *size* of a data object is the number of storage units occupied by that data object. A storage unit is taken to be the amount of storage occupied by one character; the size of an object of type char is therefore 1. (Storage units are sometimes called *bytes*, the name for a character-sized piece of memory in some computers.)

Because all data objects of a given type occupy the same amount of storage, we can also refer to the size of a *type* as the number of storage units occupied by an object of that type. The sizeof operator may be used to determine the size of a data object or type.

We say that a type is "longer" or "larger" than another type if its size is greater. Similarly we say that a type is "shorter" or "smaller" than another type if its size is less.

References   character types 5.2.3; `sizeof` operator 7.4.2

5.2 INTEGER TYPES

C provides a larger number of integer types and operators than do most programming languages. The variety reflects the different word lengths and kinds of arithmetic operators found on most computers, thus allowing a close correspondence between C programs and the underlying hardware. Integer types in C are used to represent:

1. signed or unsigned integer values, for which the usual arithmetic and relational operations are provided
2. bit vectors, with the operations AND, OR, XOR, and left and right shifts
3. boolean values, for which zero is considered "false" and all nonzero values are considered "true," with the integer 1 being the canonical "true" value
4. characters, which are represented by their integer encodings on the computer

It is convenient to divide the integer types into three classes: signed types, unsigned types, and characters. Each of these classes has a set of type specifiers that can be used to declare objects of the type.

> *integer-type-specifier* ::= *signed-type-specifier*
> | *unsigned-type-specifier*
> | *character-type-specifier*

References   assignment conversions 6.11; binary operators 7.5; bitwise and operator '&' 7.5.6; bitwise not operator '~' 7.4.5; bitwise or operator '|' 7.5.8; bitwise xor operator '^' 7.5.7; character constants 2.7.3; constant expressions 7.10; declarations 4.1; integer constants 2.7.1; relational operators 7.5.4, 7.5.5; shift operators '<<' and '>>' 7.5.3; unary minus operator '−' 7.4.3

5.2.1 Signed Integer Types

C provides the programmer with three sizes of signed integer types, denoted by the type specifiers `short`, `int`, and `long` in nondecreasing order of size.

> *signed-type-specifier* ::= `short` { `int` }?
> | `int`
> | `long` { `int` }?

The specifier `short int` is equivalent to `short` and the specifier `long int` is equivalent to `long`. Here are some examples of typical declarations of signed integers.

```
auto short i, j;
long int l;
static int k;
```

The type `int` may not be shorter than `short` and `long` may not be shorter than `int`. However, it is permitted in principle for `short` and `int` to be the same size or for `int` and `long` to be the same size. On a computer which cannot easily address memory smaller than a word, the implementor might even choose to use a single word for all three types.

The implementor's selection of representations for signed integer types is determined by what natural representations are provided by the underlying hardware, by what signed and unsigned arithmetic operators are provided, and so on. Many implementations represent characters in eight bits, short integers in 16 bits, and long integers in 32 bits, with ordinary integers being either 16 or 32 bits wide, whichever leads to greater efficiency. These particular widths technically are not specified by the C language but have become traditional; many programmers expect characters to be eight bits wide and all other integers to be at least 16 bits wide. Certainly there are many existing C programs that depend on this.

The C programmer must constantly make decisions as to which signed integer type to use for a given purpose. There are three considerations: the range of integer values required by the program, the amount of storage that may be consumed, and the speed of the program. The only way to judge these trade-offs is to check your compiler documentation, but the following general rules seem to apply for the larger computers and for all microprocessors except the small 8-bit ones.

1. The `short` type is likely to be represented in 16 or more bits. If this size is sufficient, `short` may be used for large integer arrays in order to save space. However, because C converts all `short` values to `int` in arithmetic expressions, in most cases it usually doesn't make much sense to use `short` for individual variables.

2. The `long` type is likely to be represented in at least 32 bits. It gives the largest range of signed integer values available. Operations on objects of type `long` are sometimes slower than operations on objects of type `int`, depending on the implementation.

3. The `int` type is traditionally the "standard" integer in C, and operations on it are likely to be efficient. However, it is also the type whose size is least predictable, being represented with 32 bits or more by some compilers and with only 16 bits by others. Because of this, the use of `int` is often a source of portability problems. A good rule of thumb is that `long`

is the largest *supported* integer size, while `int` is the largest *efficient* integer size. If efficiency is much more important than portability, then the `int` type may be the better one to use.

The precise range of values representable by a signed integer type may depend not only on the number of bits used in the representation but also on the encoding technique. The expectation is that on a computer using two's-complement arithmetic, a signed integer represented with n bits will have a range from -2^{n-1} through $2^{n-1}-1$. On a computer using one's-complement or sign-magnitude representations, however, the lower bound will be $-(2^{n-1}-1)$.

A useful technique for maximizing portability is to define and use your own integer types based on the range of integers needed by your application. Each of your types can then be defined in terms of one of the standard integer types depending upon the particular computer being used. For example, suppose you are writing an inventory control program and have need of integers that will be part numbers, order quantities, and purchase-order numbers. Depending on the sizes of the numbers, and the sizes of the integer types on the computer, you might want to use `short`, `int`, or `long` to represent part numbers. The solution is to use a single definition file, say `invdef.h`, to define your own integer types.

```
/* invdef.h
   Inventory definitions for the XXX computer.
*/
typedef short  part_number;
typedef int    order_quantity;
typedef long   purchase_order;
```

The source files that define processing functions would use the types defined by `invdef.h`:

```
#include "invdef.h"

purchase_order back_order(part, number)
   part_number part;
   order_quantity number;
/*
   Abstract        Make an order for 'number' units
                   of 'part'. Return the purchase
                   order number.
*/
{
     . . .
}
```

In addition to making the program more readable, this technique makes it possible to adapt to different computers with different integer sizes by changing the definitions in only one file.

References   declarations 4.1; integer constants 2.7.1; type conversions 6; `typedef` 5.11

5.2.2 Unsigned Integer Types

Unsigned integer types have values that range from 0 to some maximum that depends on the size of the type. This maximum is always one less than a power of two; that is, 2^n-1 where n is the number of bits used to represent the unsigned type.

An unsigned type occupies the same amount of storage as the corresponding signed type, but the bit patterns are interpreted differently. On a two's-complement computer, for instance, a 16-bit word with all bits equal to 1 has the value -1 when treated as a signed integer, and has the value 65,535 when treated as an unsigned integer. (The largest signed integer in the same word would be 32,767.)

The original definition of C provided a single unsigned integer type, `unsigned`. However, some compilers now provide an unsigned type corresponding to each signed integer type described in section 5.2.1. The unsigned type is specified by preceding the corresponding signed type specifier with the keyword `unsigned`.

> *unsigned-type-specifier* ::= `unsigned short` { `int` }?
> | `unsigned` { `int` }?
> | `unsigned long` { `int` }?

In each case the keyword `int` is optional and does not affect the meaning of the type specifier. Choosing among the unsigned types involves the same considerations already discussed with respect to the signed integer types.

No matter what representation is used for signed integers, an unsigned integer represented with n bits is always considered to be in straight unsigned binary notation, with values ranging from 0 through 2^n-1. Therefore, the bit pattern for a given unsigned value is predictable and portable, whereas the bit pattern for a given signed value is not predictable and not portable.

Whether an integer is signed or unsigned affects the operations performed on it. All arithmetic operations on unsigned integers behave according to the rules of modular (congruence) arithmetic mod 2^n. So, for example, adding 1 to the largest value of an unsigned type is guaranteed to produce 0.

Expressions that mix signed and unsigned integers are forced to use unsigned operations. Section 6.13 discusses the conversions performed, and chapter 7 discusses the effect of each operator when its arguments are unsigned. These conversions can be surprising. For example, because unsigned integers are always nonnegative, you would expect that the following test would always be "true":

```
unsigned int u;
...
if (u > -1) ...
```

However, it is always "false"! The (signed) -1 is converted to an unsigned integer before the comparison, yielding the largest unsigned integer, and the value of u cannot be greater than that integer.

References   conversions between integers 6.3; integer constants 2.7.1; signed integer types 5.2.1

5.2.3 Character Type

The character type in C is an integral type; that is, values of the type are integers and can be used in integer expressions.

character-type-specifier ::= { unsigned }? char

The character type has some special characteristics that sets it apart from the normal signed and unsigned types. Its representation is implementation dependent and will depend upon the nature of the character and string processing facilities on the target computer. An array of characters is C's notion of a "string." Typical declarations involving characters are:

```
static char greeting[7] = "Hello\n";
char *prompt;
auto char ch = '\0';
```

One thing that is uncertain about the char type is whether it is signed or unsigned. A C compiler is free to treat it either way, although the values of the characters in the standard character set (section 2.1) are always guaranteed to have nonnegative values. The choice is usually dictated by the computer, which may or may not sign-extend characters when the characters are stored into larger integers.

The signedness of characters is an important issue because the standard I/O library routines, which normally return characters from files, return -1 (conventionally named EOF) when the end of the file is reached. To guard against unsigned characters, the programmer must always treat these functions as returning values of type int. For example, the following program is intended to copy characters from the standard input stream to the standard output stream until an end-of-file indication is returned from getchar. The first three definitions are usually supplied in the standard header file stdio.h.

```
extern int getchar();
extern void putchar();
#define EOF -1

void copy_characters()
{
    char ch;                          /* Incorrect! */

    while ((ch = getchar()) != EOF)
        putchar(ch);
}
```

However, this function will not work when `char` is unsigned. To see this, assume the `char` type is represented in eight bits and the `int` type in 16 bits, and that two's-complement arithmetic is used. Then, when `getchar` returns −1, the assignment

```
ch = getchar()
```

assigns the value 255 (the low-order eight bits of −1) to `ch`. (Strictly speaking, the conversion is implementation dependent, but this result is usual.) The loop test is then

```
((unsigned) 255) != -1
```

or, after −1 is converted to an unsigned integer,

```
255 != 65535
```

which evaluates to "true." Thus, the loop never terminates. Changing the declaration of `ch` to

```
int ch;
```

makes everything work fine.

A common C programming technique is to define a "pseudocharacter" type to use in these cases. For example:

```
typedef int character;
...
void copy_characters()
{
    character ch;
    while ((ch = getchar() ) != EOF)
        putchar(ch);
}
```

Now the reader of the program realizes that `ch` is logically a character, although it is represented with type `int`.

An implementation that normally treats characters as signed integers may also provide an "unsigned character" type with the type specifier `unsigned char`. On the other hand, in an implementation that normally treats characters as unsigned integers, there is no way to specify a signed character; the presumption is that if characters could be conveniently implemented as signed quantities, they would have been.

A second area of vagueness about characters is their size. In the above example, we assumed they occupied eight bits, and this assumption is almost always valid (although you still can't be sure if they range from 0 to 255 or from -128 to 127). However, a few computers may use nine bits or even seven bits. This is a problem only when a programmer uses characters (especially arrays of characters) as "very short integers."

It is safe to use character arrays to implement boolean arrays, as in the following example that uses a character array to record whether or not some small integers are prime:

```
static char prime_vector[] =
        {0,0,1,1,0,1,0,1,0,0,0,1,0,1,0,0,0,1,0,1};
int is_prime(n)
   int n;
{
    if ((n > 0) && (n < sizeof(prime_vector)))
        if (prime_vector[n])
            printf("Yes.\n");
        else
            printf("No.\n");
    else
        printf("Don't know.\n");
}
```

References   character constants 2.7.3; character set 2.1; EOF 11.5.1; `getchar` 11.5.21; integer types 5.2; integer conversions 6.3; signed types 5.2.1; unsigned types 5.2.2

5.3 FLOATING-POINT TYPES

C's floating-point numbers (sometimes called "real" numbers) come in two sizes: single and double precision, or `float` and `double`.

> *floating-type-specifier* ::= `float`
> | `long float`
> | `double`

The type name `long float` is a (less popular) synonym for `double`. We recommend that you always use `double` rather than `long float`.

Here are some typical declarations of objects of floating-point type:

```
double d;
static long float pi;
auto float coefficients[10];
    /* "coefficients" is an array of
        floating-point numbers.  */
```

The use of `float` and `double` is analogous to the use of `short` and `int`. Since in expressions all values of type `float` are converted to `double` before any operations are performed (section 6.13), the use of type `float` is mainly restricted to structures and large arrays, for which the savings in storage of the shorter `float` type is important.

C does not dictate the sizes to be used for `float` and `double`. The representations used for floating-point numbers are completely machine dependent. On some computers they may have the same implementation. It is reasonable for the programmer to assume, however, that the precision and range of type `double` is at least as great as for type `float`, and thus that the set of values representable as type `float` is a subset of—possibly the same as—the set of values representable as type `double`.

Most of the arithmetic and logical operations may be applied to floating-point operands. These include arithmetic and logical negation; addition, subtraction, multiplication, and division; relational and equality tests; logical (as opposed to bitwise) AND and OR; assignment; and conversions to and from all the arithmetic types. Chapter 7 discusses the operations in more detail.

There are no requirements about the relative sizes of the floating-point and the integer or pointer types. In the past some C programs have depended on the assumption that the type `double` can accurately represent all values of type `long`; that is, that converting an object of type `long` to type `double` and then back to type `long` results in exactly the original `long` value. While this is likely to be true in many implementations of C, it is not required by the C language definition. For maximum portability of programs, the programmer should avoid depending on this assumption.

References   floating-point constants 2.7.2; floating-point conversions 6.4

5.4 POINTER TYPES

For any type T except `void`, a pointer type "pointer to T" may be formed. A value of this type is the address of an object of type T. The declaration of pointer types is discussed in section 4.5.2. For example, to declare `ip` as a pointer to an object of type `int` and `cp` as a pointer to an object of type `char`, we write

```
int *ip;
char *cp;
```

Pointers are used heavily in C programs, partly because of C's history as a systems programming language and partly because pointers and arrays are so well integrated (section 5.5.1). The two most important operators used in conjunction with pointers are the address operator, '&' (section 7.4.6), and the indirection operator, '*' (section 7.4.7). In the following example, `ip` is assigned the address of variable `i` (`&i`). After that assignment, the expression `*ip` refers to the variable `i`.

```
int i, j, *ip;
ip = &i;
i = 22;
j = *ip;
   /* j now has the value 22 */
*ip = 17;
   /* i now has the value 17 */
```

Every pointer type has a special value, "pointer to nothing," which is written as the integer constant 0. Standard header files usually define the preprocessor macro name NULL to be 0. Recalling that the integer 0 also represents "false" in boolean tests, it is no surprise that pointers may be used in logical comparisons. That is, the statement

```
if (ip) i = *ip;
```

is shorthand for

```
if (ip != NULL) i = *ip;
```

Pointers may also be subscripted as if they were arrays; see section 5.5.1.

References   address operator '&' 7.4.6; array types 5.5; `if` statement 8.5; indirection operator '*' 7.4.7; logical operators 7.6; pointer declarators 4.5.2

5.4.1 Pointer Arithmetic

A convenient feature of C is its provision for performing arithmetic on pointers. If p is an expression of type "pointer to T" and i is an integer value, then the expression

$$p + i$$

is defined to be a pointer to the ith object of type T beyond the one pointed to by *p*. Thinking in terms of computer addresses, the integer *i* must be multiplied by the size of type *T* and then added to *p* to arrive at a new address.

As a more concrete example, suppose we are on a computer that is byte addressable and on which the type `int` is allocated four bytes. Let a be an array of ten integers that begins at address `0x100000`. Let `ip` be a pointer to an integer, and assign to it the address of the first element of array a. Finally, let `i` be an integer variable currently holding the value 6. We now have the following situation:

```
int *ip, i, a[10];
ip = &a[0];
i = 6;
```

What is the value of `ip+i`? Because integers are four bytes long, the expression `ip+i` becomes

```
0x100000 + 4*6
```

or `0x100018` (24 is 18 in hexadecimal radix).

Other operations on pointer types include assignment; subtraction; relational and equality tests; logical (as opposed to bitwise) AND and OR; addition and subtraction of integers; and conversions to and from integers and other pointer types.

References   addition operator 7.5.2; assignment operators 7.8; conversions to pointers 6.7; logical operators 7.6; relational operators 7.5.4, 7.5.5; subtraction operator 7.5.2

5.4.2 Some Problems with Pointers

This section will be of interest primarily to compiler writers and advanced programmers. There is a subtle assumption in C that all pointer types (actually, all addresses) have a uniform representation. For instance, on byte-addressed computers it is usual for all pointers to be simple byte addresses occupying, say, one word. Except for alignment considerations, conversions between pointer types—and between pointers and integers—require no change in representation. When executing C programs on such computers, the C programmer will not usually encounter problems.

On some word-oriented computers, however, pointers to characters must be represented by special "field pointers" which have a different format from addresses of larger objects. On the DECSYSTEM-20 computer, for instance, a character pointer may have some high-order bits set in the address—bits that are 0 in other pointer types. As a consequence:

1. Converting from character pointers to other pointer types involves a change of representation.
2. Comparisons of pointers of different types cannot be implemented as

simple integer comparisions.

3. Conversions between integers and pointers may produce surprising results.

This problem can be even worse on computers with a capability-based address-ing structure.

A relatively common problem with some microprocessors is the presence of both short and long address formats. In order to handle the general case, the C implementor must use the longer and less efficient address form everywhere or must extend the language to allow the programmer to specify when the shorter addresses are being used.

Whatever representations are chosen for pointers, they should satisfy the following criterion, which many C programs heavily depend on (especially those that use the library function malloc): If the alignment requirement for type P is no more stringent than that for type Q, it should always be possible to cast a "pointer to Q" to a "pointer to P" and back, without losing information. For example, on a computer that requires every object of type double to have an address that is a multiple of eight characters and requires every object of type int to have an address that is a multiple of four characters, it should be pos-sible to cast a "pointer to double" to be a "pointer to int" and then back to "pointer to double" and get back the original pointer. The most important consequence is that a pointer of type "pointer to character" should be capable of holding the equivalent of a pointer to any other type without loss of infor-mation.

The programmer should always use explicit casts when converting between pointer types, and should be especially careful that pointer arguments given to functions have the correct type expected by the function.

References   cast expressions 7.4.1; conversions to pointer types 6.7; malloc function 11.4.5

5.5 ARRAY TYPES

If T is any C type except void or "function returning . . . ," the array type "array of T" may be declared. Values of this type are sequences of elements of type T. All C arrays are 0-origin; for example, the array declared

```
int A[3];
```

consists of the elements A[0], A[1], and A[2]. In the following example, an array of integers (ints) and an array of pointers (ptrs) are declared, and the each of the pointers in ptrs is set equal to the address of the corresponding integer in ints.

```
int ints[10], *ptrs[10], i;
for (i = 0; i < 10; i++)
    ptrs[i] = &ints[i];
```

The size of an array is always equal to the length of the array in elements multiplied by the size of an element.

References   array declarators 4.5.3; storage units 5.1

5.5.1 Arrays and Pointers

In C there is a close correspondence between types "array of T" and "pointer to T." First, when an array identifier appears in an expression, the type of the identifier is converted from "array of T" to "pointer to T," and the value of the identifier is converted to a pointer to the first (zeroth) element of the array. Thus, in

```
int a[10], *ip;
ip = a;
```

the value a is converted to a pointer to the first element of the array. It is exactly as if we had written

```
ip = &a[0];
```

This rule is one of the usual unary conversions. The only exception to this conversion rule is when the array identifier is used as an operand of the sizeof operator, in which case sizeof returns the size of the entire array, not the size of a pointer to the first array element.

Second, array subscripting is defined in terms of pointer arithmetic. That is, the expression

```
a[i]
```

is defined to be the same as

```
*((a) + (i))
```

which is to say the same as

```
*(&(a)[0] + (i))
```

when a is an array. This equivalence means also that pointers may be subscripted; it is up to the programmer to ensure that the pointer is pointing into an appropriate array of elements:

```
*dp;
```

```
;
```

address operator '&' 7.4.6; addition operator '+' 7.5.2; array declarators 4.5.3; 6.12; indirection operator '*' 7.4.7; pointer types 5.4; subscripting '[ ]' 7.3.4; ıns 6.12

ıensional Arrays

Multidimensional arrays are declared as "arrays of arrays," such as in the declaration

```
int matrix[10][10];
```

which declares matrix to be a 10-by-10 element array of int. The language places no limit on the number of dimensions an array may have.

Multidimensional arrays are stored such that the last subscript varies most rapidly. That is, the elements of the array

```
int t[2][3];
```

are stored (in increasing addresses) as

```
t[0][0],t[0][1],t[0][2],t[1][0],t[1][1],t[1][2]
```

The conversions of arrays to pointers happens analogously for multidimensional arrays. For example, if t is a 2-by-3 array as defined above, then the expression t[1][2] is expanded to

```
*(*(t+1)+2)
```

which is evaluated as follows:

t	a 2-by-3 array, which is converted immediately to a pointer to (the first) 3-element array
t+1	a pointer to (the second) 3-element array
*(t+1)	(the second) 3-element array of int, which is immediately converted to a pointer to (the first) int (in the second 3-element array)
*(t+1)+2	a pointer to (the third) int (in the second 3-element array)
((t+1)+2)	(the third) int (in the second 3-element array)

In general, any expression A of type "i-by-j-by- . . . -by-k array of T" is immediately converted to "pointer to j-by- . . . -by-k array of T."

References   addition operator '+' 7.5.2; array declarators 4.5.3; indirection operator '*' 7.4.7; pointer types 5.4; subscripting 7.3.4

5.5.3 Array Bounds

Any time that storage for an array is allocated, the size of the array must be known. However, because subscripts are not normally checked to lie within declared array bounds, it is possible to omit the size when declaring an external, singly dimensioned array defined in another module or when declaring a singly dimensioned array that is a formal parameter to a function. (See section 4.5.3.) For instance, the following function, sum, returns the sum of the first n elements of an external array, a, whose bounds are not specified.

```
extern int a[];

int sum(n)
  int n;
{
    int i, s = 0;
    for (i = 0; i < n; i++)
      s += a[i];
    return s;
}
```

When multidimensional arrays are used, it is necessary to specify the bounds of all but the first dimension, so that the proper address arithmetic can be calculated.

```
extern int matrix[][10]; /* ?-by-10 array of int */
```

If such bounds are not specified, the declaration is in error.

References   array declarators 4.5.3; defining and referencing declarations 4.8; indirection operator '*' 7.4.7; pointer types 5.4; subscripting 7.3.4;

5.5.4 Operations

The only operation that can be performed directly on an array value is the application of the sizeof operator. The array must be bounded. The result of such an operation is the number of storage units occupied by the array. For an n-element array of type T, the result of the sizeof operator is always equal to n times the result of sizeof applied to the type T.

In all other contexts, such as subscripting, the array value is actually treated as a pointer, and so operations on pointers may be applied to the array value.

References   array declarators 4.5.3; conversions from array to pointer 6.7.3; pointer types 5.4; `sizeof` operator 7.4.2; subscripting 7.3.4;

5.6 ENUMERATION TYPES

Enumeration types are a recent addition to C, and similar concepts occur in other languages, such as Pascal and Ada. Unfortunately, not all C compilers implement enumerations, and those that do are not all consistent in their implementations. We'll start by describing the aspects of enumerations on which everyone seems to agree.

An enumeration type in C is a set of values represented by identifiers called *enumeration constants*. The enumeration constants are specified when the type is defined. For example, the declaration

```
enum fish { trout, carp, halibut }
                    my_fish, your_fish;
```

creates a new enumeration type "enum fish," whose values are `trout`, `carp`, and `halibut`. It also declares two variables of the enumeration type, `my_fish` and `your_fish`, which can be assigned values with the assignments

```
my_fish = halibut;
your_fish = trout;
```

In addition to assigning values of enumeration types, the programmer can test two values for equality.

It happens that C's enumeration types are implemented by associating integer values with the enumeration constants, so that the assignment and comparison of values of enumeration types can be implemented as integer assignment and comparison. These integers are normally chosen automatically, but they can be specified by the programmer in the type definition:

```
enum fish { trout=1, carp=0,
            halibut=10 } my_fish, your_fish;
```

The integers chosen determine the equality and ordering relationships among values of the enumeration type. We will say more about this later.

Here is the general syntax for declaring and using enumeration types:

enumeration-type-specifier ::= *enumeration-type-definition*
                    | *enumeration-type-reference*

enumeration-type-definition ::= enum { *enumeration-tag* }?
                    '{' *enumeration-definition-list* '}'

enumeration-type-reference ::= enum *enumeration-tag*

enumeration-tag ::= *identifier*

enumeration-definition-list ::= { *enumeration-constant-definition* # ',' } +

enumeration-constant-definition ::= *enumeration-constant* { '=' *expression* } ?

enumeration-constant ::= *identifier*

Each occurrence of a type specifier that is an enumeration type definition introduces a new enumeration type, different from all other enumeration types. Variables or other objects of the enumeration type can be declared in the same declaration containing the enumeration type definition or in a subsequent declaration that mentions the enumeration type with an "enumeration type reference." For example, the single declaration

```
enum color { red, blue, green, mauve }
  favorite, acceptable, least_favorite;
```

is exactly equivalent to the two declarations

```
enum color { red, blue, green, mauve } favorite;
enum color acceptable, least_favorite;
```

and to the four declarations

```
enum color { red, blue, green, mauve };
enum color favorite;
enum color acceptable;
enum color least_favorite;
```

The enumeration tag, color, allows an enumeration type to be referenced after its definition. Although the declaration

```
enum { red, blue, green, mauve }
     favorite, acceptable, least_favorite;
```

defines the same type and declares the same variables, the lack of an enumeration tag makes it impossible to introduce more variables of the type in later declarations. Enumeration tags are in the same overloading class as structure and union tags, and their scope is the same as that of a variable declared at the same location in the source program.

Identifiers defined as enumeration constants are members of the same overloading class as variables, functions, and typedef names. Their scope is the same as that of a variable defined at the same location in the source program. In the following example, the declaration of `shepherd` as an enumeration constant hides the previous declaration of the integer variable `shepherd`. However, the declaration of the floating-point variable `collie` will cause a compilation error, because `collie` is already declared in the same scope as an enumeration constant.

```
int shepherd = 12;
{
    enum dog_breeds {shepherd, collie};
                        /* Hides outer declaration of
                           the name "shepherd" */
    float collie;    /* Illegal redefinition of
                        the name "collie" */
}
```

The size of an enumeration type is generally same as the size of type `int`, although some implementations leave open the possibility of using `short` or `long` depending on the size of the enumeration type. Integer values are associated with enumeration constants in the following way:

1. An explicit integer value may be associated with an enumeration constant by writing

   enumeration-constant = expression

   in the type definition. The expression must be a constant expression of integral type, although some compilers may also allow expressions involving previously defined enumeration constants, as in

   ```
   enum boys { Bill = 10, John = Bill+2,
               Fred = John+2 };
   ```

2. The first enumeration constant receives the value 0 if no explicit value is specified.
3. Subsequent enumeration constants without explicit associations receive an integer value one greater than the value associated with the previous enumeration constant.

For example, given the declaration

```
enum sizes { small, medium=10, pretty_big, large=20 };
```

the values of `small`, `medium`, `pretty_big`, and `large` will be 0, 10, 11, and 20, respectively.

Any signed integer value representable as type `int` may be associated with an enumeration constant. Positive and negative integers may be chosen at random, and it is even possible to associate the same integer with two different enumeration constants. For instance, the following definition is legal

```
enum people { john=1, mary=19, bill=-4, sheila=1 };
```

but then the expression

```
john == sheila
```

is "true," which is not intuitive.

References   identifiers 2.5; overloading classes 4.2.4; scope 4.2.1; structure tags 5.7; union tags 5.8

5.6.1 Detailed Semantics

Enumerations, being a recent addition to C, have not been implemented consistently by all compilers. Some compilers, including the AT&T's UNIX System V compiler, consider all enumeration types to be synonyms for the type `int`. Enumeration constants, integer constants, enumeration variables, and integer variables may be freely mixed in all integer expressions. These rules effectively reduce enumeration types to a means of defining integer constants. We refer to this as the *integer model* for enumerations.

A second implementation of enumerations treats each enumeration type definition as introducing a new and distinct data type. When an enumeration constant name appears in an expression, its type is the enumeration type in which it was defined. No mixing between different enumeration types or between enumerations and integers is possible without explicit casts. We refer to this as the *structure model* for enumerations, because the set of permissible operations is close to the set of operations allowed on structure types. (Exception: values of the same enumeration type can be compared for equality.)

The third, and—to us—most natural, model is the *pointer model* for enumerations. In this model, enumerations and integers can be mixed in the same ways as pointers and integers. This permits the use of the '++' and '−−' operators to iterate over enumerations. Equality and inequality tests are also permitted. The only difficulty with this model is the interpretation of "the next enumeration value." For example, let x be an object of enumeration type E:

```
enum E { a=0, b=4, c=8 } x = a;
```

If x presently has the value a (that is, 0), what is the value of x after the execution of x++? Is it the "next" enumeration value, b, or is it the "nonexistent" enumeration element represented by the integer 1? To properly compute the "next" enumeration value in all cases would require a table of values at run time, and therefore it is more in keeping with the spirit of C to implement x+1 as simple integer addition of 1.

Most compilers implementing enumerations allow them to be used as integers. Some compilers will issue warnings when the programmer mixes enumerations and integers, but will do "the obvious thing" anyway.

References   addition operator '+' 7.5.2; casts 7.4.1; decrement operator '--' 7.4.11; equality operator '==' 7.5.5; increment operator '++' 7.4.9; integer types 5.2; pointer types 5.4; structure type 5.7

5.7 STRUCTURE TYPES

The structure types in C are similar to the types known as "records" in other programming languages. They are collections of named *components* (also called "members" or "fields") that can have different types. One way of looking at structures is that they allow the programmer to create *abstract data types*. Structures can be defined to encapsulate related data objects—the values of the abstract type—and functions can be written to manipulate the values—the operations on the type.

For example, a programmer who wanted to implement complex numbers might define a structure complex to hold the real and imaginary parts as components real and imag. The first declaration below defines the new type, and the second declares two variables, x and y, of that type:

```
struct complex {
    double real;
    double imag;
};
struct complex x, y;
```

A function new_complex can be written to create a new object of the type. Note that the selection operator '.' is used to access the components of the structure.

```
struct complex  new_complex(r, i)
  double r, i;
{
    struct complex new;
    new.real = r;
    new.imag = i;
    return new;
}
```

Operations on the type, such as complex_multiply, can also be defined:

```
struct complex  complex_multiply(a, b)
  struct complex a,b;
{
  struct complex product;
  product.real=(a.real * b.real - a.imag * b.imag);
  product.imag=(a.real * b.imag + a.imag * b.real);
  return product;
}
```

Here is the general syntax for structure declarations:

structure-type-specifier ::= *structure-type-definition*
                     | *structure-type-reference*

structure-type-definition ::= struct { *structure-tag* }? '{' *field list* '}'

structure-type-reference ::= struct *structure-tag*

structure-tag ::= *identifier*

component-declaration-list ::= { *component-declaration* ';' }+

component-declaration ::= *type-specifier component-declarator-list* ';'

component-declarator-list ::= { *component-declarator* # ',' }+

component-declarator ::= *simple-component*
                     | *bit field*

simple-component ::= *declarator*

bit-field ::= { *declarator* }? ':' *width*

width ::= *expression*

Each structure type definition introduces a new structure type, different from all others. If present in the definition, the structure tag is associated with the new type and can be used in a subsequent structure type reference. For instance, the single declaration

```
struct complex { double real, imag; } x, y;
```

is equivalent to the two declarations

```
struct complex { double real, imag; };
struct complex x, y;
```

In order to handle the case of two structures containing pointers to each other, C allows a structure type reference to precede the corresponding structure type definition (provided the reference occurs in a context where the size of the structure is not required). For example:

```
struct P { struct Q *pq; };
struct Q { struct P *pp; };
```

However, this feature should be used cautiously. In a modification of the previous example, the same two structure definitions have a different effect:

```
struct Q { int a, b; };
...
{
    struct P { struct Q *pq; };
    struct Q { struct P *pp; };
    ...
}
```

Structure P will now have as its component pq a pointer to the structure Q defined in the outer block. This is an instance of "duplicate visibility" of tag Q.

References   declarations 4.1; declarators 4.5; duplicate visibility 4.2.6; scope 4.2.1; selection operator '.' 7.3.5 type equivalence 5.12

5.7.1 Operations on Structures

The operations provided for structures may vary from compiler to compiler. All C compilers provide the selection operators '.' and '->' on structures, and newer compilers now allow structures to be assigned, to be passed as parameters to functions, and to be returned from functions. (With older compilers, assignment must be done component by component, and only pointers to structures may be passed to and from functions.)

It is not permitted to compare two structures for equality. An object of a structure type is a sequence of components of other types. Because certain data objects may be constrained by the target computer to lie on certain addressing boundaries, a structure object may contain "holes," storage units that do not belong to any component of the structure. The holes would make equality tests implemented as a wholesale bit-by-bit comparison unreliable, and component-by-component equality tests would be too expensive. (Of course, the programmer may write component-by-component equality functions.)

In any situation where it is permitted to apply the unary address operator '&' to a structure to obtain a pointer to the structure, it is also permitted to apply the operator to a component of the structure to obtain a pointer to the component; that is, it is possible for a pointer to point into the middle of a structure. An exception to this rule occurs with components defined to be bit fields. Components defined as bit fields will in general not lie on machine-addressable boundaries, and therefore it may not be possible to form a pointer to a bit field. The C language therefore forbids such pointers.

References   address operator 7.4.6; assignment 7.8; bit fields 5.7.4; equality operator '=='
7.5.5; selection operatord '.' and '->' 7.3.5; type equivalence 5.12; type tags 5.12.2

5.7.2 *Components*

A component of a structure may have any type except "function returning . . ." and `void`. Structures may not contain instances of themselves, although they may contain pointers to instances of themselves. That is,

```
struct S {
    int a;
    struct S next;   /* illegal! */
};
```

is illegal, but

```
struct S {
    int a;
    struct S *next;
};
```

is permitted.

The names of structure components are defined in a special overloading class associated with the structure type. That is, component names within a single structure must be distinct, but they may be the same as component names in other structures and may be the same as variable, function, and type names. For example, consider the following sequence of declarations:

```
int x;
struct A { int x; double y; } y;
struct B { int y; double x; } z;
```

The identifier x has three nonconflicting declarations: it is an integer variable, an (integer) component of structure A, and a (floating-point) component of structure B. These three declarations are used, respectively, in the expressions

```
x
y.x
z.x
```

If a structure tag is defined in one of the components, as T is in

```
struct S {
    struct T {int a, b; } x;
};
```

the scope of T extends to the end of the block in which structure S is defined. (If S is defined at the top level, so is T.)

A historical note: The original definition of C specified that all components in all structures were allocated out of the same overloading class, and therefore no two structures could have components with the same name. (An exception was made when the components had the same type and the same relative position in the structures.) This interpretation is now anachronistic, but you might see it mentioned in older documentation or actually implemented in some old compilers.

> **References**   overloading classes 4.2.4; scope 4.2.1

5.7.3 Structure Component Layout

Most programmers will be unconcerned with how components are packed into structures. However, C does give the programmer some control over the packing. C compilers are constrained to assign components increasing memory addresses in a strict left-to-right order, with the first component starting at the beginning address of the structure itself. There is no difference in component layout between the structure

```
struct { int a, b, c; };
```

and the structure

```
struct { int a; int b, c; };
```

Both put a first, b second, and c last. In general, given two pointers p and q to components within the same structure, $p < q$ will be true if and only if the declaration of the component that p points to appears earlier within the declaration of the structure type than the declaration of the component that q points to. For example:

```
{
    struct vector3 { int x, y, z; } s;
    int *p, *q, *r;
    . . .
    p = &s.x;
    q = &s.y;
    r = &s.z;
    /* At this point (p < q), (q < r),
        and (p < r) are all true. */
    . . .
}
```

Holes, or padding, may appear between any two consecutive components in the layout of a structure if necessary to allow proper alignment of components in memory. The bit patterns appearing in such holes are unpredictable, and may differ from structure to structure or over time within a single structure.

5.7.4 Bit Fields

C allows the programmer to pack integer components into spaces smaller than the compiler would ordinarily allow. These integer components are called *bit fields* and are specified by following the component declarator with a colon and a constant integer expression that indicates the width of the field in bits:

```
struct S{
    unsigned  a:4;
    unsigned  b:5, c:7;
};
```

The intent is that bit fields should be packed as tightly as possible in a structure, subject to the rules discussed below.

Bit fields are typically used in machine-dependent programs that must force a data structure to correspond to a fixed hardware representation. The precise manner in which components (and especially bit fields) are packed into a structure is implementation dependent but is predictable for each implementation. The use of bit fields is therefore likely to be nonportable. The programmer should consult the implementation documentation if it is necessary to lay out a structure in memory in some particular fashion, and then verify that the C compiler is indeed packing the components in the way expected.

Here is an example of how bit fields can be used to match the format of a 32-bit virtual address.

```
/*      Format of 32-bit virtual address
        for the XBQ-43 computer.
+-+-+---------+----------+-----------------------+
|S|x| Segment |   Page   |        Offset         |
+-+-+---------+----------+-----------------------+
31   29        23         15                  bit 0
*/
/* Note: the XBQ-43 C compiler packs bit fields
                        from right to left. */
typedef struct {
    unsigned offset       : 16;
    unsigned page         : 8;
    unsigned segment      : 6;
    unsigned              : 1;   /* for future use */
    unsigned supervisor : 1;
  } virtual_address;
```

C specifies that no compiler has to allow bit fields of any type except `unsigned`, but some compilers allow signed integer types (that is, sign extension occurs when extracting the contents of the field). There would be no implementation difficulty in allowing enumeration types to be used in bit fields, but few compilers allow it. Use of any type other than `unsigned` for a bit field should therefore be considered even less portable than using bit fields at all.

Compilers are free to impose constraints on the maximum size of a bit field and to specify certain addressing boundaries that bit fields cannot cross. These limits are usually related to the natural word size of the target computer. When a field is too long for the computer, the compiler will issue an appropriate error message. When a field would cross a word boundary, it may be moved to the next word.

The grammar indicates that an unnamed bit field may be included in a structure. The intent is to allow a specific amount of padding space to be inserted into the structure. For instance, the structure

```
struct S {
    unsigned a : 4;
    unsigned   : 2;
    unsigned b : 6;
};
```

indicates that component a is to be allocated the first four bits of the structure, followed by two bits of padding, followed by the component b in six bits. Unnamed bit fields cannot be referenced and their contents at run time are not predictable.

The case of an unnamed bit field of length 0 is a special case. It indicates that the following component should begin on the next boundary appropriate to its type. ("Appropriate" is not specified further.) That is, in the structure

```
struct S {
    unsigned a : 4;
    unsigned   : 0;
    unsigned b : 6;
};
```

the component b should begin on a natural addressing boundary following component a.

The address operator '&' may not be applied to bit-field components, since many computers cannot address arbitrary-sized fields directly.

References   address operator '&' 7.4.6; enumeration types 5.6; signed types 5.2.1; unsigned types 5.2.2

5.7.5 Portability Problems

The use of bit fields is likely to be nonportable and therefore should be restricted to situations in which memory is a scarce resource or in which a hardware-defined data structure must be matched exactly. (In the latter case the program will doubtless be nonportable anyway, so using bit fields doesn't make matters any worse.)

There are several ways in which depending on packing strategies is dangerous. First, computers differ on the alignment constraints on data types. For instance, a four-byte integer on some computers must begin on a byte boundary that is a multiple of four, whereas on other computers the integer can (and will) be aligned on the nearest byte boundary.

Second, the restrictions on bit-field widths will be different. Some computers have a 16-bit word size, which limits the maximum size of the field and imposes a boundary that fields cannot cross. Other computers have a 32-bit word size, and so forth.

Third, computers differ in the way fields are packed into a word. On IBM 370-style computers, characters are packed left to right into words; that is, from the most significant bit to the least significant bit. On DEC VAX computers and many microprocessors, characters are packed right to left; that is, from the least significant bit to the most significant bit.

5.7.6 Sizes of Structures

The size of an object of a structure type is the amount of storage necessary to represent all components of that type, including any unused padding space between or after the components. The rule is that the structure will be padded out to the size the type would occupy as an element of an array of such types.

(For any type T, including structures, the size of an n-element array of T is the same as the size of T times n.) Another way of saying this is that the structure must terminate on the same alignment boundary on which it started; that is, if the structure must begin on an even byte boundary, it must also end on an even byte boundary.

For example, on a computer that starts all structures on an address that is a multiple of four characters, the length of the structure

```
struct S {
    char c1;
    char c2;
};
```

will be four, even though only two characters are actually used.

Note that the alignment requirement for a structure type will be at least as stringent as for the component having the most stringent requirements. For example, on a computer that requires all objects of type `double` to have an address that is a multiple of eight characters, the length of the structure

```
struct S {
    double value;
    char name[10];
};
```

will be 24, even though the components may be allocated contiguously and their total length is 18 units; six extra units of padding are needed to make the size of the structure a multiple of the alignment requirement. (If the padding were not used, then in an array of such structures not all of the structures would have the `value` component aligned properly to a multiple-of-eight address.)

Alignment requirements may cause padding to appear in the middle of a structure. Consider this variation on the previous example in which the two components appear in the other order:

```
struct S {
    char name[10];
    double value;
};
```

The length of this structure will also be 24. After the ten units of storage allocated for the `name` component, six units of padding are required before the `value` component so that the `value` component may be aligned to an address that is a multiple of eight characters relative to the beginning of the structure. Any object of the structure type will be required to have an address that is a multiple of eight, and so the `value` component of such an object will always be properly aligned.

5.8 *UNION TYPES*

C's union type is somewhat like a "variant record" in other languages. Like structures, unions are defined to have a number of components. Unlike structures, however, a union can hold at most one of its components at a time; the components are conceptually overlaid in the storage allocated for the union.

For example, suppose we want an object that can be *either* an integer or a floating-point number, depending on the situation. We can define union datum:

```
union datum {
    int i;
    double d;
};
```

and define a variable of the union type:

```
union datum u;
```

Then, to use the datum to hold an integer, we can say:

```
u.i = 15;
```

To use the datum to hold a floating-point number, we assign to the other component.

```
u.d = 88.9e4;
```

The programmer is responsible for remembering what kind of data is in the union at any one time.

Unions may be used in a portable fashion if certain rules are obeyed. In particular, the only time a component of a union should be referenced is if the last assignment to the union was through the same component. It is *not* portable to assign one union component and then reference another component:

```
union U { long c; double d; } x;
long l;
x.d = 1.0e10;
l = x.c;
```

C provides no way to inquire which component of a union was last assigned. The programmer can encode explicit *data tags* in unions; that is, some indication of which component is stored in the union. The union may be enclosed in a structure that includes a special tag component that is used by programming convention to indicate which component of a union is "active." For example, we might replace the union

```
union widget {
    long count;
    double value;
    char name[30];
  } x;
```

by

```
enum widget_tag { count_widget,
                  value_widget,
                  name_widget };

struct WIDGET {
    enum widget_tag tag;
    union { long count;
            double value;
            char name[30]; } data;
  } x;

/* Make "widget" a name for "struct WIDGET". */
typedef struct WIDGET widget;
```

To assign to the union, the we write either

```
x.tag = count_widget;
x.data.count = 10000;
```

or

```
x.tag = value_widget;
x.data.value = 3.1415926535897932384;
```

or

```
x.tag = name_widget;
strcpy(x.data.name, "Millard Fillmore");
```

Then we can write a portable function that can discriminate among the possibilities for the union, and call the function without regard to which component was last assigned:

```
/* Print a widget, whatever it contains. */
void print_widget(w)
  widget w;
{
    switch(w.tag) {
      case count_widget:
        printf("Count %ld\n", w.data.count);
        break;
      case value_widget:
        printf("Value %f\n", w.data.value);
        break;
      case name_widget:
        printf("Name \"%s\"\n", w.data.name);
        break;
    }
}
```

The general syntax for defining unions is:

union-type-specifier ::= *union-type-definition*
                    | *union-type-reference*

union-type-definition ::= union { *union-tag* }?
                    '{' *component-declaration-list* '}'

union-type-reference ::= union *union-tag*

union-tag ::= *identifier*

The syntax for defining components is the same as that used for structures, except that bit fields are not permitted in unions.

As with structures and enumerations, each union type definition introduces a new union type, different from all others. If present in the definition, the union tag is associated with the new type and can be used in a subsequent union type reference.

A component of a union may have any type except "function returning . . ." and void. Also, unions may not contain instances of themselves, although they may contain pointers to instances of themselves.

As in structures, the names of union components are defined in a special overload class associated with the union type. That is, component names within a single union must be distinct, but they may be the same as component names in other unions and may be the same as variable, function, and type names.

References   enumerations 5.6; overloading 4.2.4; scope 4.2.1; structures 5.7

5.8.1 Union Component Layout

Each component of a union type is allocated storage starting at the beginning of the union. An object of a union type will begin on a storage alignment boundary appropriate for any contained component.

In other words, if we have the following union type and object definitions:

```
static union U {
    ...
    int C;
    ...
} object, *P = &object;
```

then the following equalities hold:

```
(union U *) &(P->C)   ==           P
           &(P->C)   ==   (int *) P
```

Furthermore, these equalities hold no matter what the type of the component C.

5.8.2 Sizes of Unions

The size of an object of a union type is the amount of storage necessary to represent the largest component of that type, plus any padding that may be needed at the end to raise the length up to an appropriate alignment boundary. The rule is that the union will be padded out to the size the type would occupy as an element of an array of such types. (For any type T, including unions, the size of an n-element array of T is the same as the size of T times n.) Another way of saying this is that the structure must terminate on the same alignment boundary on which it started; that is, if the structure had to begin on an even byte boundary, it must end on an even byte boundary.

Note that the alignment requirement for a union type will be at least as stringent as for the component having the most stringent requirements. For example, on a computer that requires all objects of type double to have an address that is a multiple of eight characters, the length of the union

```
union U {
    double value;
    char name[10];
};
```

will be 16, even though the size of the longest component is only 10; six extra units of padding are needed to make the size of the union a multiple of the alignment requirement. (If the padding were not used, then in an array of such unions not all of the unions would have the value component aligned properly to a multiple-of-eight address.)

5.9 *FUNCTION TYPES*

The type "function returning T" is a function type, where T may be any type except "array of . . ." or "function returning . . . ." Said another way, functions may not return arrays or other functions, although they can return pointers to arrays and functions.

Objects of function type may be introduced in only two ways. First, a function *definition* can create a function object, define its parameters and return value, and supply the body of the function. For example, square is an object of function type:

```
int square(x)
   int x;
{
     return x*x;
}
```

More information about function definitions is given in section 9.1.

Second, a function *declaration* can introduce an external reference to a function object defined elsewhere, such as in this definition of square.

```
extern int square();
```

The only operation that can be applied to an expression of function type (aside from the implicit usual unary conversion to "pointer to function") is to call the function. For example, the line

```
extern int f(), (*fp)(), (*apf[])();
```

declares external identifiers f, fp, and apf to have types "function returning int," "pointer to function returning int," and "array of pointers to functions returning int," respectively. These identifiers can be used in function call expressions by writing:

```
int i;
i = f(14);
i = (*fp)(j, k);
i = (*apf[j])(k);
```

When a function is called, certain standard conversions are applied to the actual arguments, but no attempt is made to check the type or number of arguments with the type or number of formal arguments to the function, if known. See section 6.14.

A function identifier can appear by itself—that is, not in the context of a call—but the identifier is immediately converted to the type "pointer to function returning . . . ." For example,

```
extern int f();
int (*fp)();
fp = f;
```

The only expressions that can yield a value of type "function returning *T*" are the name of such a function and an indirection expression consisting of the unary indirection operator '*' applied to an expression of type "pointer to function returning . . . ."

There are only three operations that can be applied to the name of a function:

1. Call the function, by appending to the name a parenthesized, comma-separated list of argument expressions.
2. Use the function name as an actual parameter to another function, in which case a pointer to the function is passed.
3. Assign the function to a variable of the appropriate (pointer) type.

The `sizeof` operator may not be applied to functions.

All the information needed to invoke a function is assumed to be encapsulated in an object of type "pointer to function returning . . . ," which satisfies the normal pointer requirements. Although a pointer to a function is often assumed to point to the function's code in memory, on some computers a function pointer actually points to a block of information needed to invoke the function. Fortunately, such representation issues are normally invisible to the C programmer and need concern only the compiler implementor.

References   function argument conversions 6.14; function call 7.3.6; function definition 9.1; indirection operator '*' 7.4.7; `sizeof` operator 7.4.2; usual unary conversions 6.12

5.10 VOID

The type `void` is a recent addition to C. It has no values and no operations and is used mainly as the return type of a function, signifying that the function returns no value.

void-type-specifier ::= `void`

For example:

```
{
    extern void write_line();
    ...
    write_line();
    ...
}
```

The `void` type may also be used in a cast expression when it is desired to explicitly discard a value. For example:

```
{
    extern int write_line2();   /* returns error
                                       indication */
    ...
    (void) write_line2(...);    /* don't check for
                                       error */
    ...
}
```

Casting the return value to void indicates clearly that the programmer knows that `write_line2` returns a value but chooses to ignore it.

References   casts 7.4.1; discarded expressions 7.12

5.11 TYPEDEF NAMES

When a declaration is written whose "storage class" is `typedef`, the type definition facility is invoked.

typedef-name ::= *identifier*

An identifier enclosed in any declarator of the declaration is defined to be a name for a type (a "typedef name"); the type is that which would have been given the identifier if the declaration were a normal variable declaration. For example, in the declaration

```
typedef int *ptr, (*func)();
```

the name `ptr` is defined to be the type "pointer to int" and the name `func` is defined to be the type "pointer to function returning int."

Once a name has been declared as a type, it may appear anywhere a type specifier is permitted. This is useful because it allows you to create mnemonic abbreviations for complicated types. For example, after writing the above type definitions, we can write

```
ptr link, *indirect_link;
func my_routine, my_vector[10];
```

in which case

`link`	has type "pointer to `int`"
`indirect_link`	
	has type "pointer to pointer to `int`"
`my_routine`	has type "pointer to function returning `int`"
`my_vector`	has type "10-element array of pointers to functions returning `int`"

Typedef declarations do not introduce new types; the names are always considered to be synonyms for types that could be specified in other ways. For instance, after the declaration

```
typedef struct S { int a; int b; } s1type, s2type;
```

the type specifiers `s1type`, `s2type`, and `struct S` can be used interchangeably to refer to the same type.

References   type equivalence 5.12

5.11.1 Redefining Typedef Names

The language specifies that `typedef` names may be redefined in inner blocks in the same fashion as ordinary identifiers:

```
typedef int T;
T foo;
...
{
    float T;
    T = 1.0;
    ...
}
```

However, some compilers have been known to have problems with such redeclarations, probably because of the pressure typedef names put on the C language grammar. We now turn to this problem.

References   scope 4.2.1

5.11.2 *Implementation Note*

Allowing ordinary identifiers, as opposed to reserved words only, as type specifiers makes the C grammar context sensitive, and hence not LALR(1). To see this, consider the program line

```
A ( *B ) ;
```

If A has been defined as a typedef name, then the line is a declaration of a variable B to be of type "pointer to A." (The parentheses surrounding "*B" are ignored.) If A is not a type name, then the line is a call of the function A with the single parameter *B. This ambiguity cannot be resolved grammatically.

C compilers based on UNIX' YACC parser-generator—such as the Portable C Compiler—handle this problem by feeding information acquired during semantic analysis back to the lexer. In fact, most C compilers do some `typedef` analysis during lexical analysis.

5.12 *TYPE EQUIVALENCE*

Several times in the text we say that, for instance, two objects must have the same type. What do we mean?

First of all, two pointer or function types are the same if their elements are the same:

1. Two types "pointer to T" and "pointer to S" are the same only if types T and S are the same.
2. Two types "function returning T" and "function returning S" are the same only if types T and S are the same.

> **References**   array types 5.5; function types 5.9; pointer types 5.4

5.12.1 *Array Types*

Two types "n-element array of T" and "m-element array of S" are the same only if types T and S are the same and $n=m$. A consequence of this is, for instance, that the pointer types "pointer to 10-element array of `int`" and "pointer to 5-element array of `int`" are *not* the same. (Incrementing values of these types will have different effects since the pointer element sizes are different.) However, there are two clarifications to this equivalence rule.

First, in those contexts in which an array's size may be omitted, the size does not participate in computing type equivalence. (If the array is multidimensional, and if the first dimension's size may be omitted, then *only* the first dimension does not participate; the other dimensions must match.) Therefore the two external declarations

```
extern int a[10];
extern int a[];
```

effectively declare a to be of the same type.

Second, in many situations a value of type "*n*-element array of *T*" is converted to a value of type "pointer to *T*." In that case, the rules for pointer type equivalence apply; that is, the size of the array becomes irrelevant.

References   array types 5.5

5.12.2 Enumeration, Structure, and Union Types

Each occurrence of a type specifier that is a structure type definition, union type definition, or enumeration type definition introduces a new structure, union, or enumeration type that is neither the same as nor equivalent to any other type.

A type specifier that is a structure, union, or enumeration type *reference* is the same type introduced in the corresponding *definition*. The type tag is used to associate the reference with the definition, and in that sense the tag may be thought of as the name of the type. Thus, the types of x, y, and u below are all different, but the types of u and v are the same.

```
struct { int a; int b; } x;
struct { int a; int b; } y;
struct S { int a; int b; } u;
struct S v;
```

Historically, tags predate the typedef facility in C, which largely supplants them. The only facility provided by tags that cannot be duplicated with type definitions is recursive references within structures and unions:

```
struct S { int data; struct S *next; };
```

References   enumerations 5.6; structures 5.7; unions 5.8

5.12.3 Typedef Names

Names declared as types in typedef definitions are synonyms for types, not new types. Thus, in the following example, the type my_int is the same as type int, and the type my_function is the same as the type "float *()."

```
typedef int my_int;
typedef float *my_function();
```

In the more complicated example

```
struct S { int a, b; } x;
typedef struct S  t1, t2;
struct S w;
t1 y;
t2 z;
```

the variables w, x, y, and z all have the same type.

References   typedef names 5.11

5.13 TYPE NAMES AND ABSTRACT DECLARATORS

In two situations in C programming, it is necessary to write the name of a type without declaring an object of that type: when writing cast expressions and when applying the sizeof operator applied to a type. In these cases, one uses a *type name* built from an *abstract declarator*. (Don't confuse "type name" with "typedef name" described in section 5.11.)

type-name ::= *type-specifier abstract-declarator*

abstract-declarator ::= *empty-abstract-declarator*
                    | *nonempty abstract-declarator*

empty-abstract-declarator ::=

nonempty-abstract-declarator ::= ' (' *nonempty-abstract-declarator* ') '
                    | *abstract-declarator* ' (' ') '
                    | *abstract-declarator* ' [' { *expression* }? '] '
                    | '*' *abstract-declarator*

An abstract declarator resembles a regular declarator in which the enclosed identifier has been replaced by the empty string. Thus, a type name looks like a declaration from which the enclosed identifier has been omitted.

The precedences of the alternatives of the abstract declarator are the same as in the case of normal declarators. However, to resolve an ambiguity, the form

(*A*)

is permitted only if the abstract declarator *A* is nonempty.

Examples of type names:

```
int         type int
float *     type "pointer to float"
```

```
char (*)()     type "pointer to function returning char"
unsigned *[4]
               type "array of four pointers to unsigned"
int (*(*)())()
               type "pointer to function returning pointer to function return-
               ing int"
```

Such type names always appear within the parentheses that form part of the syntax of the cast or `sizeof` operator.

References   casts 7.4.1; `sizeof` operator 7.4.2

6

Type Conversions

The C language provides for values of one type to be converted to values of other types under several circumstances.

- A cast expression may be used to explicitly convert a value to another type.
- An operand may be implicitly converted to another type in preparation for performing some arithmetic or logical operation.
- An object of one type may be assigned to a location (lvalue) of another type, causing an implicit type conversion.
- An actual argument to a function may be implicitly converted to another type prior to the function call.
- A return value from a function may be implicitly converted to another type prior to the function return.

There are restrictions as to what types a given object may be converted to. Furthermore, the set of conversions that are possible on assignment, for instance, is not the same as the set of conversions that are possible with type casts.

In the following sections we will discuss the set of possible conversions and then discuss which of these conversions are actually performed in each of the circumstances listed above.

References   assignment operator 7.8.1; casts 7.4.1; function calls 7.3.6; lvalue 7.1; return statement 8.9

6.1 REPRESENTATION CHANGES

The representation of a data object is the particular pattern of bits in the storage area that holds the object; this pattern distinguishes the value of the object from all other possible values of that type.

A conversion of a value from one type to another may or may not involve a representation change. For instance, whenever the two types have different sizes, a representation change has to be made. When integers are converted to a floating-point representation, a representation change is made even if the integer and floating-point type have the same sizes. However, when a value of type `int` is converted to type `unsigned int`, a representation change may not be necessary (it isn't necessary if signed integers are represented in two's-complement form).

Some representation changes are very simple, involving merely discarding of excess bits or padding with extra 0 bits. Other changes may be very complicated, such as conversions between integer and floating-point representations. For each of the conversions discussed in the following sections, we describe the possible representation changes that may be required.

6.2 TRIVIAL CONVERSIONS

It is always possible to convert a value from a type to another type that is the same as the first type. See section 5.12 for a discussion of when types are the same. No representation change needs to occur in this case.

6.3 CONVERSIONS TO INTEGER TYPES

The types that may be converted to integers are the arithmetic types, the pointer types, and the enumeration types.

6.3.1 From Integer Types

The general rule for converting from one integer type to another is that the mathematical value of the result should equal the original mathematical value if that is possible. For example, if an unsigned integer has the value 15 and this value is to be converted to a signed type, the resulting signed value should be 15 also.

If it is not possible to represent the original value of an object of the new type, then there are two cases. If the result type is a signed type, then the conversion is considered to have overflowed and the result value is technically not defined (but see the discussion below). If the result type is an unsigned type, then the result must be that unique value of the result type that is equal (congruent) mod 2^n to the original value, where n is equal to the number of bits used in the representation of the result type.

These rules have a number of interesting consequences. When a signed integer is converted to an unsigned integer of the same size, no change of representation is needed if signed integers are represented using two's-complement notation; that is, the resulting unsigned integer will have the same bit pattern as the original signed integer. On the other hand, if signed integers are represented in some other way, such as with one's-complement or sign-magnitude representation, then a change of representation will be necessary.

When an unsigned integer is converted to a signed integer of the same size, no change of representation is needed if signed integers are represented using two's-complement notation. Technically, this conversion is considered to overflow if the original value is too large to represent exactly in the signed representation (that is, if the high-order bit of the unsigned number is 1). However, we do not doubt that many programmers and many programs depend on the conversion being performed quietly and with no change of representation to produce a negative number. If signed integers are represented in some other way, such as with one's-complement or sign-magnitude representation, then a change of representation will be necessary. Moreover, the transformation may not be mathematically straightforward. For example, when converting the value 0 there may be a choice of "+0" or "−0" in the result representation, and when converting the unsigned value 2^{n-1} it may not be clear what the result value should be. The best the implementor can do in such cases is to make some rational decision and then document it carefully.

If the destination type is longer than the source type, then the only case in which the source value will not be representable in the result type is when a negative signed value is converted to a longer, unsigned type. In that case, the conversion must necessarily behave as if the source value were first converted to a longer signed type of the same size as the destination type, and then converted to the destination type. For example, since the constant expression −1 has type int,

```
((unsigned long) -1) == ((unsigned long) ((long) -1)))
```

For many computers this two-step approach will in fact be the most efficient way to implement the conversion.

If the destination type is shorter than the source type, and both the original type and the destination type are unsigned, the conversion can be effected simply by discarding excess high-order bits from the original value; the bit pattern of the result representation will be equal to the n low-order bits of the original representation. This same rule of discarding works for converting signed integers in two's-complement form to a shorter unsigned type. The discarding rule is also one of several acceptable methods for converting signed or unsigned integers to a shorter signed type when signed integers are in two's-complement form. Note that this rule will not preserve the sign of the value in case of overflow, but the action on overflow is not officially defined anyway. When signed integers are not represented in two's-complement form, the conversions are necessarily more complicated. While the C language does not require the two's-complement representation for signed integers, it certainly favors that representation, and implementations should use it whenever feasible.

References   integer types 5.2; overflow 7.2.3; signed types 5.2.1; unsigned types 5.2.2

6.3.2 From Floating-point Types

The conversion of a floating-point value to an integral value should produce a result that is, as nearly as possible and expedient, equal in value to the value of the old object. The behavior of the conversion is undefined if the old value cannot be represented even approximately in the new type (for example, if its magnitude is much too large, or if a negative floating-point value is converted to an unsigned integer type). Questions of rounding versus truncation and the handling of overflow and underflow are left to the discretion of the implementor.

References   floating types 5.3; integer types 5.2; overflow 7.2.3

6.3.3 From Enumeration Types

Values of enumeration types have integral values determined in the definition of the enumeration type and have a representation equal to that of type int. Therefore, the conversion of an enumeration value to an integer can be reduced to a case of integer-to-integer conversion.

Converting between enumeration types and integers may be a symptom of bad program design or bad programming style. Such conversions may be necessary for certain purposes, however, such as selecting an element of an array that is conceptually indexed by enumeration type.

References   enumeration types 5.6; integer types 5.2

6.3.4 From Pointer Types

When the source value is of a pointer type, the pointer is treated as if it were an unsigned integer of a size equal to the size of the pointer. No representation change is made. Then the unsigned integer is converted to the destination type using the rules listed above.

There is one special case: If a null pointer of any type is created through assignment or initialization by the integer constant 0, then the conversion of that null pointer to an integer type must yield the value 0. This requirement may cause a change in representation in some implementations.

References   integer types 5.2; pointer types 5.4; unsigned types 5.2.2

6.4 CONVERSIONS TO FLOATING-POINT TYPES

Only arithmetic types may be converted to floating-point types.

6.4.1 From Floating-point Types

When converting from `float` to `double`, the result has the same value as the original value.

When converting from `double` to `float`, such that the original value is within the range of values representable as type `float`, the result should be one of the two `float` values closest to the original value. (Whether the original value is rounded up or down is implementation dependent.)

If the original value is outside the range of values representable as type `float`—as when the magnitude is too large or too small for the representation of `float`—the resulting value is undefined, as is the overflow or underflow behavior of the program. (However, if no trap occurs, the most desirable behavior would be for large values to map to the largest floating-point number and for small values to map to 0.0.)

> **References**   floating types 5.3; overflow 7.2.3

6.4.2 From Integer Types

If the integer value is exactly representable in the floating-point type, then the result is the equivalent floating-point value. If the integer value is not exactly representable but is within the range of values representable in the floating-point type, then one of the two closest floating-point values should be chosen as the result. If the integer value is outside the range of values representable in the floating-point type, the result is undefined.

> **References**   floating types 5.3; integer types 5.2; overflow 7.2.3

6.5 CONVERSIONS TO STRUCTURE AND UNION TYPES

An object of a structure or union type *T* may be converted only to a type that is the same as *T* (the trivial conversion). There is no change of representation, except that the bit patterns in any unused "holes" in the structure or union are not necessarily preserved.

> **References**   structure types 5.7; union types 5.8

6.6 CONVERSIONS TO ENUMERATION TYPES

The only values that can be converted to an enumeration type are those of integer or enumeration types.

6.6.1 From Enumeration Types

If the destination type has an element whose integer value is equal to the integer value of the source enumeration element, then that destination element is the result of the conversion.

If the destination type does not have such an element, the result of the conversion is undefined.

Converting between enumeration types may be a symptom of bad program design or bad programming style.

> **References**   enumeration types 5.6;

6.6.2 From Integer Types

If the destination type has an element whose value is equal to the source integer value, then that element of the enumeration is the result.

If the destination type does not have an element whose value is equal to the source integer value, the result of the conversion is undefined.

Converting between enumeration types and integers may be a symptom of bad program design or bad programming style. Such conversions may be necessary for certain purposes, however, such as selecting an element of an array that is conceptually indexed by enumeration type.

> **References**   enumeration types 5.6; integer types 5.2

6.7 CONVERSIONS TO POINTER TYPES

In general, pointers and integers may be converted to pointer types. There are special circumstances under which an array or a function will be converted to a pointer.

6.7.1 From Pointer Types

A null pointer of any type may be converted to any other pointer type and it will still be recognized as a null pointer. There may be a representation change in the conversion.

In the general case, a value of type "pointer to S" may be converted to type "pointer to D" for any types S and D. Information may be lost, depending on the relative sizes of types S and D, because of memory alignment adjustments.

If the alignment requirement for type S is at least as stringent as that for as D (that is, the "alignment modulus" for S, of which the address of any S object must be a multiple, is no smaller than the alignment modulus for D) then the conversion loses no information and the result will be the "same address." A subsequent conversion back to the original pointer type will recover the original pointer. The rationale is that if an object of type S begins at a certain address, then an object of the smaller type *D* could have the same address, since its alignment constraints cannot be more strict.

If the alignment requirement for type *S* is less stringent than that for type *D*, then the conversion to the destination pointer type may require an adjustment of the pointer to an appropriate addressing boundary. (Whether the adjustment is "forward" or "backward" in the address space is not specified.) A subsequent conversion back to the original pointer type might not recover the same pointer.

For example, suppose *S* is char (1 byte) and *D* is int (4 bytes) and that we are on a byte-addressed machine that requires integers to be aligned on addresses divisible by 4. Suppose further we have a value of type (char *) whose representation is 044521. Then if we convert this pointer to a legal value of type (int *), we might have to adjust the representation to be either 044520 or 044524. When we convert back to (char *), the value won't change and will not be the same as the original value of 044521. Alternatively, such a conversion might not perform any adjustment, but simply result in an illegal pointer for the result type. In our example, we might get a pointer of type (int *) with address 044521, and an attempt to indirect through this pointer might result in a machine trap because of an addressing fault.

It should be noted, however, that the library function malloc, which returns a value of type "pointer to char," guarantees that the returned pointer may be converted to any other pointer type without encountering any alignment problems. This is a convention that should be copied when writing other similar functions.

References   malloc function 11.4.5; pointer types 5.4

6.7.2 *From Integer Types*

The integer constant 0 may always be converted to a pointer type. The conversion may or may not involve a representation change, regardless of the relative sizes of int and the pointer type. The result of such a conversion is a "null pointer" that is different from any legal pointer to a data object. Note that null pointers of different pointer types may have different internal representations in some implementations; the results of the expressions

```
(unsigned)(int *)0
(unsigned)(char *)0
```

might be different, for example.

Other integers may be converted to pointer type, but the result is nonportable. The intent is that the pointer be considered an unsigned integer (of the same size as the pointer) and the standard integer conversions then be applied to take the source type to the destination type.

In early C implementations on the DEC VAX-11 and PDP-11 computers it happened to be the case that pointers had the same size as type `int`. Because `int` was also the default type specifier, many programmers played very fast and loose with pointer/integer conversions. In particular, they would often omit the type of functions returning pointers, knowing the type would default to `int`, which was "good enough" because of the conversion rules used in those compilers. This has proved to be a frequent source of portability problems.

> **References**   integer types 5.2; pointer types 5.4; unsigned types 5.2.2

6.7.3 From Array Types

An expression of type "array of *T*" for some type *T* is converted to a value of type "pointer to *T*" by substituting a pointer to the first element of the array for the array itself. This occurs in all contexts except when the array is an argument to `sizeof`.

> **References**   array types 5.5; pointer types 5.4; `sizeof` operator 7.4.2; usual unary conversions 6.12

6.7.4 From Function Types

An expression of type "function returning *T*" for some type *T* is converted to a value of type "pointer to function returning *T*" by substituting a pointer to the function for the function itself. The conversion occurs implicitly in all contexts except the fucntion expression in a function call. The only expression that can have type "function returning . . ." is the name of a function.

> **References**   function calls 7.3.6; usual unary conversions 6.12

6.8 CONVERSIONS TO ARRAY AND FUNCTION TYPES

No conversions to array or function types are possible.

6.9 CONVERSIONS TO THE VOID TYPE

Any value may be converted to type `void`. Of course, the result of such a conversion cannot be used for anything. Such a conversion may occur only in a context where an expression value will be discarded, such as in an expression statement.

> **References**   discarded expresions 7.12; expression statements 8.2; `void` type 5.10

6.10 THE CASTING CONVERSIONS

Any of the conversions discussed earlier in this chapter may be explicitly performed with a type cast without error. Here are some examples of legal cast expressions:

```
int i, *ip;
char c, *cp;
float f;
double d;
enum E { red=1, blue=2, green=3 } color;
...
ip = (int *)  cp;
ip = (int *)  ip;     /* Trivial conversion. */
cp = (char *) ip;
i  = (int)    color;
color = (enum E) ((int) d);
```

References   casts 7.4.1

6.11 THE ASSIGNMENT CONVERSIONS

In a simple assignment expression, the types of the expressions on the left and right sides of the assignment operator should be the same. If they are not, an attempt will be made to convert the value on the right side of the assignment to the type on the left side. The conversions that are legal—a subset of the possible conversions—are listed below.

Left Side Type	Right Side Type
any arithmetic type	any arithmetic type
any pointer type	the integer constant 0
pointer to *T*	array of *T*
pointer to function	function

Attempting any other conversion may elicit a warning or error, but some compilers permit any casting conversion.

References   assignment operator 7.8.1

6.12 THE USUAL UNARY CONVERSIONS

The usual unary conversions determine whether and how a single operand is converted before an operation is performed. The conversions are applied automatically to operands of the unary '!', '−', '~', and '*' operators. They are also applied to each of the operands of the binary '<<' and '>>' operators. (Despite the fact that '<<' and '>>' arc binary operators, they do not perform the usual binary conversions. They merely perform the usual unary conversions on each operand separately.) Finally, the usual unary conversions are applied to actual arguments in a function call before the call is performed.

The purpose of these conversions is to reduce the large number of arithmetic and pointer types to a smaller number that must be handled by the operators. The conversions are of two kinds. First, arithmetic values of narrow type are widened to a larger type with the same value. For example, `short` integers are widened to type `int` and floating-point numbers of type `float` are widened to type `double`. Second, pointerlike references to arrays and functions are converted into actual pointers.

Original Operand Type	Converted Type
char, short	int
unsigned char	unsigned
unsigned short	unsigned
float	double
"array of T"	"pointer to T"
"function returning T"	"pointer to function returning T"

An operand of any other type is unchanged.

Some implementations of C provide an optional compilation mode in which the implicit conversion of type `float` to type `double` is suppressed. This is not compatible with the true C language, but can be very useful if high-quality, efficient numerical software is to be written.

References   bitwise negation operator '~' 7.4.5; function argument conversions 6.14; function calls 7.3.6; indirection operator '*' 7.4.7; logical negation operator '!' 7.4.4; shift operators '<<' and '>>' 7.5.3; unary minus operator '−' 7.4.3

6.13 THE USUAL BINARY CONVERSIONS

The usual binary conversions determine whether and how operands are converted before a binary or ternary operation is performed. They are applied to the operands of most binary operators and to the second and third operands in a conditional expression. The purpose of these conversions is to reduce the large number of arithmetic and pointer types to a smaller number that must be handled by the operators. When two values must be operated upon in combination, they are first converted to a single common type (and typically the result is also of that same common type).

An operator that performs "the usual binary conversions" on its two operands first performs the usual unary conversions on each of the operands independently (to widen short values and to convert arrays and functions to pointers) and then effectively performs one of the following conversions on the results of the unary conversions, all this being done before the operation itself is executed:

1. If either operand is not of arithmetic type, or if the two operands have the same type, then no additional conversion is performed.

2. Otherwise, if one operand is of type `double`, then the other operand is converted to type `double`.

3. Otherwise, if one operand is of type `unsigned long int`, then the other operand is converted to type `unsigned long int`.

4. Otherwise, if one operand is of type `long int` and the other operand is of type `unsigned int`, then each of the two operands is converted to type `unsigned long int`.

5. Otherwise, if one operand is of type `long int`, then the other operand (which now must be of type `int`) is converted to type `long int`.

6. Otherwise, if one operand is of type `unsigned int`, then the other operand is converted to type `unsigned int`.

7. Otherwise, both operands must be of type `int`, and so no additional conversion is performed.

Some implementations of C provide an optional compilation mode in which the implicit conversion of type `float` to type `double` is suppressed. This is not compatible with the original C language, but can be very useful if high-quality, efficient numerical software is to be written. In this mode, the usual unary conversion of `float` to `double` is omitted, and the usual binary conversion rules are amended by adding a new rule just after rule number 2.

2a. Otherwise, if one operand is of type `float`, then the other operand is converted to type `float`.

6.14 THE FUNCTION ARGUMENT CONVERSIONS

When an expression appears as an argument in a function call, the result of the expression is adjusted using the usual unary conversions before being passed as an actual argument.

As described in the previous section, some implementations of C provide an optional compilation mode in which the implicit conversion of type `float` to type `double` is suppressed during the usual unary and binary conversions. When this mode is in effect, the conversion of function arguments of type `float` to type `double` may still be performed. None of the standard C library routines are prepared to accept arguments of type `float`, because they all expect the automatic conversion to `double` to occur.

References   function calls 7.3.6; usual unary conversions 6.12

6.15 OTHER FUNCTION CONVERSIONS

The declared types of the formal parameters of a function, and the type of its return value, are subject to certain adjustments that parallel the function argument conversions. They are discussed in section 9.4.

7

Expressions

C has an unusually rich set of operators that provide access to most of the operations provided by the underlying hardware. This chapter presents the syntax of expressions and describes the function of each of the operators.

7.1 OBJECTS AND LVALUES

An *object* is a region of memory that can be examined and stored into. An *lvalue* (pronounced "ell-value") is an expression that refers to an object in such a way that the object may be altered as well as examined. Sometimes we also speak of the result computed by such an expression as being an lvalue. (An expression or result is called an lvalue because it may be used on the left-hand side of an assignment. Similarly, an expression that permits examination but not alteration of a value is sometimes called an *rvalue*, because it can be used on the right-hand side of an assignment.)

Some names are lvalues: names of variables declared to be of arithmetic, pointer, enumeration, structure, or union type. Names of functions, names of arrays, and enumeration constants, on the other hand, are not lvalues. Some operations on non-lvalues can produce lvalues. For example, the name of an array is not an lvalue but references to elements of the array using subscripting expressions are lvalues. (In other words, one cannot modify an entire array variable using assignment, but one can modify individual elements.) Besides names, the following forms of expressions may produce lvalues:

1. Every subscript expression $e[k]$ is an lvalue, regardless of whether or not the expressions e and k are lvalues.

2. A parenthesized expression is an lvalue if and only if the contained expression is an lvalue.

3. A direct component selection expression *e.name* is an lvalue if and only if the expression *e* is an lvalue.

4. An indirect component selection expression *e−>name* is always an lvalue, regardless of whether *e* is an lvalue.

5. An indirection expression *∗e* is always an lvalue, regardless of whether *e* is an lvalue.

No other form of expression can produce an lvalue. In particular, the result of an assignment expression is never an lvalue, and a function call cannot produce an lvalue.

Some operators require certain of their operands to be lvalues:

1. The operand of a unary address operator '&' must be an lvalue.

2. The operand of a unary '++' or '−−' operator, whether prefix or postfix, must be an lvalue.

3. The left operand of any assignment operator must be an lvalue.

No other operator requires an lvalue as an operand.

7.2 EXPRESSIONS AND PRECEDENCE

7.2.1 Kinds of Expressions

The full syntax of expressions is begun below. The individual kinds of expressions are discussed in the following sections.

        expression ::= *comma-expression*
                      | *no-comma-expression*

        no-comma-expression ::= *assignment-expression*
                      | *conditional-expression*
                      | *logical-expression*
                      | *binary-expression*
                      | *unary-expression*
                      | *primary-expression*

A distinction is drawn between "comma expressions," in which the main operator is the comma operator, and "no comma expressions," in which the main operator is not the comma operator. In contexts where an expression is required but the comma is used for other purposes (such as function calls and initializers), only "no comma expressions" are permitted, because otherwise ambiguity might result as to the meaning of a given comma.

References   assignment expressions 7.8; binary expressions 7.5; comma expressions 7.9; conditional expressions 7.7; function calls 7.3.6; logical expressions 7.6; primary expressions 7.3; unary expressions 7.4

7.2.2 *Precedence and Associativity of Operators*

Each expression operator in C has a precedence level and a rule of associativity. Where parentheses do not explicitly indicate the grouping of operands with operators, it may appear that an operand could be grouped with either of two operators. In such cases the grouping is determined by the rules of precedence and associativity: The operand is grouped with the operator having higher precedence, but if the two operators have the same precedence, the operand is grouped with the left or right operator according to whether the operators are left-associative or right-associative. (All operators having the same precedence level always have the same associativity.) For example, in the expression

```
a * b + c
```

the operand b is grouped with the multiplication operator '*', because '*' has higher precedence than '+', and so the expression is treated as if it had been written

```
(a * b) + c
```

Similarly, in the expression

```
a += b != c
```

the operand b is grouped with the operator '!=', because '!=' has higher precedence than '+=', and so the expression is treated as if it had been written

```
a += (b != c)
```

In the case of the expression

```
a - b + c
```

the two operators '−' and '+' have the same precedence and are left-associative, so the operand b is grouped with the operator to its left, resulting in the interpretation

```
(a - b) + c
```

rather than

```
a - (b + c)
```

On the other hand, in the case of the expression

```
a = b += c
```

the two operators '=' and '+=' have the same precedence and are right-associative, so the operand b is grouped with the operator to its right, resulting in the interpretation

```
a = (b += c)
```

Table 7-1 contains a concise list of the C operators in order from the highest to the lowest precedence. The operators are presented in this chapter in decreasing order of precedence.

All of the binary and ternary operators are left-associative except for the conditional and assignment operators, which are right-associative. The unary operators are sometimes described as being right-associative, but this is needed only to express the idea that an expression such as *x++ is interpreted as *(x++) rather than as (*x)++. We prefer simply to state that the postfix unary operators have higher precedence than the prefix unary operators.

The rules of precedence and associativity are, for the most part, not reflected in the grammar for expressions shown in this chapter. (It is possible to construct a grammar that reflects these rules, but such a grammar is much more difficult to read. See appendix C.)

References   assignment operators 7.8; binary operators 7.5; conditional operator 7.7; postfix operators 7.4.9, 7.4.11

7.2.3 Overflow and Other Arithmetic Exceptions

For certain operations in C such as addition and multiplication, it may be that the true mathematical result of the operation cannot be represented as a value of the expected result type (as determined by the usual conversion rules). This condition is called overflow (or, in some cases, underflow).

In general, the C language does not specify the consequences of overflow. One possibility is that an incorrect value (of the correct type) is produced. Another possibility is that program execution is terminated. A third possibility is that some sort of machine-dependent trap or exception occurs that may be detected by the program in some implementation-dependent manner.

For certain other operations, the C language explicitly specifies that the effects are unpredictable for certain operand values or (more stringently) that a value is always produced but the value is unpredictable for certain operand values. If the right-hand operand of the division operator '/' or the remainder operator, '%', is zero, then the effects are unpredictable, as for overflow. If the right-hand operand of a shift operator '<<' or '>>' is too large or negative, then an unpredictable value is produced.

Traditionally, all implementations of C have ignored the question of signed primary expressions

16	*names literals*	simple tokens
16	$a[k]$	subscripting
16	$f(\ldots)$	function call
16	.	direct selection
16	->	indirect selection

unary operators

15	++ --	postfix increment/decrement
14	++ --	prefix increment/decrement
14	sizeof	size
14	(*type name*)	casts (type conversion)
14	~	bitwise not
14	!	logical not
14	−	arithmetic negation
14	&	address of
14	*	indirection

binary and ternary operators

13L	* / %	multiplicative
12L	+ −	additive
11L	<< >>	left and right shift
10L	< > <= >=	inequality
9L	== !=	equality/inequality
8L	&	bitwise and
7L	^	bitwise xor
6L	|	bitwise or
5L	&&	logical and
4L	||	logical or
3R	? :	conditional (ternary)
2R	= += −= *= /= %=	assignment
2R	<<= >>= &= ^= |=	
1L	,	sequential evaluation

The numbers on the left indicate relative precedence; larger numbers indicate higher precedence. "L" indicates left-associative operators and "R" indicates right-associative operators.

Table 7-1:   C Operators in Order of Precedence

integer overflow, in the sense that the result is whatever value is produced by the machine instruction used to implement the operation. (Many computers that use a two's-complement representation for signed integers handle overflow of addition and subtraction simply by producing the low-order bits of the true two's-complement result. No doubt many existing C programs depend on this fact, but such code is technically not portable.) Floating-point overflow and underflow is usually handled in whatever convenient way is supported by the machine; if the machine architecture provides more than one way to handle exceptional floating-point conditions, a library function may be provided to give the C programmer access to such options.

For unsigned integers the C language is quite specific on the question of overflow: Every operation on unsigned integers always produces a result value that is congruent mod 2^n to the true mathematical result of the operation (where n is the number of bits used to represent the unsigned result). This amounts to computing the correct n low-order bits of the true result (of the true two's-complement result if the true result is negative, as when subtracting a big unsigned integer from a small one).

As an example, suppose that objects of type `unsigned` are represented using 16 bits; then subtracting the unsigned value 7 from the unsigned value 4 would produce the unsigned value `65533`; that is, $2^{16}-3$, because this value is congruent mod 2^{16} to the true mathematical result -3.

An important consequence of this rule is that operations on unsigned integers are guaranteed to be completely portable between two implementations that use representations having the same number of bits; moreover, any implementation can easily simulate the unsigned arithmetic of another implementation using some smaller number of bits.

Despite the explicit rule for the handling of overflow, the operations of division and remainder on unsigned integers nevertheless have unpredictable effects, as for signed integers, when the the right-hand operand is 0.

References   division operator '/' 7.5.1; floating-point types 5.3; remainder operator '%' 7.5.1; shift operators '<<' and '>>' 7.5.3; signed types 5.2.1; unsigned types 5.2.2

7.3 PRIMARY EXPRESSIONS

There are seven kinds of primary expressions: names (identifiers), literal constants, parenthesized expressions, subscripting expressions, two forms of component selection (direct and indirect), and function calls.

primary-expression ::= *name*
      | *literal*
      | *parenthesized-expression*
      | *subscript-expression*
      | *component-selection-expression*
      | *function-call*

7.3.1 Names

The value of a name depends on its type. The type of a name is determined by the declaration of that name (if any), as discussed in chapter 4.

The name of a variable declared to be of arithmetic, pointer, enumeration, structure, or union type evaluates to an object of that type; the name, considered as an expression, is an lvalue.

An enumeration constant evaluates to the integer value associated with that enumeration constant; it is not an lvalue. In the example below, the six color names are enumeration constants. The `switch` statement (described in section 8.7) selects one of six statements to execute based on the value of the variable `color`.

```
typedef enum { red, blue, green, cyan,
               yellow, magenta } colortype;

static colortype complementary(color)
  colortype color;
{
    switch (color) {
      case red:            return cyan;
      case blue:           return yellow;
      case green:          return magenta;
      case cyan:           return red;
      case yellow:         return blue;
      case magenta:        return green;
    }
}
```

The name of an array evaluates to that array; it is not an lvalue. In contexts where the result is subject to the usual conversions, the array value is immediately converted to a pointer to the first object in the array. This occurs in all contexts except as the argument to the `sizeof` operator, in which case the size of the array is returned, rather than the size of a pointer.

```
{
    extern void PrintMatrix();
    int Matrix[10][10], total_length, row_length;

    total_length = sizeof Matrix;
    row_length = sizeof Matrix[0];
    PrintMatrix(Matrix);    /* pointer to first
                               element is passed */
}
```

The name of a function evaluates to that function; it is not an lvalue. In contexts where the result is subject to the usual conversions, the function value is immediately converted to a pointer to the function. This occurs in all contexts but two: as the argument to the sizeof operator, where a function is illegal, and as the function in a function call expression, in which case the function itself is desired, and not a pointer to it.

```
#include <math.h>
        /* Declares sin and cos functions. */

void PlotFunction(f, x0, x1)
    double (*f)(), x0, x1;
{
    ...
}

double fn(x)    /* Function to be plotted. */
    double x;
{
    return (sin(x) - 2.0 * cos(x));
}

void main()
{
    PlotFunction(fn, 0.01, 100.0);
                        /* fn becomes a pointer */
}
```

It is not possible for a name, as an expression, to refer to a label, typedef name, struct component name, union component name, structure tag, union tag, or enumeration tag. Names used for those purposes reside in name spaces separate from the names that can be referred to by a name in an expression. Some of these names may be referred to within expressions by means of special constructs. For example, structure and union component names may be referred to using the '.' or '->' operators, and typedef name may be used in casts and as an argument to the `sizeof` operator.

References   array types 5.5; casts 7.4.1; enumeration types 5.6; function calls 7.3.6; function types 5.9; lvalue 7.1; name space 4.2.4; selection operators '.' and '->' 7.3.5; `sizeof` operator 7.4.2; typedef names 5.11; usual unary conversions 6.12

7.3.2 Literals

A literal (lexical constant) is a numeric constant, and when evaluated as an expression yields that constant as its value. A literal expression is never an lvalue. See section 2.7 for a discussion of literals and their types and values.

7.3.3 Parenthesized Expressions

A parenthesized expression consists of a left parenthesis, any expression, and then a right parenthesis.

> *parenthesized-expression* ::= ' (' *expression* ')'

The type of a parenthesized expression is identical to the type of the enclosed expression; no conversions are performed. The value of a parenthesized expression is the value of the enclosed expression, and will be an lvalue if and only if the enclosed expression is an lvalue.

The purpose of the parenthesized expression is simply to delimit the enclosed expression for grouping purposes, either to defeat the default precedence of operators or to make code more readable. For example:

```
x1 = (-b + discriminant)/(2.0 * a)
```

Parentheses do not necessarily force a particular evaluation order. See section 7.11.

Some compilers—incorrectly, we think—use parentheses to force the usual unary conversions on the operand within the parentheses. For instance, one compiler treats

```
sizeof("abcdef")
```

as being equal to 7 (the size of the string) but

```
sizeof(("abcdef"))
```

as being equal to 4 (which happens to be the size of a pointer to the string in that implementation). This treatment contradicts the specifications in the original description of C.

References   lvalue 7.1; `sizeof` operator 7.4.2

7.3.4 Subscripting Expressions

A subscripting expression consists of a primary expression, a left bracket, an arbitrary expression, and a right bracket. This construction is usually used for array subscripting, where the primary expression evaluates to a pointer and the other expression to an integer.

> *subscript-expression* ::= *primary-expression* '[' *expression* ']'

In C, the expression $e_1[e_2]$ is by definition precisely equivalent to the expression $*((e_1)+(e_2))$. The usual binary conversions are applied to the two operands, and the result is always an lvalue. Note that the operand for the '$*$' operator must be a pointer, and the only way that the result of the '+' operator can be a pointer is for one operand to be a pointer and the other an integer, and therefore it follows that for $e_1[e_2]$ one operand must be a pointer and the other an integer. It is conventional for the first operand to be the pointer.

```
char buffer[100], *bptr = buffer;
int i = 99;
buffer[0] = '\0';
bptr[i] = bptr[0];
```

A consequence of the definition of subscripting is that arrays use 0-origin indexing. In the example above, the first element allocated for the 100-element array `buffer` is referred to as `buffer[0]`, and the last element as `buffer[99]`. The names `buffer` and `bptr` both point to the same place, namely `buffer[0]`, the first element of the `buffer` array, and they can be used in identical ways within subscripting expressions. However, `bptr` is a variable (an lvalue), and thus can be made to point to some other place:

```
bptr = &buffer[6];
```

after which the expression `bptr[-4]` refers to the same place as the expression `buffer[2]`. (This illustrates the fact that negative subscripts make sense in certain circumstances.) An assignment can also make `bptr` point to no place at all:

```
bptr = NULL; /* Store a null pointer into bptr. */
```

On the other hand, the array name `buffer` is not an lvalue and cannot be modified; considered as a pointer, it always points to the same fixed place.

Multidimensional array references are formed by composing subscripting operators, not by putting multiple expressions within the brackets.

```
{
#define SIZE 10
    double matrix[SIZE][SIZE];
    int i, j;
    /* Set up an identity matrix.  Note: this
       method is clear, but is not the fastest
       way to set up such a matrix. */
    for (i = 0; i < SIZE; i++)
        for (j = 0; j < SIZE; j++)
            matrix[i][j] = ((i == j) ? 1.0 : 0.0);
    ...
}
```

It is bad programming style to use a comma expression within the subscripting brackets, because it might mislead a reader familiar with other programming languages to think that it means subscripting of a multidimensional array. For example, the expression

```
commands[k=n+1, 2*k]
```

might appear to be a reference to an element of a two-dimensional array named commands with subscript expressions k=n+1 and 2*k, whereas its actual interpretation in C is as a reference to a one-dimensional array named commands with subscript 2*k after k has been assigned n+1. If a comma expression is really needed (and it is hard for us to think of a plausible example), enclose it in parentheses to indicate that it is something unusual:

```
commands[(k=n+1, 2*k)]
```

It is possible to use pointers and casts to refer to a multidimensional array as if it were a one-dimensional array. This may be desirable for reasons of efficiency. It must be kept in mind that arrays in C are stored in row-major order. Here is an example of such trickery:

```
{
#define SIZE 10
    double matrix[SIZE][SIZE];
    int i;
    /* Set up an identity matrix.  Tricky but fast.
       First clear the matrix, treating it as a
       one-dimensional array of length SIZE*SIZE.
     */
    for (i = 0; i < (SIZE * SIZE); i++)
        ((double *) matrix)[i] = 0.0;
    /* Now install the 1.0 elements. */
    for (i = 0; i < (SIZE * SIZE); i += (SIZE + 1))
        ((double *) matrix)[i] = 1.0;
    ...
}
```

References   addition operator '+' 7.5.2; array types 5.5; comma expressions 7.9; indirection operator '*' 7.4.7; integral types 5.2; lvalue 7.1; pointer types 5.4

7.3.5 *Component Selection*

Component selection operators are used to access fields (components) of structure and union types.

> *component-selection-expression* ::= *direct-component-selection*
> | *indirect-component-selection*

> *direct-component-selection* ::= *primary-expression* '.' *name*

> *indirect-component-selection* ::= *primary-expression* '->' *name*

A direct component selection expression consists of a primary expression, a period '.', and a name. The primary expression must be of a structure or union type, and the name must be the name of a component of that type. The value of the selection operation is the named member of the union or structure and is an lvalue if and only if the expression before the period is an lvalue. (A structure or union value can fail to be an lvalue only when it is the result of a function call.)

In the original definition of C, the expression "*e1.e2*" always yielded an lvalue and was legal only if *e1* was itself an lvalue. Recent extensions to C now allow functions to return structures and unions, and these returned values are not lvalues but their components can be selected, as in this code:

```
{
    extern struct {int a, b;} f();
    int x;
    x = f().a;      /* Only component "a" of the
                       result is needed here. */

    ...
}
```

Experiments indicate, however, that some compilers permitting structure-returning functions still require the left operand of a selection to be an lvalue, and these compilers reject the above example. We regard this as a deficiency of those compilers.

An indirect component selection expression consists of a primary expression, the operator '->', and a name. The value of the primary expression must be a pointer to a structure or union type, and the name must be the name of a component of that structure or union type. The value is the named member of the union or structure and is an lvalue. The expression *e->name* is by definition precisely equivalent to the expression (*e*) . *name*.

```
{
    static struct {float x, y; } Point, *Point_Ptr;
    /* Set both components of Point to 0.0 in a
       roundabout fashion to demonstrate "->". */
    Point.x = 0.0;              /* Sets x to 0.0 */
    Point_Ptr = &Point;
    Point_Ptr->y = 0.0;   /* Sets y to 0.0 */
}
```

References   indirection operator '*' 7.4.7; lvalue 7.1; structure types 5.7; union types 5.8

7.3.6 Function Calls

A function call consists of a primary expression (the *function expression*), a left parenthesis, a possibly empty sequence of expressions (the *argument expressions*) separated by commas, and then a right parenthesis.

function-call ::= *primary-expression*
           '(' { *no-comma-expression* # ',' }* ')'

Because commas are used to separate the argument expressions, the comma operator may not be used in argument expressions unless enclosed by parentheses to prevent mistaking it for an argument separator. We are hard pressed to think of a plausible example of an argument expression containing a comma operator; the left operand of the comma operator can almost always be made into a separate statement preceding the statement containing the function call. We therefore offer this implausible example:

```
void f(x,y)
  int x,y;
{
    ...
}

void main()
{
    int i, j;
    f((i=1, i), (j=1, j)); /* legal, but strange */
    ...
}
```

Conceivably a plausible example might arise from expansion of a preprocessor macro.

The type of the function expression must be "function returning T" for some type T, in which case the result of the function call is of type T. The result is not an lvalue. If T is `void`, however, then the function call produces no result and may not be used in a context that requires the call to yield a result.

One other case is permitted in some compilers but is not strictly permitted by the language: If the function expression is the name of a formal parameter declared to be of type "function returning T," this is considered correct despite the fact that the type of the parameter is really "pointer to function returning T" (after the usual adjustments to parameter types, which are discussed in section 9.4). Such compilers insert an implicit indirection operator to make this case work.

The arguments are each converted according to the usual argument conversions, but no other conversions or checks are required of the compiler. In particular, the compiler is not required to issue any warning message or take any other special action if the number of actual arguments does not match the number of formal parameters of the function being called, or if the (converted) type of an actual argument does not match the (promoted) type of the corresponding formal parameter. The reason is that in the general case information about the formal parameters is not available to the compiler, because declarations of external functions do not necessarily contain any information about the formal parameters. On the other hand, the compiler is not forbidden to issue warnings when the information needed to make such checks happens to be available.

After the actual arguments have been evaluated and converted, they are copied for transmission to the called function; thus, all arguments are passed by value. Within the called function the names of formal parameters are lvalues, but assigning to a formal parameter changes only the value of the formal parameter and has no effect on any actual argument that may happen to be an lvalue. For example, consider this code:

```
/* Computes y to the fourth power. */
double power4(y)
  double y;
{
    y *= y;               /* Square the value of y. */
    return (y * y);       /* Square again. */
}

void main()
{
    double x, z;
    . . .
    x = 3.0;
    z = power4(x);
    . . .
}
```

The function `power4` uses its formal parameter to hold an intermediate result (the square of the original argument). The motivation for this method is that it requires only two multiplications, whereas computing y*y*y*y would require three.

When the function `power4` is called from routine `main`, the assignment to y in the function power4 changes the value of y but does not change the value of the variable x within `main`. After the assignment to z, z has the value 81.0 and x has the value 3.0 (not 9.0).

It should be noted, however, that when a pointer is passed as an argument, the pointer itself is copied but the object pointed to is not copied. By using pointers, a function and its caller can cooperate in allowing the called function to modify an object supplied by the caller.

If a function whose return type is not `void` is called in a context where the value of the function would be discarded, the compiler may issue a warning to that effect. The intent to discard the result of the function call may be made explicit by using a cast:

```
{
    . . .
    (void) strcat(word, suffix);
                        /* Discard result of strcat. */
}
```

References   comma operator 7.9; discarded expressions 7.12; function types 5.9; indirection operator '*' 7.4.7; lvalue 7.1; pointer types 5.4; void type 5.10

7.4 UNARY OPERATOR EXPRESSIONS

There are four kinds of unary operator expressions, according to the operator involved: casts, `sizeof`, prefix operators, and postfix operators.

> *unary-expression* ::= *cast-expression*
> | *sizeof-expression*
> | *prefix-expression*
> | *postfix-expression*
>
> *prefix-expression* ::= *unary-minus-expression*
> | *logical-negation-expression*
> | *bitwise-negation-expression*
> | *address-expression*
> | *indirection-expression*
> | *preincrement-expression*
> | *predecrement-expression*
>
> *postfix-expression* ::= *postincrement-expression*
> | *postdecrement-expression*

The unary operators have precedence lower than the primary expressions but higher than all binary and ternary operators. Among the unary operators, postfix operators have higher precedence than prefix operators. For example, the expression `*x++` is interpreted as `*(x++)`, not as `(*x)++`.

References precedence 7.2.2

7.4.1 Casts

A cast expression consists of a left parenthesis, a type name, a right parenthesis, and an operand expression.

> *cast-expression* ::= '(' *type-name* ')' *prefix-expression*

The cast causes the operand value to be converted to the type named within the parentheses. Any permissible conversion may be invoked by a cast expression. The result is not an lvalue.

```
extern char *alloc();
struct S *p;
p = (struct S *) alloc(sizeof(struct S));
```

Some implementations of C incorrectly ignore certain casts whose only effect is to make a value "narrower" than normal. For example, suppose that type `unsigned short` is represented in 16 bits and type `unsigned` is represented in 32 bits. Then the value of the expression

```
(unsigned)(unsigned short)0xFFFFFF
```

ought to be 0xFFFF, because the cast (unsigned short) should cause truncation of the value 0xFFFFFF to 16 bits, and then the cast (unsigned) should widen that value back to 32 bits. Deficient compilers fail to implement this truncation effect and generate code that passes the value 0xFFFFFF through unchanged. Similarly, for the expression

```
(double)(float)3.14159265358979323384
```

deficient compilers do not produce code to reduce the precision of the approximation to pi to the that of a float, but pass through the double-precision value unchanged. For maximum portability, we advise programmers to truncate values by storing them into variables or performing explicit masking operations (such as with the binary bitwise AND operator '&') rather than relying on narrowing casts.

> **References**   bitwise AND operator 7.5.6; type conversions 6; type names 5.13

7.4.2 Sizeof Operator

The sizeof operator is used to obtain the size of a type or data object.

sizeof-expression ::= sizeof '(' *type-name* ')'
                 | sizeof *prefix-expression*

The sizeof expression has two forms: the operator sizeof followed by a parenthesized type name, or the operator sizeof followed by an operand expression.

Applying the sizeof operator to a parenthesized type name yields the size of an object of the specified type; that is, the amount of memory (measured in storage units) that would be occupied by an object of that type. The type name may not name an array type with no explicit length, or a function type, or the type void.

Applying the sizeof operator to an expression yields the same result as if it had been applied to the name of the type of the expression. The sizeof operator does not of itself cause any of the usual conversions to be applied to the expression in determining its type, but if the expression contains operators that do perform usual conversions, then those conversions are considered when determining the type. For example, applying sizeof to the name of an array produces the total size of the array; this is possible because the sizeof operator does not cause the array to be converted to a pointer first. Likewise, if the variable v is of type short, then sizeof(v) is the same as sizeof(short). However, sizeof(v+0) is the same as sizeof(int), which might not be the same as `sizeof(short)`. This is because the operator '+' performs the usual conversions, causing the sum of v and 0 to have type `int`.

The result of applying `sizeof` to an expression can always be deduced at compile time by examining the types of the objects in the operand expression. The result of `sizeof` never depends on the particular values of the objects at run time (except insofar as the value of an integer literal may determine whether or not it is considered to be a `long` constant, but then again the value of a literal is determinable at compile time).

When `sizeof` is applied to an expression, the expression is analyzed at compile time to determine its type, but the expression itself is not compiled into executable code. This means that any side effects that might be produced by execution of the expression will not take place. For example, execution of the expression

```
k = sizeof(j++)
```

will assign some value to k *but will not increment* j.

Applying the `sizeof` operator to a structure member that is a bit field produces the size of the declared type of the member; the size of the field in bits does not affect the result. This usage is probably misleading and should be avoided.

The original definition of C did not specify the type of the result of the `sizeof` operator. We recommend that the result of the `sizeof` operator be either of type `unsigned int` or of type `unsigned long` at the discretion of the implementor. Normally it will be `unsigned int` unless `unsigned int` is too small to represent a pointer in the particular implementation, in which case `unsigned long` must be used. Some implementations of C use `int` or `long int` as the type of the result of `sizeof`, but this is an inferior choice because it may be impossible to represent the size of a very large array, say one that spans more than half the total address space.

There is, on the face of it, a syntactic ambiguity in an expression such as

```
sizeof(long)-2
```

It could be interpreted as three unary operators (unary negation '-', the cast '(long)', and 'sizeof') to be applied successively to the value 2:

```
sizeof((long)(-2))
```

Alternatively, it could be interpreted as a binary subtraction operator '-' whose operands are `sizeof(long)` and 2:

```
(sizeof(long))-2
```

This ambiguous case is resolved quite arbitrarily by declaring that the latter interpretation shall be used.

References   array types 5.5; function types 5.9; storage units 5.1; type names 5.13; unsigned types 5.2.2; usual binary conversions 6.13; void type 5.10

7.4.3 Unary Minus

The prefix operator '−' computes the arithmetic negation of its operand. The operand may be of any arithmetic type. The usual unary conversions are performed on the operand. The result is not an lvalue.

unary-minus-expression ::= '−' *unary-expression*

A unary minus expression "$-e$" may be considered to be a shorthand notation for "$0-(e)$"; the two expressions in effect always perform the same computation. This computation may produce unpredictable effects if the operand is a signed integer or floating-point number and overflow occurs.

For an unsigned integer operand k, the result is always unsigned and equal to 2^n-k, where n is the number of bits used to represent the result. Because the result is unsigned, it can never be negative. This may seem strange. Note, however, that $(-x)+x$ is equal to 0 for any unsigned integer x. (This identity also holds for any signed integer x for which $-x$ is well defined.)

References   floating types 5.3; integer types 5.2; lvalue 7.1; overflow 7.2.3; subtraction operator '−' 7.5.2; unsigned types 5.2.2; usual unary conversions 6.12

7.4.4 Logical Negation

The prefix operator '!' computes the logical negation of its operand. The operand may be of any scalar type.

logical-negation-expression ::= '!' *unary-expression*

The usual unary conversions are performed on the operand. The result of the '!' operator is of type int; the result is 1 if the operand is zero (null in the case of pointers, 0.0 in the case of floating-point values) and 0 if the operand is not zero (nonnull, not 0.0). The result is not an lvalue. The expression $!(x)$ is identical in meaning to $(x)==0$.

```
/* Assume that assertion_failure accepts a string
   and reports it as a message to the user. */
#define assert(x,s) if (!(x)) assertion_failure(s)
...
assert(num_cases > 0, "No test cases.");
average = total_points/num_cases;
...
```

References   equality operator '==' 7.5.5; floating types 5.3; integer types 5.2; lvalue 7.1; pointer types 5.4; scalar types 5; usual unary conversions 6.12

7.4.5 Bitwise Negation

The prefix operator '~' computes the bitwise negation of its operand.

bitwise-negation-expression ::= '~' *unary-expression*

The operand may be of any integral type. The usual unary conversions are performed on the operand. Every bit in the binary representation of the result is the inverse of what it was in the (converted) operand. The result is not an lvalue.

```
#define LOW_ADDRESS_BITS 3L
long address;
...
/* Clear the low-order address bits.  For a 32-bit
   address this performs a bitwise AND of the
   address with 037777777774. However, the use of
   '~' allows the code to work properly
   no matter what the size of the address is.
*/
address &= ~LOW_ADDRESS_BITS ;
```

Because different implementations may use different representations for signed integers, the result of applying the bitwise NOT operator '~' to signed operands may not be portable. We recommend using '~' only on unsigned operands for portable code.

References   integer types 5.2; lvalue 7.1; signed types 5.2.1; unsigned types 5.2.2; usual unary conversions 6.12

7.4.6 Address Operator

The prefix operator '&' returns a pointer to its operand, which must be an lvalue.

address-expression ::= '&' *unary-expression*

If the type of the operand for '&' is "*T*," then the type of the result is "pointer to *T*." None of the usual conversions are relevant to the '&' operator.

The original description of C specified that it was illegal to apply the unary address operator '&' to a `register` variable, and some compilers still enforce this restriction. However, since `register` is treated only as a hint to the compiler and not a mandatory requirement, it seems appropriate to allow such usage, inasmuch as on some computers the registers really are addressable as if they were memory locations. On the other hand, when the target computer does not have addressable registers, applying '&' to a `register` variable may simply defeat the declaration of the variable as `register`, forcing it to be of class `auto` instead. We recommend that new compilers take this latter approach and perhaps also issue a warning message. In any case, such usage should be regarded as nonportable.

It is incorrect for the operand expression to be the name of a function or the name of an array, because such a name is not an lvalue. (Some compilers permit the '&' operator to be applied to a function or array and consider it to have no effect, but this is confusing at best. At the very least, a warning message should be issued.) Recall that in most contexts a function value is implicitly converted to a pointer to that function anyway, in exactly the same manner as if '&' had been used, and an array value is implicitly converted to a pointer to the first element.

```
extern int i, f();
int *ip, (*fp)();
ip = &i;          /* '&' needed */
fp = f;           /* '&' not needed or permitted */
```

References   array type 5.5; function type 5.9; lvalue 7.1; pointer type 5.4; register storage class 4.3

7.4.7 Indirection

The prefix operator '*' performs indirection through a pointer. Thus the '&' and '*' operators are each the inverse of the other.

indirection-expression ::= '*' *unary-expression*

The usual unary conversions are performed on the operand, but the only relevant conversions are from arrays and functions to pointers. The (converted) operand must be a pointer, and the result is an lvalue referring to the object to which the operand points. If the type of the operand is "pointer to T," then the type of the result is simply "T."

```
int i,*p;
p  = &i;          /* p now points to variable i */
*p = 10;          /* sets value of i to 10 /*
```

The run-time effects of applying the indirection operator to a null pointer are undefined. It may return an unpredictable error, cause a trap, or perform some completely unpredictable action.

References   array types 5.5; function types 5.9; lvalue 7.1; pointer types 5.4; usual unary conversions 6.12

7.4.8 Preincrement Operator

The prefix operator '++' performs "preincrementation," a side effect-producing operation.

> *preincrement-expression* ::= '++' *unary-expression*

The operand must be an lvalue and may be of any scalar type. The constant 1 is added to the operand and the result stored back in the lvalue. The result is the new (incremented) value of the operand but is not an lvalue. The expression ++(x) is identical in meaning to (x)+=1. (The operator '+=', a compound assignment operator, is described in section 7.8.2.) The usual binary conversions are performed on the operand and the constant 1 before the addition is performed, and the usual assignment conversions are performed when storing the sum back into the operand. The type of the result is that of the lvalue operand before conversion.

```
static int uniqueint()
/* uniqueint: Successive calls to this routine
   return the integers 1, 2, ... without check for
   overflow. */
{
    static int count = 0;
    return ++count;
}
```

This operation may produce unpredictable effects if overflow occurs and the operand is a signed integer or floating-point number. The result of incrementing the largest representable value of an unsigned type is 0.

If the operand is a pointer, say of type "pointer to T" for some type T, the effect is to move the pointer forward beyond the object pointed to, as if to move the pointer to the next element within an array of objects of type T.

Whether an enumeration value is a legitimate operand for the preincrement operator in a given implementation depends on which model of enumeration types is adopted by that implementation. See section 5.6.

References   addition 7.5.2; array types 5.5; assignment conversions 6.11; compound assignment 7.8.2; enumeration types 5.6; floating types 5.3; integer types 5.2; lvalue 7.1; overflow 7.2.3; pointer types 5.4; scalar types 5; signed types 5.2.1; unsigned types 5.2.2; usual binary conversions 6.13

7.4.9 Postincrement Operator

The postfix operator '++' performs "postincrementation," a side effect-producing operation.

> *postincrement-expression* ::= *primary-expression* '++'

The operand must be an lvalue and may be of any scalar type. The constant 1 is added to the operand, modifying the operand. The result is the *old* value of the operand, before it was incremented. The result is not an lvalue. The usual binary conversions are performed on the operand and the constant 1 before the addition is performed, and the usual assignment conversions are performed when storing the sum back into the operand. The type of the result is that of the lvalue operand before conversion.

This operation may produce unpredictable effects if overflow occurs and the operand is a signed integer or floating-point number. The result of incrementing the largest representable value of an unsigned type is 0.

If the operand is a pointer, say of type "pointer to *T*" for some type *T*, the effect is to move the pointer forward beyond the object pointed to, as if to move the pointer to the next element within an array of objects of type *T*. However, the value of the expression is the pointer before modification.

```
int strlen(cp)
/* strlen: count the characters in a string.
   The argument "cp" should be a pointer to
   the first character of the string.
 */
  char *cp;
{
    int count = 0;
    while (*cp++)     /* "*cp++" means "*(cp++)" */
        count++;
    return count;
}
```

Whether an enumeration value is a legitimate operand for the postincrement operator in a given implementation depends on which model of enumeration types is adopted by that implementation. See section 5.6.

References   addition 7.5.2; array types 5.5; assignment conversions 6.11; enumeration types 5.6; floating types 5.3; integer types 5.2; lvalue 7.1; overflow 7.2.3; pointer types 5.4; scalar types 5; signed types 5.2.1; unsigned types 5.2.2; usual binary conversions 6.13

7.4.10 *Predecrement Operator*

The prefix operator '−−' performs "predecrementation," a side-effect producing operation.

> *predecrement-expression* ::= '−−' *unary-expression*

The operand must be an lvalue and may be of any scalar type. The constant 1 is subtracted from the operand and the result stored back in the lvalue. The result is the new (decremented) value of the operand but is not an lvalue. The expression $--(x)$ is identical in meaning to $(x)-=1$. (The operator '$-=$', a compound assignment operator, is described in section 7.8.2.) The usual binary conversions are performed on the operand and the constant 1 before the subtraction is performed, and the usual assignment conversions are performed when storing the difference back into the operand. The type of the result is that of the lvalue operand before conversion.

This operation may produce unpredictable effects if overflow occurs and the operand is a signed integer or floating-point number. The result of decrementing the value 0 of an unsigned integer type is the largest representable value of that type.

If the operand is a pointer, say of type "pointer to T" for some type T, the effect is to move the pointer back over an object of type T preceding the one originally pointed to, as if to move the pointer to the previous element within an array of objects of type T.

```
int strrev(s1, s2)
/* strrev: copy string s2 in reversed form into
            string s1.  s2 should be a pointer to
            the first character of a null-terminated
            string.  s1 should point to an area that
            will receive a null-terminated string
            of the same length but with reversed
            contents. */
  char *s1, *s2;
{
    char *p = s1;
    while (*p++);    /* Locate end of first string. */
    --p;             /* Overshot: back up to the null. */
    /* Now copy the characters in reverse order. */
    while (p > s1)
        *s2++ = *--p;
    *s2 = '\0';      /* Terminate the result string. */
}
```

Whether an enumeration value is a legitimate operand for the predecrement operator in a given implementation depends on which model of enumeration types is adopted by that implementation. See section 5.6.

References   array types 5.5; assignment conversions 6.11; compound assignment 7.8.2; enumeration types 5.6; floating types 5.3; integer types 5.2; lvalue 7.1; overflow 7.2.3; pointer types 5.4; scalar types 5; signed types 5.2.1; subtraction 7.5.2; unsigned types 5.2.2; usual binary conversions 6.13

7.4.11 *Postdecrement Operator*

The postfix operator '$--$' performs "postdecrementation," a side effect-producing operation.

> *postdecrement-expression* ::= *primary-expression* '$--$'

The operand must be an lvalue and may be of any scalar type. The constant 1 is subtracted from the operand and the result stored back into the lvalue. The result is the *old* value of the operand, before it was decremented. The result is not an lvalue. The usual binary conversions are performed on the operand and the constant 1 before the subtraction is performed, and the usual assignment conversions are performed when storing the difference back into the operand. The type of the result is that of the lvalue operand before conversion.

This operation may produce unpredictable effects if overflow occurs and the operand is a signed integer or floating-point number. The result of decrementing the value 0 of an unsigned integer type is the largest representable value of that type.

If the operand is a pointer, say of type "pointer to T" for some type T, the effect is to move the pointer back over an object of type T preceding the one originally pointed to, as if to move the pointer to the previous element within an array of objects of type T. However, the value of the expression is the pointer before modification.

Whether an enumeration value is a legitimate operand for the postdecrement operator in a given implementation depends on which model of enumeration types is adopted by that implementation. See section 5.6.

References   array types 5.5; assignment conversions 6.11; enumeration types 5.6; floating types 5.3; integer types 5.2; lvalue 7.1; overflow 7.2.3; pointer types 5.4; scalar types 5; signed types 5.2.1; subtraction 7.5.2; unsigned types 5.2.2; usual binary conversions 6.13

7.5 *BINARY OPERATOR EXPRESSIONS*

A binary operator expression consists of two expressions separated by a binary operator. The various operators have different levels of precedence, as described in section 7.2.2.

> *binary-expression* ::= *multiplicative-expression*
> | *additive-expression*
> | *shift-expression*
> | *inequality-expression*
> | *equality-expression*
> | *bitwise-and-expression*
> | *bitwise-xor-expression*
> | *bitwise-or-expression*

All of the binary operators described in this section are left-associative. For example, the operators '`*`' and '`%`' have the same level of precedence, and therefore the expression `x*y%z` is treated as `(x*y)%z`, not as `x*(y%z)`; similarly, the expression `x%y*z` is treated as `(x%y)*z`, not as `x%(y*z)`.

For each of the binary operators described in this section, both operands are fully evaluated (but in no particular order) before the operation is performed.

References   order of evaluation 7.11; precedence 7.2.2

7.5.1 *Multiplicative Operators*

The three multiplicative operators, '`*`', '`/`', and '`%`', have the same precedence and are left-associative.

multiplicative-expression ::= *multiplication*
                              | *division*
                              | *remainder*

multiplication ::= *expression* '`*`' *expression*

division ::= *expression* '`/`' *expression*

remainder ::= *expression* '`%`' *expression*

References   precedence 7.2.2

Multiplication The binary operator '`*`' indicates multiplication.   The operands may each be of any arithmetic type. The usual binary conversions are performed on the operands, and the type of the result is that of the converted operands. The result is not an lvalue. For integral operands, integer multiplication is performed; for floating-point operands, floating-point multiplication is performed.

The multiplication operator may produce unpredictable effects if overflow occurs and the operands (after conversion) are signed integers or floating-point numbers. If the operands are unsigned integers, the result is congruent mod 2^n to the true mathematical result of the operation (where n is the number of bits used to represent the unsigned result).

The '`*`' operator is assumed to be commutative and associative, and the compiler is permitted to rearrange an expression with several multiplications, even in the presence of parentheses and without regard to avoiding overflow. For example, the compiler may freely interpret the expression `a*(b*c)*d` as if it were `(c*a)*(b*d)`, subject to the restrictions discussed in section 7.11.

References   arithmetic types 5; floating types 5.3; integer types 5.2; lvalue 7.1; order of evaluation 7.11; overflow 7.2.3; signed types 5.2.1; unsigned types 5.2.2; usual binary conversions 6.13

Division The binary operator '/' indicates division. The operands may each be of any arithmetic type. The usual binary conversions are performed on the operands, and the type of the result is that of the converted operands. The result is not an lvalue.

For floating-point operands, floating-point division is performed.

For integral operands, if the mathematical quotient of the operands is not an exact integer, then the result will be one of the two integers closest to the mathematical quotient of the operands. Of those two integers, the one closer to 0 must be chosen if both operands are positive (that is, division of positive integers is truncating division). Note that this completely specifies the behavior of division for unsigned operands. If either operand is negative, then the choice is left to the discretion of the implementor. For maximum portability, programs should therefore avoid depending on the behavior of the division operator when applied to negative integral operands.

The division operator may produce unpredictable effects if overflow occurs and the operands (after conversion) are signed integers or floating-point numbers. Note that overflow can occur for signed integers represented in two's-complement form if the most negative representable integer is divided by -1; the mathematical result is a positive integer that cannot be represented. Overflow cannot occur if the operands are unsigned integers.

The consequences of division by zero, whether integer or floating-point, are machine dependent.

References   arithmetic types 5; floating types 5.3; integer types 5.2; lvalue 7.1; overflow 7.2.3; signed types 5.2.1; unsigned types 5.2.2; usual binary conversions 6.13

Remainder The binary operator '%' computes the remainder when the first operand is divided by the second. The operands may each be of any integral type. The usual binary conversions are performed on the operands, and the type of the result is that of the converted operands. The result is not an lvalue.

It is always true that (a/b)*b + a%b is equal to a if b is not 0, so the behavior of the remainder operation is coupled to that of integer division. When both operands are positive, the remainder operation will always be equivalent to the mathematical "mod" operation. Note that this completely specifies the behavior of the remainder operation for unsigned operands. If either operand is negative, the behavior will be machine dependent in a manner corresponding to the machine dependence of integer division. For maximum portability, programs should therefore avoid depending on the behavior of the remainder operator when applied to negative integral operands.

The remainder operator may produce unpredictable effects if performing division on the two operands would produce overflow. Note that overflow can occur for signed integers represented in two's-complement form if the most negative representable integer is divided by -1; the mathematical result of the division is a positive integer that cannot be represented, and therefore the results are unpredictable, even though the remainder itself (zero) is representable. Overflow cannot occur if the operands are unsigned integers.

The consequences of taking a remainder with a second operand of zero are machine dependent.

```
/* Compute the greatest common divisor by Euclid's
   algorithm.  The result is the largest integer
   that evenly divides x and y.
 */
unsigned gcd(x, y)
  unsigned x, y;
{
    while ( y != 0 ) {
        unsigned temp = y;
        y = x % y;
        x = temp;
    }
    return x;
}
```

References integer types 5.2; lvalue 7.1; overflow 7.2.3; signed types 5.2.1; unsigned types 5.2.2; usual binary conversions 6.13

7.5.2 Additive Operators

The two additive operators, '+' and '−', have the same precedence and are left-associative.

additive-expression ::= *addition-expression*
　　　　　　　　　　　| *subtraction-expression*

addition-expression ::= *expression* '+' *expression*

subtraction-expression ::= *expression* '−' *expression*

References precedence 7.2.2

Addition The binary operator '+' indicates addition. The usual binary conversions are performed on the operands. The operands may both be arithmetic or one may be a pointer and the other an integer or one may be an enumeration type and the other an integer. No other operand types are allowed. The result is not an lvalue.

When the operands are arithmetic, the type of the result is that of the converted operands. For integral operands, integer addition is performed; for floating-point operands, floating-point addition is performed.

When adding a pointer p and an integer k, it is assumed that the object that p points to lies within an array of such objects, and the result is a pointer to that object within the presumed array that lies k objects away from the one p points to. For example, $p+1$ (or $1+p$) points to the object just after the one p points to, and $p+(-1)$ (or $(-1)+p$) points to the object just before. It is illegal for p to be of type "pointer to function." (Functions cannot be elements of arrays.)

Whether an enumeration value is a legitimate operand for the addition operator in a given implementation depends on which model of enumeration types is adopted by that implementation. See section 5.6. If the "pointer model" of enumerations is used, then when adding an enumeration value e and an integer k, the result is that enumeration constant of the same type as e whose value is equal to the sum of k and the value of e. If there is more than one such enumeration constant, then it doesn't matter which is selected. If there is no such enumeration constant in the enumeration type in question, then the result value is undefined.

The addition operator may produce unpredictable effects if overflow occurs and the operands (after conversion) are signed integers or floating-point numbers, or if either operand is a pointer or enumeration value. If the operands are both unsigned integers, the result is congruent mod 2^n to the true mathematical result of the operation (where n is the number of bits used to represent the unsigned result).

The '+' operator is assumed to be commutative and associative, and the compiler is permitted to rearrange an expression with several additions, even in the presence of parentheses and without regard to avoiding overflow. For example, the compiler may freely interpret the expression a+(b+c)+d as if it were (c+a)+(b+d), subject to the restrictions discussed in section 7.11.

References   array types 5.5; enumeration types 5.6; floating types 5.3; integer types 5.2; lvalue 7.1; order of evaluation 7.11; overflow 7.2.3; pointer types 5.4; scalar types 5; signed types 5.2.1; unsigned types 5.2.2; usual binary conversions 6.13

Subtraction The binary operator '−' indicates subtraction. The usual binary conversions are performed on the operands. The operands may both be arithmetic or may both be of the same pointer type or may both be of the same enumeration type, or the left operand may a pointer and the other an integer, or the left operand may be an enumeration value and the other an integer. No other operand types are permitted. The result is not an lvalue.

If the operands are both arithmetic, the type of the result is that of the converted operands. For integral operands, integer subtraction is performed; for floating-point operands, floating-point subtraction is performed. Note that the result of subtracting one unsigned integer from another is always unsigned and therefore cannot be negative. However, unsigned numbers always obey such identities as `(a+(b-a))==b` and `(a-(a-b))==b`.

Subtraction of an integer from a pointer is analogous to addition of an integer to a pointer. When subtracting an integer k from a pointer p, it is assumed that the object that p points to lies within an array of such objects, and the result is a pointer to that object within the presumed array that lies $-k$ objects away from the one p points to. For example, $p-1$ points to the object just before the one p points to, and $p-(-1)$ points to the object just after. It is illegal for p to be of type "pointer to function." (Functions cannot be elements of arrays.)

Given two pointers p and q of the same type, the difference $p-q$ is an integer k such that adding k to q yields p. The type of the difference may be either `int` or `long`, depending on the implementation. The result is well defined and portable only if the two pointers point to objects in the same array, or at least are aligned as if they did. If either of the pointers is null, the result is undefined. It is illegal for either pointer to be of type "pointer to function."

Whether an enumeration value is a legitimate operand for the subtraction operator in a given implementation depends on which model of enumeration types is adopted by that implementation. See section 5.6. If the "pointer model" of enumerations is used, then subtraction of an integer from an enumeration constant is analogous to addition of an integer to an enumeration constant. When subtracting an integer k from an enumeration constant e, the result is that enumeration constant of the same type as e whose value is equal to the result of subtracting k from the value of e. If there is no such enumeration constant in the enumeration type in question, then the result value is undefined.

Given two enumeration constants e and d of the same type, the difference $e-d$ (if permitted at all by the implementation) is that integer k such that adding k to d yields e. The type of the result is `int`.

The subtraction operator may produce unpredictable effects if overflow occurs and the operands (after conversion) are signed integers or floating-point numbers, or if either operand is a pointer or enumeration value. If the operands are both unsigned integers, the result is congruent mod 2^n to the true mathematical result of the operation (where n is the number of bits used to represent the unsigned result).

References   array types 5.5; enumeration types 5.6; floating types 5.3; integer types 5.2; lvalue 7.1; overflow 7.2.3; pointer types 5.4; scalar types 5; signed types 5.2.1; unsigned types 5.2.2; usual binary conversions 6.13

7.5.3 *Shift Operators*

The binary operator '<<' indicates shifting to the left and the binary operator '>>' indicates shifting to the right.

shift-expression ::= *left-shift-expression*
　　　　　| *right-shift-expression*

left-shift-expression ::= *expression* '<<' *expression*

right-shift-expression ::= *expression* '>>' *expression*

Each operand must be of integral type. The usual unary conversions are performed *separately* on each operand (the usual binary conversions are *not* used for the shift operators), and the type of the result is that of the converted left operand. The result is not an lvalue.

The first operand is a quantity to be shifted, and the second operand specifies the number of bit positions by which the first operand is to be shifted. The direction of the shift operation is controlled by which operator ('<<' or '>>') is used. The operator '<<' shifts the value of the left operand to the left; excess bits shifted off to the left are discarded, and 0-bits are shifted in from the right. The operator '>>' shifts the value of the left operand to the right; excess bits shifted off to the right are discarded. The bits shifted in from the left for '>>' depend on the type of the converted left operand: If it is unsigned, then 0-bits are shifted in from the left; but if it is signed, then at the implementor's option either 0-bits or copies of the leftmost bit of the left operand are shifted in from the left.

Table 7-2 shows, as an example, how unsigned shift operations may be used to compute the greatest common divisor of two integers by the binary algorithm. Although this method is a bit more complicated than the Euclidean algorithm, it may also be also faster, because in some implementations of C the remainder operation is rather slow, especially for unsigned operands.

The result value is undefined if the value of the right operand is negative, so specifying a negative shift distance does *not* (necessarily) cause '<<' to shift to the right or '>>' to shift to the left. The result value is also undefined if the value of the right operand is greater than or equal to the width (in bit positions) of the value of the converted left operand. Note, however, that the right operand may be 0, in which case no shift occurs and the result value is identical to the value of the converted left operand.

The two shift operators have the same precedence and are left-associative. One can exploit this fact to write expressions that are visually pleasing but semantically confusing:

```
b << 4 >> 8
```

```
/* Compute the greatest common divisor by the so-called
   binary algorithm.  The result is the largest integer
   that evenly divides x and y.  Only subtraction,
   shifts, and bitwise operations are used; the remain-
   der operation (which may be expensive) is not used.
 */
unsigned binary_gcd(x, y)
  unsigned x, y;
{
    unsigned temp;
    unsigned common_power_of_two = 0;

    /* Special cases: if either argument is zero,
       then return the other one. */
    if (x == 0) return y;
    if (y == 0) return x;
    /* Determine the largest power of two that
       divides both x and y. */
    while ((((x | y) & 1) == 0) {
        x = x >> 1;   /* One could write "x >>= 1;" */
        y = y >> 1;
        ++common_power_of_two;
    }
    while ((x & 1) == 0)   x = x >> 1;
    while (y) {
        /* At this point x is guaranteed odd,
           and y is nonzero. */
        while ((y & 1) == 0)   y = y >> 1;
        /* At this point both x and y are odd. */
        temp = y;
        if (x > y)  y = x - y;
        else        y = y - x;
        x = temp;
        /* Now x has the old value of y; y was odd, so
           now x is odd.  Now y is even, because it
           was computed as the difference of two odd
           numbers; therefore it will be right-shifted
           at least once on the next iteration. */
    }
    return (x << common_power_of_two);
}
```

Table 7-2: Computing the Greatest Common Divisor by the Binary Method

If b is a 16-bit quantity, this expression extracts the middle eight bits. As always, it is better to use parentheses when there is any possibility of confusion:

```
(b << 4) >> 8
```

The original description of C specified that the '>>' operator with a signed left operand might shift in *either* 0-bits or copies of the leftmost bit of the left operand, at the discretion of the implementor. The intent was to permit the implementor the freedom to implement a right shift efficiently, but the effect has been to discourage any use of '>>' on a signed left operand. If a new compiler is to use a two's-complement or one's-complement representation for signed integers, we strongly recommend that right shifts on signed integers be performed by replicating the sign bit. This is the most consistent with the definition and use of signed integer types. The programmer can always cast the left operand to an unsigned type to force the shifting in of 0-bits.

Because different implementations may use different representations for signed integers, and because implementations using the same representation may nevertheless differ in their handling of right shifts on signed integers, the result of applying the shift operators '<<' and '>>' to signed operands may not be portable. We recommend using '<<' and '>>' only on unsigned operands for portable code.

References   integer types 5.2; lvalue 7.1; precedence 7.2.2; signed types 5.2.1; unsigned types 5.2.2; usual unary conversions 6.12

7.5.4 *Inequality Operators*

The binary operators '<', '<=', '>', and '>=' indicate comparison.

inequality-expression ::= *expression inequality-operator expression*

inequality-operator ::= '<' | '<=' | '>' | '>='

The usual binary conversions are performed on the operands. The operands may both be of arithmetic types or may both be of the same pointer type or may both be of the same enumeration type. The result is always of type int and has the value 0 or 1. The result is not an lvalue.

For integral operands, integer comparison is performed (signed or unsigned as appropriate). For floating-point operands, floating-point comparison is performed. For pointer operands, the result depends on the relative locations within the address space of the two objects pointed to; the result is portable only if the objects pointed to lie within the same array, or at least are aligned as if they did, in which case "greater than" means "having a higher index in the array."

Whether an enumeration value is a legitimate operand for the inequality operators in a given implementation depends on which model of enumeration types is adopted by that implementation. See section 5.6. If such comparison is permitted, then in effect the integer values of the elements of the enumeration type are compared.

The operator '<' tests for the relationship "is less than"; '<=' tests "is less than or equal to"; '>' tests "is greater than"; and '>=' tests "is greater than or equal to." The result is 1 if the stated relationship holds for the particular operand values and 0 if the stated relationship does not hold.

The binary inequality operators all have the same precedence and are left-associative. It is therefore permitted to write an expression such as 3<x<7. This does not have the meaning it has in usual mathematical notation, however; by left-associativity it is interpreted as (3<x)<7. Because the result of (3<x) is 0 or 1, either of which is less than 7, the result of 3<x<7 is always 1. One must express the meaning of the usual mathematical notation by using a bitwise AND operator, as in 3<x & x<7, or a logical AND operator, as in 3<x && x<7.

The programmer should exercise care when using inequality operators on mixed types. A particularly confusing case is this expression:

```
-1 < (unsigned) 0
```

One might think that this expression would always produce 1 (true), because −1 is less than 0. However, the usual binary conversions cause the value −1 to be converted to a (large) unsigned value before the comparison, and such an unsigned value cannot be less than 0. Therefore, the expression always produces 0 (false).

References   arithmetic types 5; array types 5.5; bitwise AND operator '&' 7.5.6; enumeration types 5.6; floating types 5.3; integer types 5.2; logical AND operator '&&' 7.6.1; lvalue 7.1; pointer types 5.4; precedence 7.2.2; signed types 5.2.1; unsigned types 5.2.2; usual binary conversions 6.13

7.5.5 Equality Operators

The binary operators '==' and '!=' indicate comparison.

equality-expression ::= *expression equality-operator expression*

equality-operator ::= '==' | '!='

In this they are similar to the binary inequality operators discussed in section 7.5.4; they differ in testing different relationships and in having a different level of precedence. The usual binary conversions are performed on the operands. The result is always of type int and has the value 0 or 1. The result is not an lvalue.

The operands may both be of arithmetic types or may both be of the same pointer type or may both be of the same enumeration type, or one of the operands may be a pointer and the other a constant integer expression with value 0.

For integral operands, integer comparison is performed. For floating-point operands, floating-point comparison is performed. Pointer operands are considered equal if they point to the same object or if they are both null. Enumeration operands are equal if their values are enumeration elements with the same value. A pointer is equal to the integer constant 0 if and only if it is a null pointer.

The operator '==' tests for the relationship "is equal to"; '!=' tests "is not equal to." The result is 1 if the stated relationship holds for the particular operand values and 0 if the stated relationship does not hold.

The programmer should be very careful not to confuse the '==' operator with the '=' operator. The '==' operator performs equality comparison; the '=' operator performs simple assignment. Several other programming languages use '=' for equality comparison. As a matter of style, if it is necessary to use an assignment expression in a context that will test the value of the expression against zero, it is best to write "!= 0" explicitly to make the intent clear. For example, consider this code:

```
while (x = next_item()) {
    . . .
}
```

It is unclear whether this is correct or whether it contains a typographical error that should be corrected to

```
while (x == next_item()) {
    . . .
}
```

The intent can be made explicitly clear in this manner:

```
while ((x = next_item()) != 0) {
    . . .
}
```

The binary equality operators both have the same precedence (but lower precedence than '<', '<=', '>', and '>=') and are left-associative. It is therefore permitted to write an expression such as x==y==7. This does not have the meaning it has in usual mathematical notation, however; by left-associativity it is interpreted as (x==y)==7. Because the result of (x==y) is 0 or 1, neither of which is equal to 7, the result of x==y==7 is always 0. One must express the meaning of the usual mathematical notation by using a bitwise AND operator, as in x==y & y==7, or a logical AND operator, as in x==y && y==7.

There is a bitwise XOR operator as well as bitwise AND and OR operators, but there is no logical XOR operator to go along with the logical AND and OR operators. The '!=' operator serves the purpose of a logical XOR operator: One may write a<b != c<d for an expression that yields 1 if exactly one of a<b and c<d yields 1, and 0 otherwise. If either of the operands might have a value other than 0 or 1, then the unary '!' operator can be applied to both operands: !x != !y yields 1 if exactly one of x and y is nonzero, and yields 0 otherwise. In a similar manner, '==' serves as a logical equivalence (EQV) operator.

References   arithmetic types 5; array types 5.5; bitwise AND operator '&' 7.5.6; bitwise OR operator '|' 7.5.8; bitwise XOR operator '^' 7.5.7; enumeration types 5.6; floating types 5.3; integer types 5.2; logical AND operator '&&' 7.6.1; logical NOT operator '!' 7.4.4; logical OR operator '||' 7.6.2; lvalue 7.1; pointer types 5.4; precedence 7.2.2; signed types 5.2.1; simple assignment operator '=' 7.8.1; unsigned types 5.2.2; usual binary conversions 6.13

7.5.6 Bitwise AND Operator

The binary operator '&' indicates the bitwise AND function.

  bitwise-and-expression ::= *expression* '&' *expression*

The operands must both be integral and the usual binary conversions are performed on the operands. The type of the result is that of the converted operands. The result is not an lvalue.

Each bit of the result is equal to the AND function of the two corresponding bits of the two (converted) operands. The AND function yields a 1-bit if both arguments are 1-bits, and otherwise yields a 0-bit.

The bitwise AND operator '&' may be used to combine logical (integer 0 or 1) values, yielding the integer value 1 if both operands are the integer value 1, and yielding the integer value 0 if either operand is the integer value 0. For this purpose it differs from the logical AND operator '&&' in that both operands for '&' are always fully evaluated, whereas the right operand of '&&' is not evaluated if the left operand is zero.

Of course, the operators '&' and '&&' also differ in that the result of '&&' is *always* 0 or 1, no matter what the values of the operands, while this is not so for '&'.

The '&' operator is commutative and associative, and the compiler is permitted to rearrange an expression with several bitwise AND operators, even in the presence of parentheses. For example, the compiler may freely interpret the expression a&(b&c)&d as if it were (c&a)&(b&d), subject to the restrictions discussed in section 7.11.

Because different implementations may use different representations for signed integers, the result of applying the bitwise AND operator '&' to signed operands may not be portable. For portable code we recommend using '&' only on unsigned operands or on signed 0/1 values such as result from inequality operators.

References   integer types 5.2; lvalue 7.1; order of evaluation 7.11; signed types 5.2.1; unsigned types 5.2.2; usual binary conversions 6.13

7.5.7 *Bitwise XOR Operator*

The binary operator '^' indicates the bitwise XOR function.

> *bitwise-xor-expression* ::= *expression* '^' *expression*

The operands must both be integral and the usual binary conversions are performed on the operands. The type of the result is that of the converted operands. The result is not an lvalue.

Each bit of the result is equal to the XOR function of the two corresponding bits of the two (converted) operands. The XOR function yields a 1-bit if one argument is a 1-bit and the other is a 0-bit, and yields a 0-bit if both arguments are 1-bits or if both arguments are 0-bits.

The '^' operator is commutative and associative, and the compiler is permitted to rearrange an expression with several bitwise XOR operators, even in the presence of parentheses. For example, the compiler may freely interpret the expression a^(b^c)^d as if it were (c^a)^(b^d), subject to the restrictions discussed in section 7.11.

Because different implementations may use different representations for signed integers, the result of applying the bitwise XOR operator '^' to signed operands may not be portable. For portable code we recommend using '^' only on unsigned operands or on signed 0/1 values such as result from inequality operators.

References   integer types 5.2; lvalue 7.1; order of evaluation 7.11; signed types 5.2.1; unsigned types 5.2.2; usual binary conversions 6.13

7.5.8 *Bitwise OR Operator*

The binary operator '|' indicates the bitwise OR function.

> *bitwise-or-expression* ::= *expression* '|' *expression*

The operands must both be integral and the usual binary conversions are performed on the operands. The type of the result is that of the converted operands. The result is not an lvalue.

Each bit of the result is equal to the OR function of the two corresponding bits of the two (converted) operands. The OR function yields a 1-bit if either argument is a 1-bit, and otherwise yields a 0-bit.

The bitwise OR operator '|' may be used to combine logical (integer 0 or 1) values, yielding the integer value 1 if either operand is the integer value 1 and the other operand is the integer value 0 or 1, and yielding the integer value

0 if both operands are the integer value 0. For this purpose it differs from the logical OR operator '⎮⎮' in that both operands for '⎮' are always fully evaluated, whereas the right operand of '⎮⎮' is not evaluated if the left operand is nonzero.

Of course, the operators '⎮' and '⎮⎮' also differ in that the result of '⎮⎮' is *always* 0 or 1, no matter what the values of the operands, while this is not so for '⎮'.

The '⎮' operator is commutative and associative, and the compiler is permitted to rearrange an expression with several bitwise OR operators, even in the presence of parentheses. For example, the compiler may freely interpret the expression a⎮(b⎮c)⎮d as if it were (c⎮a)⎮(b⎮d), subject to the restrictions discussed in section 7.11.

Because different implementations may use different representations for signed integers, the result of applying the bitwise OR operator '⎮' to signed operands may not be portable. For portable code we recommend using '⎮' only on unsigned operands or on signed 0/1 values such as result from inequality operators.

Tables 7-3 through 7-6 show a library that defines a "set" package. It uses the bitwise operators to implement sets as bit vectors. Table 7-7 shows a program that uses certain facilities in the set package to enumerate and print certain sets. Table 7-8 shows the output produced by that program.

References   integer types 5.2; lvalue 7.1; order of evaluation 7.11; signed types 5.2.1; unsigned types 5.2.2; usual binary conversions 6.13

7.6 LOGICAL OPERATOR EXPRESSIONS

logical-operator-expression ::= *logical-and-expression*
                              ⎮ *logical-or-expression*

A logical operator expression consists of two expressions separated by one of the logical operators '&&' and '⎮⎮'. The two operators have different levels of precedence; '&&' has higher precedecne than '⎮⎮'.

Both of the logical operators described in this section are described as being syntactically left-associative, though this doesn't matter much to the programmer because the operators happen to be fully associative semantically and no two operators have the same level of precedence. (Implementors find the fact of syntactic left-associativity useful because it tends to make it easier for relatively simple compilers to produce good code for these operators than right-associativity would.)

For each of the logical operators described in this section, the second operand is *not evaluated at all* if the value of the first operand provides sufficient information to determine the result of the logical operator expression.

References   precedence 7.2.2

```
/* A set package, suitable for sets of small integers
   in the range 0 (inclusive) to the number of bits in
   an 'unsigned int' type (exclusive).  Each integer is
   represented by a bit position; if the bit is 1, the
   integer is in the set; if the bit is 0,  the integer
   is not in the set.  The low-order bit represents
   the element 0.
*/

/* Maximum bits per set (implementation dependent). */
#define SET_BITS 32

typedef unsigned SET;   /* A type to represent sets. */

/* check: true if i can be a set element. */
#define check(i)          ( ((unsigned) (i)) < SET_BITS )

/* emptyset: a set with no elements. */
#define emptyset                ((SET) 0)

/* add: add a single integer to a set. */
#define add(set,i)              ((set) | singleset(i))

/* singleset: return a set with one element in it. */
#define singleset(i)            (((SET) 1) << (i))

/* intersect: return intersection of two sets. */
#define intersect(set1,set2)    ((set1) & (set2))

/* union: return the union of two sets. */
#define union(set1,set2)        ((set1) | (set2))

/* setdiff: symmetric set difference; return a set of
   those elements that appear in either argument set
   but not both. */
#define setdiff(set1,set2)      ((set1) ^ (set2))

/* element: true if integer i is in the set. */
#define element(i,set)          (singleset((i)) & (set))
```

Table 7-3:   A Package for Manipulating Sets of Integers (Part 1)

```
/* forallelements: perform the following statement
   once for every element of the set s, with the
   variable j set to that element.  For example, to
   print all the elements in a set z, just write
        {
             int k;
             forallelements(k, z)
                  printf("%d ", k);
        }
 */
#define forallelements(j,s) \
 for ((j)=0; (j)<SET_BITS; ++(j)) if (element((j),(s)))

/* cardinality: return the number of elements in x. */
int cardinality(x)
   SET x;
{
    int count = 0;
    /*  At this point one could simply write
                int j;
                forallelements(j, x) ++count;
        which would obviously count all the elements of
        the set. However, the following loop is faster
        (but trickier).
     */
    while (x != emptyset) {
        /* The body of this loop is executed once for
           every 1-bit in the set x. Each time through,
           the smallest remaining element is removed
           from x (and counted).  The trick is that the
           expression (x & -x) yields a set that
           contains  the smallest element in x and no
           others.  This trick exploits properties of
           binary representation and unsigned negation.
         */
        x ^= (x & -x);
        ++count;
    }
    return count;
}
```

Table 7-4:   A Package for Manipulating Sets of Integers (Part 2)

```
/* Produce a set of size n whose elements are the
   integers from 0 to n-1 (inclusive).  This is a bit
   tricky, and exploits the properties of unsigned
   subtraction. */
#define first_set_of_n_elements(n)   (SET)((1<<(n))-1)



/* Given a set of n elements, produce a new set of n
   elements.  If you start with the result of
   first_set_of_n_elements(k), and then at each step
   apply next_set_of_n_elements to the previous result,
   and keep going until a set is obtained containing
   m as a member, you will have obtained sets
   representing all possible ways of choosing k things
   from m things.
 */
SET next_set_of_n_elements(x)
  SET x;
{
    /* This code exploits many unusual properties of
       unsigned arithmetic.  As an illustration,
       suppose that the bit pattern 001011001111000
       is given as the argument x. */
    SET smallest = (x & -x);
    /* The value of "smallest" is   000000000001000 */
    SET ripple = x + smallest;
    /* The value of "ripple" is      001011010000000 */
    SET new_smallest = (ripple & -ripple);
    /* Now "new_smallest" is         000000010000000 */
    SET ones = ((new_smallest / smallest) >> 1) - 1;
    /* Now "ones" is                 000000000000111 */
    return (ripple | ones);
    /* The returned value is         001011010000111 */
    /* The overall idea is that you find the rightmost
       contiguous group of 1-bits.  Of that group, you
       slide the leftmost 1-bit to the left one place,
       and slide all the others back to the extreme
       right.  (This code was adapted from HAKMEM.) */
}
```

Table 7-5:   A Package for Manipulating Sets of Integers (Part 3)

```
/* Print a set in the form "{1, 2, 3, 4}". */
void printset(z)
  SET z;
{
    int first = 1;
    int e;
    /* Print the elements, with leading punctuation. */
    forallelements(e, z) {
        if (first) printf("{");
        else printf(", ");
        printf("%d", e);
        first = 0;
    }
    /* Take care of the empty set. */
    if (first) printf("{");
    /* Print trailing punctuation. */
    printf("}");
}
```

Table 7-6:   A Package for Manipulating Sets of Integers (Part 4)

```
#define LINE_WIDTH 54

/* Print all the sets of size k having elements less
   than n.  Try to print as many as will fit on each
   line of the output.  Also print the total number of
   such sets; it should equal n!/(k!*(n-k)!) where "!"
   is the factorial symbol (5! = 1*2*3*4*5 = 120). */
void print_k_of_n(k, n)
   int k, n;
{
    int count = 0;
    /* Estimate how wide each printed set will be. */
    int printed_set_width = k * ((n > 10) ? 4 : 3) + 3;
    int sets_per_line = LINE_WIDTH / printed_set_width;
    SET z - first_set_of_n_elements(k);

    printf("\nAll the size-%d subsets of ", k);
    printset(first_set_of_n_elements(n));
    printf(":\n");
    do {                        /* Enumerate all the sets. */
        printset(z);
        if ((++count) % sets_per_line) printf ("    ");
        else printf("\n");
        z = next_set_of_n_elements(z);
    } while ((z != emptyset) && !element(n, z));
    if ((count) % sets_per_line) printf ("\n");
    printf("The total number of such subsets is %d.\n",
           count);
}

/* The main program merely tries some examples. */
void main()
{
    print_k_of_n(0, 4);
    print_k_of_n(1, 4);
    print_k_of_n(2, 4);
    print_k_of_n(3, 4);
    print_k_of_n(4, 4);
    print_k_of_n(3, 5);
    print_k_of_n(3, 6);
}
```

Table 7-7:   A Program for Enumerating Subsets of a Given Set

```
All the size-0 subsets of {0, 1, 2, 3}:
{}
The total number of such sets is 1.

All the size-1 subsets of {0, 1, 2, 3}:
{0}    {1}    {2}    {3}
The total number of such sets is 4.

All the size-2 subsets of {0, 1, 2, 3}:
{0, 1}    {0, 2}    {1, 2}    {0, 3}    {1, 3}    {2, 3}
The total number of such sets is 6.

All the size-3 subsets of {0, 1, 2, 3}:
{0, 1, 2}    {0, 1, 3}    {0, 2, 3}    {1, 2, 3}
The total number of such sets is 4.

All the size-4 subsets of {0, 1, 2, 3}:
{0, 1, 2, 3}
The total number of such sets is 1.

All the size-3 subsets of {0, 1, 2, 3, 4}:
{0, 1, 2}    {0, 1, 3}    {0, 2, 3}    {1, 2, 3}
{0, 1, 4}    {0, 2, 4}    {1, 2, 4}    {0, 3, 4}
{1, 3, 4}    {2, 3, 4}
The total number of such sets is 10.

All the size-3 subsets of {0, 1, 2, 3, 4, 5}:
{0, 1, 2}    {0, 1, 3}    {0, 2, 3}    {1, 2, 3}
{0, 1, 4}    {0, 2, 4}    {1, 2, 4}    {0, 3, 4}
{1, 3, 4}    {2, 3, 4}    {0, 1, 5}    {0, 2, 5}
{1, 2, 5}    {0, 3, 5}    {1, 3, 5}    {2, 3, 5}
{0, 4, 5}    {1, 4, 5}    {2, 4, 5}    {3, 4, 5}
The total number of such sets is 20.
```

Table 7-8: Sample Output from Enumerating Subsets of a Given Set

7.6.1 Logical AND Operator

The logical AND operator '&&' is called "conditional and" in other programming languages.

> *logical-and-expression* ::= *expression* '&&' *expression*

The logical operator '&&' accepts operands of any scalar type. There is no constraint between the types of the two operands. The type of the result is always int and has the value 0 or 1. The result is not an lvalue.

The left operand of '&&' is fully evaluated first. If the left operand is equal to zero (in the sense of the '==' operator), then the right operand is not evaluated and the result value is 0. If the left operand is not equal to zero, then the right operand is evaluated; if the right operand is equal to zero, then the result value is 0 and otherwise is 1.

Unlike the binary bitwise AND operator '&', the logical operator '&&' guarantees left-to-right conditional evaluation.

> **References**   bitwise AND operator '&' 7.5.6; enumeration types 5.6; floating types 5.3; integer types 5.2; lvalue 7.1; pointer types 5.4; scalar types 5

7.6.2 Logical OR Operator

The logical OR operator '||' is called "conditional or" in other programming languages.

> *logical-or-expression* ::= *expression* '||' *expression*

The logical operator '||' accepts operands of any scalar type. There is no constraint between the types of the two operands. The type of the result is always int and has the value 0 or 1. The result is not an lvalue.

The left operand of '||' is fully evaluated first. If the value of the left operand is not equal to zero (in the sense of the '==' operator), then the right operand is not evaluated and the result value is 1. If the left operand is equal to zero, then the right operand is evaluated; if the right operand is not equal to zero, then the result value is 1 and otherwise is 0.

Unlike the binary bitwise OR operator '|', the logical operator '||' guarantees left-to-right conditional evaluation.

> **References**   bitwise OR operator '|' 7.5.8; enumeration types 5.6; floating types 5.3; integer types 5.2; lvalue 7.1; pointer types 5.4; scalar types 5

7.7 CONDITIONAL EXPRESSIONS

> *conditional-expression* ::= *expression* '?' *expression* ':' *expression*

A conditional expression consists of three expressions, with the first and second expressions separated by '?' and the second and third expressions separated by ':'.

The first operand is used to determine which of the other two operands should be evaluated. The first operand is fully evaluated. If the first operand is not equal to zero (in the sense of the '==' operator), then the second operand is evaluated and the third operand is not evaluated; the result value is the value of the (possibly converted) second operand. If first operand is equal to zero, then the second operand is not evaluated and the third operand is evaluated; the result value is the value of the (possibly converted) third operand. In either case, the result is not an lvalue.

Conditional expressions are right-associative with respect to their first and third operands, so that

```
a ? b : c ? d : e ? f : g
```

is interpreted as

```
a ? b : (c ? d : (e ? f : g))
```

Here is one example where this might be useful:

```
/* Return 1, -1, or 0 if x is positive,
   negative, or zero, respectively. */
int signum(x)
  int x;
{
    return (x > 0) ? 1 : (x < 0) ? -1 : 0;
}
```

Anything more complicated than this is probably better done with one or more if statements.

The second operand of a conditional expression may be any expression whatsoever and may use operators that have lower precedence. There is no possibility of confusion, because the tokens '?' and ':' effectively bracket the second operand like parentheses. However, the third operand cannot involve operators of lower precedence without the use of parentheses. As an example, the expression

```
a ? b = c : c = b
```

is not legal. The first assignment is all right, but the second assignment causes a problem. Because the assignment operator has lower precedence than the conditional operator, the expression must be interpreted as

```
(a ? b = c : c) = b
```

However, a conditional expression cannot produce an lvalue, and so the assignment is illegal. When there is any doubt, it is better to use too many parentheses than too few:

    a ? (b = c) : (c = b)

The first operand of a conditional expression may be of any scalar type. There are four possibilities for the second and third operands:

1. They may both be arithmetic. The usual binary conversions are performed on the second and third operands, and the type of the result is the common type to which the operands are converted.
2. They may be pointers of the same type, after application of the usual unary conversions, if necessary, to convert functions and arrays to pointers. The result is a pointer of this same type.
3. They may have identical types (structure, union, enumeration, or void). The result has this same type.
4. One may be a pointer (after the usual unary conversions) and the other a constant integer expression with value 0. The result is of the same type as the pointer operand.

As a matter of style, it is a good idea to enclose the first operand of a conditional expression in parentheses, but this is not required.

Not all existing implementations of C permit the result of a conditional expression to have structure, union, enumeration, or void types. New implementations should permit them.

References   arithmetic types 5; array types 5.5; enumeration types 5.6; floating types 5.3; integer types 5.2; lvalue 7.1; pointer types 5.4; precedence 7.2.2; scalar types 5; signed types 5.2.1; structure types 5.7; union types 5.8; unsigned types 5.2.2; usual binary conversions 6.13; usual unary conversions 6.12; `void` type 5.10

7.8 ASSIGNMENT EXPRESSIONS

assignment-expression ::= *expression assignment-operator expression*

assignment-operator ::= '=' | '+=' | '−=' | '*=' | '/=' | '%='
          | '<<=' | '>>=' | '&=' | '^=' | '|='

An assignment expression consists of two expressions separated by an assignment operator. The operator '=' is called the *simple* assignment operator; all the others are *compound* assignment operators.

Assignment operators are all of the same level of precedence and are right-associative (all other operators in C that take two operands are left-associative).

For example, the expression `x*=y=z` is treated as `x*=(y=z)`, not as `(x*=y)=z`; similarly, the expression `x=y*=z` is treated as `x=(y*=z)`, not as `(x=y)*=z`. The right-associativity of assignment operators allows "multiple assignment expressions" to have the "obvious" interpretation; the expression

```
a = b = c = d + 7
```

is interpreted as

```
a = (b = (c = d + 7))
```

and therefore assigns the value of d+7 to c then to b then to a.

Every assignment operator requires an lvalue as its left operand and modifies that lvalue by storing a new value into it; the operators are distinguished by how they compute the new value to be stored. The result of an assignment expression is never an lvalue.

> **References**   lvalue 7.1; precedence 7.2.2

7.8.1 Simple Assignment

The simple assignment operator '=' indicates simple assignment. The value of the right operand is stored into the left operand. The two operands may each be of any arithmetic type, in which case the usual assignment conversions are used to convert the right operand to the type of the left operand before assignment. The two operands may also be of the same pointer, enumeration, structure, or union type. Finally, it is permitted for the left operand to be of any pointer type and the right operand to be the integer constant 0; this has the effect of assigning a null pointer to the pointer lvalue, guaranteed not to point at any object.

The type of the result is equal to the (unconverted) type of the left operand. The result is the value stored into the left operand. The result is not an lvalue.

The simple assignment operator '=' cannot be used to copy the entire contents of one array into another, for two reasons. First, the name of an array is not an lvalue and so cannot appear on the left-hand side of an assignment. Second, the name of an array appearing on the right-hand side of an assignment would be converted (by the usual conversions) to be a pointer to the first element, and so the assignment would copy the pointer, not the contents of the array. The '=' operator can, therefore, be used to copy the address of an array into a pointer variable:

```
{
    int a[20], *p;
    p = a;
    ...
```

In this example, a is an array of integers and p is of type "pointer to integer." The assignment causes p to point to (the first element of) the array a.

It is possible to get the effect of copying an entire array by embedding the array within a structure or union, because simple assignment can copy an entire structure or union:

```
struct matrix {double contents[10][10]; };

struct matrix a, b;
...
{
    /* Copy structure containing a 10x10 array. */
    a = b;
    /* Clear the diagonal elements. This
       illustrates how the array is accessed. */
    for (j = 0; j < 10; j++)
        a.contents[j][j];
}
```

In the original description of C, assignment of structure and union objects was not permitted. Nearly all C compilers now permit structure and union assignment.

References   arithmetic types 5; array types 5.5; assignment conversions 6.11; enumeration types 5.6; floating types 5.3; integer types 5.2; lvalue 7.1; pointer types 5.4; scalar types 5; signed types 5.2.1; structure types 5.7; union types 5.8; unsigned types 5.2.2

7.8.2 Compound Assignment

The compound assignment operators may be informally understood by taking the expression "*a op= b*" to be equivalent to "*a = a op b*," with the proviso that the expression *a* is evaluated only once. More precisely, the left and right operands of '*op=*' are evaluated, and the left operand must be an lvalue. The operation indicated by the operator '*op*' is then applied to the two operand values; this includes any "usual conversions" performed by the operator. The resulting value is then stored into the left operand lvalue, after performing the usual assignment conversions.

For the operators '+=' and '−=', the two operands may each be of any arithmetic type. It is also permitted for the left operand to be of pointer type and the right operand to be of integral type. Whether an enumeration value is a legitimate operand for the operators '+=' and '−=' in a given implementation depends on which model of enumeration types is adopted by that implementation. See section 5.6. If the "pointer model"is used, then it is permitted for the left operand to be of enumeration type and the right operand to be of integral type.

For the operators '∗=' and '/=', the two operands may each be of any arithmetic type.

For the operator '%=', the two operands may each be of any integral type.

For the operators '<<=', '>>=', the two operands may each be of any integral type. For portable code we recommend that only unsigned operands be used as the left operand for each of these operators.

For the operators '&=', '^=', and '|=', the two operands may each be of any integral type. For portable code we recommend that only unsigned operands be used with these operators.

For the compound assignment operators, as for the simple assignment operator, the type of the result is equal to the (unconverted) type of the left operand. The result is the value stored into the left operand. The result is not an lvalue.

In the original definition of C, all of the assignment operators except '=' were considered to consist syntactically of two distinct tokens, the operator and then the associated equal sign. The effect of this was to permit white space or comments between the two parts of an assignment operator:

```
pattern & = mask;   /* This means the same as
                       ``pattern &= mask.''*/
```

While this does not cause any syntactic ambiguities, it does make it much more difficult to write an LALR(1) grammar for C expressions. Requiring assignment operators to be written as a single syntactic token eliminates this difficulty. From the programmer's point of view, it also increases portability, because some C compilers in fact may not permit such separation into two tokens. Most programmers have treated the compound assignment operators as being single tokens anyway, considering it poor style to separate them with white space.

Historical note: In the earliest versions of C, the compound assignment operators were written in the reverse form: '=+', '=−', '=∗', '=/', '=%', '=<<', '=>>', '=&', '=^', and '=|'. This led to syntactic ambiguities. For example, the expression

```
x=−1
```

might,on the face of it, be interpreted either as

```
x = (−1)
```

or as

```
x  =-  ( 1 )
```

While the ambiguity was arbitrarily resolved by requiring the latter interpretation, this was found to be quite prone to subtle programming errors in practice.
The newer form ('+=' instead of '=+') eliminates these difficulties. While a few
compilers continue to support the older forms for the sake of compatibility, they
were officially considered to be obsolete even in the original description of C
and should not be used in new C programs nor supported by new compiler implementations.

> **References**   arithmetic types 5; assignment conversions 6.11; enumeration types 5.6; float-
> ing types 5.3; integer types 5.2; pointer types 5.4; signed types 5.2.1; unsigned types 5.2.2; usual
> binary conversions 6.13; usual unary conversions 6.12

7.9 SEQUENTIAL EXPRESSIONS

A comma expression consists of two expressions separated by a comma. The
comma operator is described here as being syntactically left-associative, though
this doesn't matter much to the programmer because the operator happens to be
fully associative semantically.

> *comma-expression* ::= *expression* ' , ' *expression*

The left operand of ' , ' is fully evaluated first. It need not produce any
value; if it does produce a value, that value is discarded. The right operand is
then evaluated. The type and value of the result of the comma expression are
equal to the type and value of the right operand. The result is not an lvalue.
The comma operator is associative, and so one may write a single expression consisting of any number of expressions separated by commas; the subexpressions will be evaluated in order, and the value of the last one will become
the value of the entire expression.
In certain contexts the comma character is used for another syntactic purpose. Expressions written within these contexts may not use the comma
operator lest ambiguity arise. This restriction can always be circumvented by
using parentheses to enclose the comma operator expression. For example, the
expression

```
f(a,  b = 5,  2*b,  c)
```

is always treated as a call to the function f with four arguments. If it is desired
to treat the second comma as the comma operator, and to call f with three arguments, additional parentheses should be inserted, thus:

```
f(a,  (b = 5,  2*b),  c)
```

The contexts where the comma operator may not be used because of potential ambiguity include argument expressions in function calls; field-length expressions in structure and union declarator lists; enumeration value expressions in enumeration declarator lists; and initialization expressions in declarations and initializers. Note that the comma character is also used as a separator in preprocessor macro calls.

The comma operator guarantees that its operands will be evaluated in left-to-right order, but other uses of the comma character do not make this guarantee. For example, the argument expressions in a function invocation need not be evaluated in left-to-right order.

The most important application of the comma operator is in `for` statements; it allows several assignment expressions to be combined into a single expression for the purpose of initializing or stepping several variables in a single loop.

References discarded expressions 7.12; enumeration types 5.6; `for` statement 8.6.3 function calls 7.3.6; initializers 4.6; lvalue 7.1; macro calls 3.3.2; structure types 5.7; union types 5.8

7.10 CONSTANT EXPRESSIONS

In several contexts the C language permits an expression to be written that must evaluate to a constant at compile time (or, in some situations, at link time, but in any case before execution of the program proper). These contexts are:

1. the tested value in the `#if` preprocessor control statement
2. array bounds
3. `case` labels in `switch` statements
4. bit-field lengths in structure declarators
5. explicit enumerator values
6. initializers for static and external variables

Each context imposes slightly different restrictions on what forms of expression are permitted.

In all cases the result of evaluating a constant expression is identical to the result of evaluating the same expression at run time. For the compiler implementor, this consistency requirement is particularly important in the case of cross-compilation, where the computer being used to execute the compiler does not necessarily have the same architecture as the computer used to execute the compiled program. Although most kinds of integer arithmetic can be simulated well enough, floating-point arithmetic—even simply converting a floating-point constant from character form to internal form—may be difficult enough that the implementor may choose to do the evaluation of constant floating-point expressions at run time.   (C requires no compile-time floating-point arithmetic capability.)

All constant expressions may contain integer constants (including character constants). Casts to integral types may also be used. The binary operators

```
*    /    %    +    -    <<    >>    ==    !=
<    <=   >    >=   &    ^     |     &&    ||
```

may be used. The unary operators

```
-    ~    !
```

may be used. The conditional operator

```
?  :
```

may be used. Parentheses may be freely used for grouping. Function calls are not permitted.

Other constants and operations may be permitted in constant expressions according to context.

1. Preprocessor #if statements permit the use of the operator defined.
2. Array bounds, case labels, field lengths, and explicit enumerator values permit the use of enumeration constants and the sizeof operator. The operators, listed above, that are permitted in all constant expressions, may be applied to enumeration values (where appropriate) as well as to integers.
3. Initializers for static and external variables permit the use of enumeration constants, floating-point constants, and the sizeof operator. The operators, listed above, that are permitted in all constant expressions, may be applied to enumeration values (where appropriate) as well as to integers. The unary '&' operator is permitted when applied to the name of a static or external object or to the result of subscripting a static or external array by a constant expression. It is also permitted to use the name of a function to refer to its address, or to the name of a static or external array to refer to its address. Semantically, an initializer for a static or external variable must evaluate either to a constant or to the address of a previously declared static or external object plus or minus an integer constant.

The original description of C did not mention that the operator '!' is allowed in constant expressions, but this obviously was an oversight or typographical error. All C implementations should support this operator in constant expressions.

Some compilers do not permit casts of any kind in constant expressions. Others allow casts other than casts to integral types. When writing portable code, it is best for the programmer to avoid casts in constant expressions.

Some compilers permit the comma operator ',' in constant expressions. We don't see the use of it, inasmuch as the left operand of the comma operator is useful only for its side effects, and constant expressions may not have side effects.

References   address operator '&' 7.4.6; array types 5.5; bit fields 5.7.4; character constant 2.7.3; comma operator 7.9; defined operator 3.5.5; enumeration constants 5.6; enumeration types 5.6; floating-point constant 2.7.2; #if preprocessor command 3.5.1; initializers 4.6; integer constant 2.7.1; sizeof operator 7.4.2; structure types 5.7; switch statement 8.7

7.11 ORDER OF EVALUATION

In general, the compiler is free to rearrange the order in which an expression is evaluated with the following restrictions.

The rearrangement may consist only of evaluating the arguments of a function call, or the two operands of a binary operator, in some particular order other than the obvious left-to-right order. (The compiler is under no compulsion ever to use left-to-right order for such operators.) There is one additional rule: The binary operators '+', '*', '&', '^', and '|' are assumed to be completely associative and commutative, and a compiler is permitted to exploit this assumption. For instance, addition is assumed to be commutative and associative, so the compiler is free, for example, to evaluate "(a+b)+(c+d)" as if it were written "(a+d)+(b+c)" (assuming all variables have the same arithmetic type).

The assumption of commutativity and associativity is indeed always true for '&', '^', and '|' on unsigned operands. It may not be true for '&', '^', and '|' on signed operands because of potential problems with certain signed representations. It may not be true for '*' and '+' because of the possibility that the order indicated by the expression as written might avoid overflow but another order might not. Nevertheless, the compiler is allowed to exploit the assumption. In such situations the programmer must use assignments to temporary variables to force a particular evaluation order:

```
{
    int temp1, temp2;
    ...
    /* Compute q=(a+b)+(c+d), exactly that way. */
    temp1 = a+b;
    temp2 = c+d;
    q = temp1 + temp2;
}
```

The original description of C placed no restrictions on the exploitation of the assumption of the associativity and commutativity of '*', '+', '&', '^', and '|'. However, the following restriction seems to be very important and should be observed by every compiler: Any rearrangement of expressions involving these operators must not alter the implicit type conversions of the operands. In the example below, the two assignment statements are not equivalent and the compiler is not free to substitute one for the other, despite the fact that one is obtained from the other "merely by reassociating the additions."

```
x = (1.0 + -3) + (unsigned) 1;    /* Result is -1.0 */
x = 1.0 + (-3 + (unsigned) 1);    /* Result is large */
```

The first assignment is straightforward and produces the expected result. The second produces a large result, because the usual binary conversions cause the signed value -3 to be converted to a large unsigned value 2^n-3, where n is the number of bits used to represent an unsigned integer. This is then added to the unsigned value 1, the result converted to floating-point representation and added to 1.0, resulting in the value 2^n-3 in a floating-point representation. Now, this result may or may not be what the programmer intended, but the compiler must not confuse the issue further by capriciously rearranging the additions.

When evaluating the actual arguments in a function call, the order in which the arguments are evaluated is not specified; but the program must behave as if it chose one argument, evaluated it fully, then chose another argument, evaluated it fully, and so on, until all arguments were evaluated. That is, the arguments may be evaluated in any order, but their computations may not appear to be interleaved. Consider this example:

```
#define SIZE 100
{
    char *x[10], **p=x;
    ...
    if ( strcmp(*p++, *p++) == 0 ) printf("Same.");
    ...
}
```

The variable x is an array of pointers to characters and is to be regarded as an array of strings. The variable p is a pointer to a pointer to a character and is to be regarded as a pointer to a string. The purpose of the if statement is to determine whether the string pointed to by p (call it *s1*) and the next string after that (call it *s2*) one are equal (and, in passing, to step the pointer p beyond those two strings in the array). It is, of course, bad programming style to have two side effects on the same variable in the same expression, because the order of the side effects is not defined; but the all-too-clever programmer here has reasoned that the order of the side effects doesn't matter, because the two strings in question may be given to `strcmp` in either order.

If it were permitted for the compiler to evaluate the two expressions in an interleaved manner, it might generate code something like this:

1. Fetch what p points to for first argument.
2. Fetch what p points to for second argument.
3. Increment p for first argument.
4. Increment p for second argument.

The net result would be that *s1* would be passed as both arguments to `strcmp` and *s2* would not be passed at all. The restriction against interleaving prohibits such behavior. Our too-clever programmer is therefore justified in believing the program will behave as intended. (However, we would not want to have to maintain that code!)

A similar restriction holds for binary operators: The two operands may be evaluated in either order, but the program must behave as if one of the two operands were evaluated completely before commencement of the evaluation of the other operand.

The original description of C specified that subexpressions may be evaluated in any order and that the arguments to a function may be evaluated in any order. The matter of interleaving was not discussed, nor the question of whether rearranging may alter the implicit type conversions. We advise implementors to adhere rigidly to the restrictions outlined here (which actually are quite sensible and not terribly restrictive). We also advise programmers not to exploit these restrictions too cleverly (as in the example above using `strcmp`). The entire purpose of the restrictions is to make the behavior of a program more understandable.

> **References**   addition operator '+' 7.5.2; binary operators 7.5; bitwise AND operator '&' 7.5.6; bitwise OR operator 'ı' 7.5.8; bitwise XOR operator '^' 7.5.7; function calls 7.3.6; multiplication operator '*' 7.5.1; `strcmp` function 11.2.3; usual binary conversions 6.13

7.12 DISCARDED VALUES

There are three contexts in which an expression can appear but its value is not used:

1. an expression statement
2. the first operand of a comma expression
3. the initialization and incrementation expressions in a `for` statement

In these contexts we say that the expression's value is *discarded*.

When the value of an expression without side effects is discarded, the compiler may presume that an error has been made and issue a warning. Side effect-producing operations include assignment and function calls. For example:

```
{
      extern void f();
      f(x);        /*  These expressions do not   */
      i++;         /*  justify any warning about  */
      a = b;       /*  discarded values.          */
}
```

The compiler may issue a warning message if the main operator of a discarded expression has no side effect. For example, these statements, though legal, may elicit warning messages:

```
{
      extern int g();
      g(x);     /* The call to g may have side effects
                   but it also returns a value that is
                   discarded. */
      x + 7;    /* Addition has no defined
                   side effects. */
      x + (a *= 2);
                /* The expression has a side effect,
                   but the last operation to be
                   performed, "+", does not, and its
                   value is discarded. */
}
```

The programmer may avoid warnings about discarded values by using a cast to type void to indicate that the value is purposely being discarded:

```
{
      extern int g();
      (void) g(x);    /* The returned value is
                         purposely discarded. */

      (void)(x + 7);  /* This is pretty silly, but
                         presumably the programmer
                         has a purpose. */
}
```

A compiler that does not implement the void type should not issue warnings when the value of a function call is discarded, because it is likely that the function being called is conceptually of type "function returning void," even though the programmer has no way to say this to the compiler.

If a compiler determines that the main operator of a discarded expression has no side effect, it may choose not to generate code for that operator (whereupon its operands become discarded values and may be recursively subjected to the same treatment).

References   assignments 7.8; casts 7.4.1; comma operator 7.9; `for` statement 8.6.3; function calls 7.3.6; expressions statements 8.2; `void` type 5.10

7.13 COMPILER OPTIMIZATION OF MEMORY ACCESSES

As a general rule, a compiler is free to generate any code equivalent in computational behavior to the program as written. The compiler is explicitly granted certain freedoms to rearrange code, as described in section 7.11. It may also generate no code for an expression when the expression has no side effects and its value is discarded, as described in section 7.12.

Some compilers may also reorganize the code in such a way that it does not always refer to memory as many times, or in the same order, as specified in the program. For example, if a certain array element is referred to more than once, the compiler may cleverly arrange to fetch it only once to gain speed; in effect, it might rewrite this code:

```
{
     int x;
     x = a[j] * a[j] * a[j];
                    /* Cube the table entry. */
}
```

causing it to be executed as if it had been written like this:

```
{
     int x;
     register temp;
     temp = a[j];
     x = temp * temp * temp;
                    /* Cube the table entry. */
}
```

For most applications, including nearly all portable applications, such optimization techniques are a very good thing, because the speed of a program may be improved by a factor of two or better without altering its effective computational behavior.

However, this may be a problem when writing certain machine-dependent programs in C, such as operating systems. On some computers the status registers of I/O devices may be accessed as if they were memory locations, and accessing such a register may have side effects. The way to read a character from a terminal might be to access a specific "memory location"; every time the location is read, a new character is obtained.

Consider this code to read characters in such a manner:

```
/* Address of the keyboard input register. */
#define KEYBOARD ((char *) 0177614)
...
c1 = *KEYBOARD;     /* Get first character. */
...
c2 = *KEYBOARD;     /* Get next character. */
```

It would be disastrous if this code were to be compiled as if it had been written this way:

```
/* Address of the keyboard input register. */
#define KEYBOARD ((char *) 0177614)
...
temp = *KEYBOARD;
c1 = temp;
...
c2 = temp;
```

A similar difficulty might arise when doing output by writing successive characters to a special "memory location": The compiler might notice that the location is written into and then written into again without being accessed, and therefore cleverly eliminate the first write operation. This is a good optimization for ordinary memory locations, but disastrous when an I/O register is involved.

We emphasize that this kind of problem does not arise in most applications, and it need not concern most programmers. The programmer who is writing low-level machine-dependent programs, such as operating systems, should carefully study the documentation for the specific C compiler to be used to determine whether problems like this may arise. Ideally, there will be a way to prohibit memory-access optimizations when compiling programs for which such optimizations would be incorrect.

8

Statements

The C language provides the usual assortment of statement forms found in most algebraic programming languages, including conditional statements, loops, and the ubiquitous "goto."

```
statement ::= expression-statement
        | labeled-statement
        | compound-statement
        | conditional-statement
        | iterative-statement
        | switch-statement
        | break-statement
        | continue-statement
        | return-statement
        | goto-statement
        | null-statement

conditional-statement ::= if-statement
                  | if-else-statement

iterative-statement ::= do-statement
                | while-statement
                | for-statement
```

We describe each of the statements in turn after some general comments about the syntax of statements.

References break statement 8.8; compound statement 8.4; continue statement 8.8; do statement 8.6.2; expression statement 8.2; for statement 8.6.3; goto statement 8.10; if statement 8.5; labeled statement 8.3; null statement 8.11; return statement 8.9; switch statement 8.7; while statement 8.6.1

8.1 GENERAL SYNTACTIC RULES FOR STATEMENTS

Although C statements will be familiar to programmers used to Algol-like languages, there are a few syntactic differences that are often the cause of confusion and errors.

8.1.1 Semicolons

As in Pascal or Ada, semicolons typically appear between consecutive statements in C. However, in C the semicolon is not a statement separator, but rather simply a part of the syntax of certain statements. The only C statement that does not require a terminating semicolon is the compound statement (or block), which is delimited by braces ('{' and '}') instead of the more usual begin and end keywords. For example, the Pascal (or Ada or Algol) statements

```
t := b;
begin b := a end;
a := t;
```

are written in C as

```
t = b;
{ b = a; }
a = t;
```

Note that in C a semicolon follows "b = a" but not '}', whereas the situation is reversed in the other languages.

8.1.2 Control Expressions

Another rule for C statements is that "control" expressions, appearing in conditional or iterative statements, must be enclosed in parentheses. These parentheses obviate the need for a keyword following the expression, such as "then" or "do." For example, the Pascal statement

```
if x = y then
    while x = z do
        process(x);
```

is rendered in C as

```
if ( x == y )
    while (x == z)
        process(x);
```

In all cases, if the control expression is 0, it is taken to be "false"; if it is nonzero, it is taken to be "true." More precisely, the type of a control expression e must be such that the expression

```
( e )  != 0
```

may be legally evaluated. If the result of this last expression is 1, e is said to be nonzero; otherwise, e is said to be zero. In practice, this means that e may have integral, pointer, or floating-point type. Values of enumeration types may also be permitted depending on the semantics chosen for enumerations.

References   '!=' operator 7.5.5; conditional statements 8.5; enumeration type 5.6; iterative statements 8.6

8.2 EXPRESSION STATEMENTS

Any expression can be treated as a statement by writing the expression followed by a semicolon.

expression-statement ::= *expression* '; '

The statement is executed by evaluating the expression and then discarding the value, if any.

An expression statement is useful only if evaluation of the expression involves a side effect, such as assigning a value to a variable or performing input or output. Usually the expression is an assignment, an incrementation or decrementation operation, or a function call. Here are some examples of expression statements:

```
speed = distance / time; /* Assign quotient to speed. */
++event_count;           /* Add 1 to event_count.     */
printf("Another game?"); /* Call the function printf. */
pattern &= mask;         /* Mask out some bits of
                                        the pattern. */
(x < y) ? ++x : ++y;     /* Increment the smaller of
                                          x and y. */
```

The last example, though legal, might be written more clearly with an if statement:

```
if (x < y) ++x; else ++y;
```

The compiler is not obliged to evaluate an expression, or a portion of an expression, that has no side effects and whose result is discarded. This is discussed in more detail in section 7.12.

References   assignment expressions 7.8; decrementation expressions 7.4.10, 7.4.11; discarded expressions 7.12; expressions 7.2.1; function call 7.3.6; incrementation expressions 7.4.8, 7.4.9

8.3 LABELED STATEMENTS

A label can be used to mark any statement so that control may be transferred to the statement by a `goto` or `switch` statement. There are three kinds of labels. A named label may appear on any statement and is used in conjunction with the `goto` statement. A `case` label or `default` label may appear only on a statement within the body of a `switch` statement.

labeled-statement ::= *label* ':' *statement*

label ::= *named-label*
       | *case-label*
       | *default-label*

A label cannot appear by itself but must always be attached to a statement. If it is desired to place a label by itself, for example at the end of a compound statement, it may be attached to a null statement.

Named labels are discussed further in the description of the `goto` statement. `case` labels and `default` labels are discussed further in the description of the `switch` statement.

References   goto statement 8.10; null statement 8.11; switch statement 8.7

8.4 COMPOUND STATEMENT

A compound statement—also called a block—consists of a (possibly empty) sequence of declarations followed by a (possibly empty) sequence of statements, all enclosed in braces.

compound-statement ::= '{' { *declaration* }* { *statement* }* '}'

A compound statement may appear anywhere a statement may appear. When the compound statement has no declarations, it just represents a group of statements. When the compound statement has declarations, it brings into existence a new scope.

A compound statement is normally executed by first processing all the declarations one at a time, in sequence, and then executing all the statements one at a time, in sequence. Execution ceases when the last statement has been executed or when control is transferred out of the compound statement through execution of a `goto`, `return`, `continue`, or `break` statement.

It is also possible to jump to a labeled statement within a compound statement by using a `goto` or `switch` statement outside the compound statement. When that happens, storage is allocated for any `auto` or `register` variables declared in the compound statement, but any initialization expressions for those variables are not evaluated and no initialization occurs. Execution then begins at the statement to which control was transferred and continues in sequence until the last statement has been executed or until control is transferred out of the compound statement through execution of a `goto`, `return`, `continue`, or `break` statement.

An unlabeled compound statement used as the body of a `switch` statement cannot be executed normally but only through transfer of control to labeled statements within it. Therefore, initializations of `auto` and `register` variables in such a compound statement never occur and their presence is a priori an error.

References   `auto` storage class 4.3; `break` statement 8.8; `continue` statement 8.8; declarations 4; `goto` statement 8.10; `register` storage class 4.3; `return` statement 8.9; scope 4.2.1

8.4.1 Declarations within Compound Statements

Each identifier declared at the beginning of a compound statement has a scope that extends from its declaration point to the end of the block. It is visible throughout that scope except when hidden by a declaration of the same identifier in an inner block.

An identifier declared at the beginning of a compound statement without a storage class specifier is assumed to have storage class `extern` if the type of the identifier is "function returning . . .", and is assumed to have storage class `auto` in all other cases. It is illegal for an identifier of function type to have any storage class except `extern` when it is declared at the beginning of a block.

If a variable or function is declared in a compound statement with storage class `extern`, then no storage is allocated and no initialization expression is permitted. The declaration refers to an external variable or function defined elsewhere, either in the same source file or a different source file.

If a variable is declared in a compound statement with storage class `auto` or `register`, then it is effectively reallocated every time the compound statement is entered and deallocated when the compound statement is exited. If there is an initialization expression for the variable, then the expression is reevaluated and the variable reinitialized every time the compound statement is entered normally. (The initialization expression is not evaluated and the variable not initialized when control is passed to a statement within the compound statement via a `goto` or `switch` statement from outside.) If there is no initialization expression for the variable, then the value of the variable is initially undefined every time the compound statement is executed; the value of the variable does not carry over from one execution of the compound statement to the next.

If a variable is declared in a compound statement with storage class `static`, then it is effectively allocated once, prior to program execution, just like any other static variable. If there is an initialization expression for the variable, then the expression is evaluated only once, prior to program execution, and the variable retains its value from one execution of the compound statement to the next.

References   auto storage class 4.3; extern storage class 4.3; goto statement 8.10; initial values 4.2.8; initializers 4.6; register storage class 4.3; scope 4.2.1; static storage class 4.3; switch statement 8.7; visibility 4.2.2

8.4.2 Use of Compound Statements

Compound statements without declarations are particularly useful as parts of other control statements, so that more than one statement can be executed conditionally or in a loop:

```
if (error_seen) {
    ++error_count;
    print_error_message();
}
```

With declarations, compound statements can also introduce additional variables with reduced visibility. This often helps to make a program clearer by restricting the area over which a variable is accessible:

```
if (first_time) {
    /* Clear the array. */
    int i;
    for (i = 0; i < 10; i++)
        a[i] = 0;
    /* Reset first-time flag. */
    first_time = 0;
}
```

C permits unrestricted jumps into compound statements, but we feel this is bad programming style. In fact, none of the languages Ada, Algol 60, Modula-2, Pascal, or PL/I permit jumps into blocks. The particular danger in C is not having initializations occur. For example, the following code fragment is unlikely to work if the statement labeled L: is jumped to from outside the compound statement, because the variable sum will not be initialized. Furthermore,

it is not possible to tell if any such jump does occur without examining at least
the entire body of the enclosing function.

```
{
    extern int a[100];
    int i, sum = 0;
  L:
    for (i = 0; i < 100; i++)
        sum += a[i];
    ...
}
```

References   declarations 4; goto statement 8.10; labeled statement 8.3

8.5 CONDITIONAL STATEMENT

There are two forms of conditional statement: with or without an else clause.
Each begins with the keyword if, followed by a control expression in parentheses, followed by a statement; there may be appended to this the keyword
else and then another statement. Note that C, unlike other programming languages such as Pascal, does not use the keyword then as part of the syntax of
its if statement.

  conditional-statement ::= *if-statement* | *if-else-statement*

  if-statement ::= if '(' *expression* ')' *statement*

  if-else-statement ::= if '(' *expression* ')' *statement* else *statement*

For each form of if statement the expression within parentheses is first
evaluated. If this value is nonzero (section 8.1.2), then the statement immediately following the parentheses is executed. If the value of the control expression is zero and there is an else clause, then the statement following the
keyword else is executed instead; but if the value of the control expression is
zero and there is no else clause, then execution continues immediately with
the statement following the conditional statement.

  References   control expression 8.1.2

8.5.1 Multiway Conditional Statements

A multiway decision can be expressed as a cascaded series of if-else statements, where each if statement but the last has another if statement in its
else clause. Such a series looks like this:

```
if  (expression1)
     statement1
else if  (expression2)
     statement2
else if  (expression3)
     statement3
...
else
     statementn
```

Here is an example of a three-way decision: The function `signum` returns one of three results depending on its argument.

```
/* Return 1, -1, or 0 if x is positive,
   negative, or zero, respectively. */
int signum(x)
  int x;
{
    if (x > 0) return 1;
    else if (x < 0) return -1;
    else return 0;
}
```

Compare this with the version of `signum` that uses conditional expressions shown in section 7.7.

The `switch` statement handles the specific kind of multiway decision where the value of an expression is to be compared against a fixed set of constants.

References   switch statement 8.7

8.5.2 The Dangling Else Problem

An ambiguity arises because a conditional statement may contain another conditional statement: In some situations it may not be apparent to which of several conditional statements an `else` might belong. Consider this example:

```
/* Warning: this example is indented
                 in a misleading fashion. */
if ((k >= 0) & (k < TABLE_SIZE))
    if (table[k] >= 0)
      printf("Entry %d is %d\n", k, table[k]);
  else printf("Error: index %d out of range.\n",k);
```

Inspection of the code might lead one to assume that whoever wrote this code intended the `else` part to be an alternative to the outer `if` statement: The error message should be printed when the test

```
(k >= 0) & (k < TABLE_SIZE)
```

is false. However, if we change the wording of the last error message to

```
else printf("Error: entry %d is negative.\n", k);
```

then one might assume that the programmer intended the `else` part to be executed when the test

```
table[k] >= 0
```

is false.

The C language does not require the compiler to interpret the meanings of error messages and make assumptions about the programmer's intentions. Instead, the ambiguity is resolved in an arbitrary but customary way: An `else` part is always assumed to belong to the *innermost* `if` statement possible. From this rule we see that the second interpretation of the code fragment above will work as intended, while the first will not. The first fragment can be made to work as intended by introducing a compound statement:

```
if (k >= 0 & k < TABLE_SIZE) {
    if (table[k] >= 0)
        printf("Entry %d is %d\n", k, table[k]);
}
else printf("Error: index %d out of range.\n", k);
```

To reduce confusion, the second interpretation could also use a compound statement:

```
if (k >= 0 & k < TABLE_SIZE) {
    if (table[k] >= 0)
        printf("Entry %d is %d\n", k, table[k]);
    else printf("Error: entry %d is negative.\n",k);
}
```

Confusion can be eliminated entirely if braces are always used to surround statements controlled by an `if` statement. However, this conservative rule can clutter a program with unnecessary braces. It seems to us that a good stylistic compromise between confusion and clutter is to use braces with an `if` statement whenever the statement controlled by the `if` is anything but an expression statement.

Appendix C contains a grammar for C that resolves the dangling `else` problem explicitly.

References   compound statement 8.4

8.6 ITERATIVE STATEMENTS

Three kinds of iteration statements are provided in C.

> *iterative-statement* ::= *while-statement*
> | *do-statement*
> | *for-statement*

The `while` statement tests an exit condition *before* each execution of a statement. The `do` statement tests an exit condition *after* each execution of a statement. The `for` statement provides a special syntax that is convenient for initializing and updating one or more control variables as well as testing an exit condition. The statement embedded within an iteration statement is sometimes called the *body* of the statement.

8.6.1 While Statement

A `while` statement consists of the keyword `while`, followed by a control expression in parentheses, followed by a statement.

> *while-statement* ::= `while` '(' *expression* ')' *statement*

Note that C, unlike other programming languages such as Pascal, does not use the keyword "do" as part of the syntax of its `while` statement.

The `while` statement is executed by first evaluating the control expression. If the result is not zero, then the statement is executed. The entire process is then repeated, alternately evaluating the expression and then, if the value is not zero, executing the statement. The value of the expression can change from time to time because of side effects in the statement or in the expression itself.

The execution of the `while` statement is complete when the control expression evaluates to zero, or when control is transferred out of the body of the `while` statement by a `return`, `goto`, or `break` statement. Also, the `continue` statement can modify the execution of a `while` statement.

As an example, the following code fragment uses a `while` loop to raise an integer x to the power specified by the nonnegative integer y (with no checking for overflow):

```
/* Compute x to the power y by repeated squaring. */
{
    int base = x;
    int exponent = y;
    int z = 1;
    while (exponent > 0) {
        if ( exponent % 2 )  /* If exponent is odd,   */
            z *= base;       /*   multiply z by base. */
        base *= base;        /* Square the base.       */
        exponent /= 2;       /* Divide exponent by 2. */
    }
    /* Now z is equal to x raised to the power y. */
}
```

The method used is that of repeated squaring of the base and decoding of the exponent in binary notation to determine when to multiply the base into the result. (To see why this works, note that the while loop maintains the invariant condition that z times base raised to the exponent power is equal to x raised to the y power. When eventually the exponent is 0, this condition degenerates to simply z equals x raised to the y power, which is the desired result.)

This while loop has a null statement for its body:

```
while ( *char_pointer++ );
```

The character pointer is advanced along by the '++' operator until a null character is found, and it is left pointing to the character after the null. This is a compact idiom for locating the end of a string. (Notice that the test expression depends on the fact that the postfix operator '++' has higher precedence than the indirection operator '*'. The test expression is interpreted as *(char_pointer++), not as (*char_pointer)++, which would increment the character pointed to by char_pointer.)

A variation on this idea uses two pointers to copy a character string from one place to another:

```
while ( *dest_pointer++ = *source_pointer++ );
```

Characters are copied until the terminating null character is found (and also copied). Of course, in writing this the programmer should have reason to believe that the destination area will be large enough to contain all the characters to be copied.

References   break statement 8.8; continue statement 8.8; control expression 8.1.2; goto statement 8.10; null statement 8.11; return statement 8.9

8.6.2 Do Statement

A do statement consists of the keyword do, followed by a statement, followed by the keyword while, followed by a control expression in parentheses, followed by a semicolon.

> *do-statement* ::= do *statement* while '(' *expression* ')' ';'

The do statement is executed by first executing the embedded statement. Then the control expression is evaluated; if the value is not zero, then the entire process is then repeated, alternately executing the statement, evaluating the control expression, and then, if the value is not zero, repeating the process. Note that the value of the expression can change from time to time because of side effects in the statement or in the expression itself.

The execution of the do statement is complete when the control expression evaluates to zero or when control is transferred out of the body of the while statement by a return, goto, or break statement. Also, the continue statement can modify the execution of a do statement.

The do statement differs from the while statement in that the do statement always executes the body at least once, whereas the while statement may never execute its body at all.

The C do statement is similar in function to what is often called a "repeat-until" statement in other programming languages such as Pascal. The C do statement is unusual in that it terminates execution when the control expression is false, whereas a Pascal repeat-until statement terminates if its control expression is true. C is more consistent in this regard: all iteration constructs in C (while, do, and for) terminate when the control expression is false.

As an example of the use of the do statement, consider this program fragment that reads and processes characters, halting after a newline character has been processed.

```
int ch;
do {
    ch = getchar();
    process(ch);
} while (ch != '\n');
```

The same effect could have been obtained by moving the computations into the control expression of a while statement, but the intent would be less clear:

```
int ch;
while( ch = getchar(ch),
       process(ch),
       ch != '\n' );
```

It is possible to write a do statement whose body is a null statement:

    do ; while (*expression*);

It is silly to do so, however, because such a do statement is identical in meaning to a while statement whose body is a null statement:

    while (*expression*);

References   break statement 8.8; continue statement 8.8; control expression 8.1.2; goto statement 8.10; null statement 8.11; return statement 8.9; while statement 8.6.1

8.6.3 For Statement

C's for statement is considerably more general than the "increment and test" statements found in most other languages. After explaining the execution of the for statement, we give several examples of how it can be used.

> *for-statement* ::= for *for-expressions statement*

> *for-expressions* ::= '(' { *expression* }? ';'
>   { *expression* }? ';'
>   { *expression* }? ')'

A for statement consists of the keyword for, followed by three expressions separated by semicolons and enclosed in parentheses, followed by a statement. Each of the three expressions within the parentheses is optional and may be independently omitted, but the two semicolons separating them and the parentheses surrounding them are mandatory.

Typically, the first expression is used to initialize a loop variable, the second tests whether the loop should continue or terminate, and the third updates the loop variable (for example, by incrementing it). However, in principle the expressions may be used to perform any computation that is useful within the framework of the for control structure.

The for statement is executed as follows:

1. If present, the first expression is evaluated and the value is discarded.
2. If present, the second expression is evaluated like a control expression. If the result is zero, then execution of the for statement is complete. Otherwise (if the value is not zero or if the second expression was omitted), proceed to step 3.
3. The body of the for statement is executed.
4. If present, the third expression is evaluated and the value is discarded.
5. Return to step 2.

The execution of a `for` statement is terminated when the second (control) expression evaluates to zero or when control is transferred outside the `for` statement by a `return`, `goto`, or `break` statement. The execution of a `continue` statement within the body of the `for` statement has the effect of causing a jump to step 4 above.

Stated another way, a `for` loop of the form

> `for` (*expression1*; *expression2*; *expression3*) *statement*

is similar (except for the action of the `continue` statement) to

```
{
      expression1;
      while (expression2) {
            statement
            expression3;
      }
}
```

where if *expression1* or *expression3* is not present in the `for` statement, then it is simply omitted in the expansion also, and if *expression2* is not present in the `for` statement, then the constant 1 is used for it in the expansion (and so the `while` loop never terminates due to the control expression becoming zero).

> **References**   break statement 8.8; continue statement 8.8; control expression 8.1.2; discarded expressions 7.12; goto statement 8.10; return statement 8.9; while statement 8.6.1

8.6.4 Using the For Statement

The standard way in C to write a loop that "never terminates" (sometimes known as a "do forever" loop) is as a `for` loop with no expressions:

> `for` (;;) *statement*

Of course, the loop can still be terminated by a `break`, `goto`, or `return` statement within the body. Of course, one can write a "do forever" loop in other ways, such as

> `while` (1) *statement*

but the idiom using `for` with no expressions is customary.

Typically, the first expression in a `for` statement is used to initialize a variable, the second expression to test the variable in some way, and the third to modify the variable toward some goal. For example, to print the integers from 0 to 9 and their squares, one might write

```
for (j = 0; j < 10; j++)
    printf("%d  %d\n", j, j*j);
```

Here the first expression initializes j; the second expression tests whether it has reached 10 yet (if it has, the loop is terminated); and the third expression increments j by 1.

The example of raising an integer to an integer power given above to illustrate the while statement can be rewritten using a for statement:

```
/* Compute x to the power y by repeated squaring. */
{
    int base = x;
    int exponent;
    int z = 1;
    for (exponent = y; exponent > 0; exponent /= 2) {
        if ( exponent % 2 ) /* If exponent is odd,  */
            z *= base;       /*   multiply z by base. */
        base *= base;        /* Square the base.      */
    }
    /* Now z is equal to x raised to the power y. */
}
```

This form stresses the fact that the loop is controlled by the variable exponent as it begins at the value y and progresses toward 0 by repeated divisions by 2. Note that the loop variable exponent still had to be declared outside the for statement. The for statement itself does not include the declaration of any variables. A common programming error is to forget to declare a variable such as i or j used in a for statement, only to discover that some other variable named i or j elsewhere in the program is inadvertently modified by the loop.

The for statement need not be used only for counting over integer values. Here is an example of scanning down a linked chain of structures, where the loop variable is a pointer:

```
struct intlist {
    struct intlist *link;
    int data;
};

void print_duplicates(p)
struct intlist *p;
{
    for (; p; p = p->link) {
        struct intlist *q;
        for (q = p->link; q; q = q->link)
            if (q->data == p->data) {
                printf("Duplicate data %d", p->data);
                break;
            }
    }
}
```

The structure intlist is used to implement a linked list of records, each record containing some data. Given such a linked list, the function print_duplicates prints the data for every redundant record in the list. A record is considered to be redundant if some other record after it in the list contains the same data. (If several records in the list have the same data, all but the last one are considered redundant.) The first for statement cleverly (perhaps too cleverly) uses the formal parameter p as its loop variable; it scans down the given list. The loop terminates when a null pointer is encountered. For every record, all the records following it are examined by the inner for statement, which scans a pointer q along the list in the same fashion. If the record pointed to by p is discovered to be redundant, the break statement is used to terminate the inner loop, to prevent the data for p from being printed more than once.

As another example of nested for loops, here is a simple sorting routine that uses the insertion sort algorithm.

```
/* Sort v[0]...v[n-1] into increasing order. */
void insertsort(v, n)
  register int v[], n;
{
    register int i, j, temp;
    for (i = 1; i < n; i++) {
        temp = v[i];
        for (j = i-1; j >= 0 && v[j] > v[j+1]; j--)
            v[j] = v[j+1];
        v[j+1] = temp;
    }
}
```

The outer for loop counts i up from 1 (inclusive) to n (exclusive). At each step, elements v[0] through v[i-1] have already been sorted, and elements v[i] through v[n-1] remain to be sorted. The inner loop counts j down from i-1, moving elements of the array up one at a time, until the right place to insert v[i] has been found. (That is why this is called "insertion sort.") Notice that the termination test for the inner loop uses the '&&' operator. This prevents the array reference v[j] from being executed when j is less than 0.

Insertion sort is a simple and efficient sorting method for small arrays (for n less than, say, 20) or for arrays that are already almost sorted. It is not a good method for very large unordered arrays, because in the worst case the time to perform the sort is proportional to the square of the number of items to be sorted.

A simple modification to insertion sort can make it astonishingly more efficient by wrapping a third loop around the first two! The following sort routine, using the shell sort algorithm, is similar to one called shell that appeared as an example in the original description of C. The original shell routine was a good example of the use of three different nested for loops in a practical setting. However, we have modified it here in four ways, two of them suggested by Knuth and Sedgewick, to make it faster.

```
/* Sort v[0]...v[n-1] into increasing order. */
void shellsort(v, n)
  register int v[], n;
{
    register int gap, i, j, temp;

    gap = 1;
    do (gap = 3*gap + 1); while (gap <= n);
    for (gap /= 3; gap > 0; gap /= 3)
        for (i = gap; i < n; i++) {
            temp = v[i];
            for (j=i-gap; (j>=0)&&(v[j]>temp); j-=gap)
                v[j+gap] = v[j];
            v[j] = temp;
        }
}
```

In the older version, shell, the value of gap started with n/2, and gap was divided by two each time through the outer loop; in this version, shellsort, gap is initialized by finding the smallest number in the series 1, 4, 13, 40, 121, . . . that is not greater than n, and gap is divided by three each time through the outer loop. This is the first improvement. It makes the sort run about 20% to 30% faster on the average. (This is an empirical result; it is not yet completely understood theoretically why this should be so. Experiments also show that one should *not* initialize gap to n and then divide by three each time; such a strategy produces a very poor sorting routine. It is important to start with an element from the series 1, 4, 13, 40, 121, ...)

The second improvement is that the number of assignments is reduced because the inner loop of shellsort contains only one assignment, compared with three assignments in the inner loop of shell.

The third improvement is the introduction of register declarations into shellsort; these make no difference in some implementations of C, but in other implementations these declarations provide a dramatic performance improvement (40% in one case).

The fourth improvement is the use of the void type specifier to indicate explicitly that shellsort returns no value.

Notice that the two inner loops of shellsort are almost identical to the two loops of insertsort; the only change is that the variable gap has replaced the constant 1 in a few places. Despite the fact that shellsort has three nested loops instead of two, experiments show that it executes in time roughly proportional to $n^{1.25}$ instead of n^2.

References   pointer types 5.4; register storage class 4.3; selection operator '->' 7.3.5; structure types 5.7

8.6.5 *Multiple Control Variables*

Sometimes it is convenient to have more than one variable controlling a `for` loop. In this connection the comma operator is especially useful, because it can be used to group several assignment expressions into a single expression:

```
/* Returns 1 if the two string arguments
   are equal, 0  otherwise. */
int string_equal(s1, s2)
    char s1[], s2[];
{
    char *p1, *p2;
    for (p1=s1, p2=s2; *p1 && *p2; p1++, p2++)
        if (*p1 != *p2) return 0;
    return *p1 == *p2;
}
```

The example function `string_equal` accepts two strings and returns 1 if they are equal and 0 otherwise. The `for` statement is used to scan two pointer variables in parallel down the two strings. The expression `p1++, p2++` causes each of the two pointers to be advanced to the next character. If the strings are found to differ at some position, the `return` statement is used to terminate execution of the entire function and return 0. (This is probably a little faster than using `break` to terminate the loop and letting the following `return` redo the comparison.) If a null character is found in either string, as determined by the expression `*p1 && *p2`, then the loop is terminated normally, whereupon the second `return` statement determines whether or not both strings ended with a null character in the same place. (The function would still work correctly if the expression `*p1` were used instead of `*p1 && *p2`. Do you see why? It would also be a bit faster, though not as pleasantly symmetrical.)

As another example of using more than one control variable in a `for` loop, this function takes a linked list and reverses it by modifying the links in place so as to chain it in reverse order:

```
struct intlist {
    struct intlist *link;
    int data;
};

/* Reverse the linked list rooted at p */
struct intlist *reverse(p)
  struct intlist *p;
{
    struct intlist *this, *previous, *next;
    for ( this = p, previous = 0;
          this;
          next = this->link,
            this->link = previous,
              previous = this,
                this = next
        );
    return previous;
}
```

The idea is that the variable this scans down the linked list and the variable previous trails behind it by one record. At each step the record indicated by this, which started out pointing to the next record, is altered to point to the previous record. Notice that the first expression contains two assignments, the third expression contains *four* assignments, and the body of the loop is an empty statement!

References   break statement 8.8; comma operator 7.9; continue statement 8.8; pointer types 5.4; selection operator '->' 7.3.5; structure types 5.7

8.7 *SWITCH STATEMENT; CASE AND DEFAULT LABELS*

The switch statement is a multiway branch based on the value of a control expression. In use, it is similar to the "case" statement in Pascal or Ada, but it is implemented more like the FORTRAN "computed goto" statement.

switch-statement ::= switch '(' *expression* ')' *statement*

case-label ::= case *constant-expression*

default-label ::= default

A switch statement consists of the keyword switch, followed by a control expression enclosed in parentheses, followed by a statement. The parentheses surrounding the expression are mandatory. The statement embedded within a `switch` statement is sometimes called the *body* of the `switch` statement. The body is usually a compound statement but need not be.

A `case` label consists of the keyword `case` followed by a constant expression. A `default` label consists of the keyword `default`. A `case` label or `default` label is said to *belong* to the innermost `switch` statement that contains it. Any statement within the body of a `switch` statement—or the body itself—may be labeled with a `case` label or a `default` label. In fact, the same statement may be labeled with several `case` labels and a `default` label.

The `case` and `default` labels that belong to a `switch` statement must satisfy the following rules:

1. All of the `case` labels (if any) must have constant expressions that—after the usual unary conversions—are of the same type as the expression in the `switch` statement.
2. No two `case` labels belonging to the same `switch` statement may have expressions that produce the same value.
3. At most one `default` label may belong to any one `switch` statement.

A `case` label or `default` label is not permitted to appear other than within the body of a `switch` statement.

The control expression of a `switch` statement is subject to the usual unary conversions, but there is some uncertainty in the types permitted for that expression. The original definition of C specified that the type had to be `int`, and this type is always permitted. Compilers that implement enumeration types will generally allow expressions of enumeration types in `switch` statements and enumeration constants in `case` labels. Type `long` may also be permitted in some implementations. However, the use of pointer or floating-point types is not permitted.

A `switch` statement is executed as follows:

1. The control expression is evaluated.
2. If the value of the expression is equal to that of the constant expression in some `case` label belonging to the `switch` statement, then program control is transferred to the point indicated by that `case` label as if by a `goto` statement; the statement labeled by that `case` label is executed next.
3. If the value of the control expression is not equal to any `case` label, but there is a `default` label that belongs to the `switch` statement, then program control is transferred to the point indicated by that `default` label; the statement labeled by the `default` label is executed next.
4. If the value of the control expression is not equal to any `case` label and there is no `default` label, no statement of the body of the `switch` statement is executed; program control is transferred to whatever follows

the `switch` statement.

After control is transferred to a `case` or `default` label, execution continues through successive statements, ignoring any additional `case` or `default` labels that are encountered, until the end of the `switch` statement is reached or until control is transferred out of the `switch` statement by a `goto`, `return`, `break`, or `continue` statement.

References   `break` statement 8.8; constant expressions 7.10; `continue` statement 8.8; enumeration types 5.6; floating-point types 5.3; `goto` statement 8.10; integer types 5.2; labeled statement 8.3; pointer types 5.4; `return` statement 8.9

8.7.1 Use of Switch Statements

The usual style in which the `switch` statement is used calls for the body to be a compound statement, statements within which are labeled by `case` and `default` labels. It should be noted that `case` and `default` labels do not themselves alter the flow of program control; execution proceeds unimpeded by such labels. The `break` statement can be used within the body of a `switch` statement to terminate its execution.

As an example, consider this program fragment:

```
switch (x) {
    case 1: printf("*");
    case 2: printf("**");
    case 3: printf("***");
    case 4: printf("****");
}
```

If the value of x is 2, then nine asterisks will be printed. The reason for this is that the `switch` statement transfers control to the `case` label with the expression 2. The call to `printf` with argument "**" is executed; next the call to `printf` with argument "***" is executed; and finally the call to `printf` with argument "****" is executed. If it is desired to terminate execution of the `switch` body after a single call to `printf` in each case, then the `break` statement should be used:

```
switch (x) {
    case 1: printf("*");
            break;
    case 2: printf("**");
            break;
    case 3: printf("***");
            break;
    case 4: printf("****");
            break;
}
```

While the last `break` statement in this example is logically unnecessary, it is a good thing to put in as a matter of style. It will help to prevent program errors in the event that a fifth case is later added to the `switch` statement.

While it is considered good style to use the `switch` statement in the manner exemplified above, the language definition itself does not require that the body be a compound statement, or that `case` and `default` labels appear only at the "top level" of the compound statement, or that `case` and `default` labels appear in any particular order or on different statements. Since a `switch` statement is effectively a multiway computed `goto` statement, the same stylistic guidelines apply as for `goto` statements. (See section 8.10.)

Here is an example of how the best intentions can lead to chaos. The intent was to implement this simple program fragment as efficiently as possible:

```
if (prime(x)) process_prime(x);
else process_composite(x);
```

The function `prime` was assumed to return 1 if its argument is a prime number and 0 if the argument is a composite number. Program measurements indicated that most of the calls to `prime` were being made with small integers, so to avoid the overhead of calls to `prime` the code was changed to this:

```
switch(x) {
    case 2: case 3: case 5: case 7:
        process_prime(x);
        break;
    case 4: case 6: case 8: case 9: case 10:
        process_composite(x);
        break;
    default:
        if (prime(x)) process_prime(x);
        else process_composite(x);
        break;
}
```

The final step was to realize that C provided a way to compress this even further:

```
switch (x)
  default:
    if (prime(x))
      case 2: case 3: case 5: case 7:
        process_prime(x);
    else
      case 4: case 6: case 8: case 9: case 10:
        process_composite(x);
```

This is, frankly, the most bizarre `switch` statement we have ever seen that still has pretenses to being purposeful. Not only is it unstructured and difficult to understand, but good compilers can generate the same code from the well-structured `switch` statement above.

We strongly recommend sticking to this simple rule of style for `switch` statements: The body should always be a compound statement, and all labels belonging to the `switch` statement should appear on "top level" statements within that compound statement. Furthermore, every `case` (or `default`) label but the first should be preceded by one of two things: either a `break` statement that terminates the code for the previous case or a comment explicitly noting that the previous code is intended to drop in:

```
enum error_type {info, warn, error, fatal} errflag;
    ...
    /* Print the appropriate prefix for issuing the */
    /* next error message, and also increment the   */
    /* appropriate counter.                         */
    switch (errflag) {
        case info:
            printf("Info");
            ++info_count;
            break;
        case warn:
            printf("Warning");
            ++warn_count;
            break;
        case fatal:
            disaster_flag = 1;
            printf("Fatal ");
            /* Drops through. */
        case error:
            printf("Error");
            ++error_count;
            break;
    }
    print_error_message();
```

8.8 BREAK AND CONTINUE STATEMENTS

The break and continue statements are used to alter the flow of control inside loops and—in the case of break—in switch statements. It is better to use these statements than to use the goto statement to accomplish the same purpose.

break-statement ::= break ';'

continue-statement ::= continue ';'

The break statement consists of just the word break followed by a semicolon. Execution of a break statement causes execution of the smallest enclosing while, do, for, or switch statement to be terminated. Program control is immediately transferred to the point just beyond the terminated statement. It is an error for a break statement to appear where there is no enclosing iterative or switch statement.

The continue statement consists of just the word continue followed by a semicolon. Execution of a `continue` statement causes execution of the body of the smallest enclosing `while`, `do`, or `for` statement to be terminated. Program control is immediately transferred to the end of the body, and the execution of the affected iterative statement continues from that point with a reevaluation of the loop test (and the increment expression, in the case of the `for` statement). It is an error for a `continue` statement to appear where there is no enclosing iterative statement.

The `continue` statement, unlike the `break` statement, has no interaction whatever with `switch` statements. A `continue` statement may appear within a `switch` statement, but it will only affect the smallest enclosing iteration statement, not the `switch` statement.

The `break` and `continue` statements can be explained in terms of the `goto` statement as follows. Consider the statements affected by a `break` or `continue` statement:

> `while` (*expression*) *statement*

> `do` *statement* `while` (*expression*) ;

> `for` (*expression1*; *expression2*; *expression3*) *statement*

> `switch` (*expression*) *statement*

Imagine that all such statements were to be rewritten in this manner:

> { `while` (*expression*) {*statement* C:;} B:;}

> { `do` {*statement* C:;} `while` (*expression*); B:;}

> { `for` (*expression1*; *expression2*; *expression3*) {*statement* C:;} B:;}

> { `switch` (*expression*) *statement* B:; }

where in each case *B* and *C* are labels that appear nowhere else in the enclosing function. Then any occurrence of a `break` statement within the body of any of these statements is equivalent to

> `goto` *B*;

and any occurrence of a `continue` statement within the body of any of these statements (except `switch`) is equivalent to

> `goto` *C*;

(This assumes that the loop bodies do not contain yet another loop containing the `break` or `continue`.)

References   do statement 8.6.2; for statement 8.6.3; goto statement 8.10; switch statement 8.7; while statement 8.6.1

8.8.1 Using `break` and `continue`

The `break` statement is frequently used in two very important contexts: to terminate the processing of a particular case within a `switch` statement, and to terminate a loop prematurely. The first use is illustrated in conjunction with `switch` in section 8.7. The second use is illustrated by this example of filling an array with input characters:

```
/* Fill "array" with input characters, stopping
   when the array is full or when the input is
   exhausted.
 */
{
    static char array[100] = {0};
    int i, c;
    for (i = 0; i < 100; i++) {
        c = getchar();
        if (c == EOF)
            break;        /* Quit if end-of-file. */
        array[i] = c;
    }
    /* Now "i" has the actual number of
       characters read. */
}
```

Note how `break` is used to handle the abnormal case. It is generally better style to handle the normal case in the loop test itself.

Most uses of `continue` can be avoided by using a more carefully constructed `if` statement; this usually results in clearer code. Here is an example of poor use of the `continue` statement:

```
extern char command_buffer[];
    ...
    for (;;) {
        /* Process all nonempty lines that do
           not start with "#". */
        gets(command_buffer));
        if (!command_buffer[0]) continue;
        if (command_buffer[0] = '#') continue;
        process_command();
    }
```

This can be rewritten to make it much more clear that the call to process_command is conditional:

```
extern command_buffer[];
    ...
for (;;) {
    /* Process all nonempty lines that do
        not start with "#". */
    gets(command_buffer));
    if (command_buffer[0] &
            (command_buffer[0] != '#'))
        process_command();
}
```

While continue statements are usually not as confusing as goto statements, a similar amount of thought should go into the decision to use one. Indiscriminate use of continue (or break, for that matter) can make programs much more difficult to understand and maintain.

Here is an example of the use of a break statement within a "do forever" loop. The idea is to find the largest element in the array a (whose length is n) as efficiently as possible. It is assumed that the array may be modified temporarily.

```
{
    int temp = a[0];
    register int smallest = a[0];
    register int *ptr = &a[n];
    for (;;) {
        while (*--ptr > smallest);
        if (ptr == &a[0]) break;
        a[0] = smallest = *ptr;
    }
    a[0] = temp;
}
```

The point is that most of the work is done by a very tight while loop. The while loop scans the pointer ptr backwards through the array, skipping elements that are larger than the smallest one found so far. (If the elements are in a random order, then once a reasonably small element has been found, most elements will be larger than that and so will be skipped.) The while loop cannot fall off the front of the array because the smallest element so far is also stored in the first array element. When the while loop is done, if the scan has reached the front of the array, then the break statement terminates the outer loop. Otherwise smallest and a[0] are updated and the while loop is entered again. At the end of the computation, element a[0] is restored to its original value.

Compare the code above with a simpler, more obvious approach:

```
{
    register int smallest = a[0];
    register int j;
    for (j = 1; j < n; ++j)
        if (a[j] < smallest)
            smallest = a[j];
}
```

This version is certainly easier to understand. However, on every iteration of the loop an explicit check ($j < n$) must be made for falling off the end of the array, as opposed to the implicit check made by the more clever code. Under certain circumstances where efficiency is paramount, the more complicated code may be justified; otherwise, the simpler, clearer loop should be used.

8.9 RETURN STATEMENT

A `return` statement is used to terminate the current function, perhaps returning a value.

> *return-statement* ::= `return` { *expression* }? ';'

A `return` statement consists of the keyword `return`, optionally followed by an expression, followed by a semicolon. Execution of a `return` statement causes execution of the current function to be terminated; program control is transferred to the caller of the function at the point immediately following the call.

If program control should "drop off the end" of a function, then the effect is as if a `return` statement with no expression were executed.

If no expression appears in the `return` statement, then no value is returned from the function; if the function was called from a context requiring a value, then the value returned is undefined. If an expression appears in the `return` statement, then it is converted, if necessary, as if by simple assignment, to the type of the return value of the function in which the statement appears.

The rules governing the agreement of the actual value returned with the declared return value in the function definition are discussed in section 9.8.

8.10 GOTO STATEMENT AND NAMED LABELS

A `goto` statement may be used to transfer control from any statement in a function to any other statement.

> *goto-statement* ::= `goto` *identifier* '`;`'

> *named-label* ::= *identifier*

A `goto` statement consists of the keyword `goto`, followed by an identifier, followed by a semicolon. The identifier must be the same as a named label on some statement within the current function. Execution of the `goto` statement causes an immediate transfer of program control to the point in the function indicated by the label; the statement labeled by the indicated name is executed next.

References   labeled statement 8.3

8.10.1 Using the `goto` *statement*

C permits a `goto` statement to transfer control to any other statement within a function, but certain kinds of branching can result in confusing programs, and the branching may hinder compiler optimizations.

The following rules should result in a more clear use of the `goto`:

1. Do not branch into the "then" or "else" arm of an if or if-else statement from outside the if or if-else statement.
2. Do not branch from the "then" arm to the "else" arm or back.
3. Do not branch into the body of a `switch` or iteration statement from outside the statement.
4. Do not branch into a compound statement from outside the statement.

Such branches should be avoided not only when using the `goto` statement, but also when placing `case` and `default` labels in a `switch` statement (which, in effect, executes a `goto` statement to get to the appropriate `case` label). Branching into the middle of a compound statement from outside it can be especially confusing, because such a branch bypasses the initialization of any variables declared at the top of the compound statement.

It is good programming style to use the `break`, `continue`, and `return` statements in preference to `goto` whenever possible, and better still to avoid them all by appropriate use of conditional and iteration statements.

Finally, the programmer wanting to produce a C program that executes as rapidly as possible should remember that the presence of *any* label—whether explicit, named labels or implicit labels required by `break` and `continue`—may inhibit compiler optimizations and therefore may slow down the C program.

References   break statement 8.8; continue statement 8.8; control expression 8.1.2; if statement 8.5; labeled statement 8.3; return statement 8.9; switch statement 8.7

8.11 NULL STATEMENT

The null statement consists of just a semicolon:

null-statement ::= ';'

It is useful primarily in two situations. First, a null body is often desired for an iterative statement (while, do, or for), as in

```
char *p;
. . .
while ( *p++ );   /* find the end of the string */
```

The second case is where a label is desired just before the right brace that terminates a compound statement. (A label cannot simply precede the right brace, but must always be attached to a statement.) For example:

```
if (e) {
    . . .
    goto L;  /* terminate this arm of the 'if' */
    . . .
L:;}
else ...
```

References   do statement 8.6.2; for statement 8.6.3; labeled statement 8.3; while statement 8.6.1

9

Functions

This chapter discusses the definition of functions in C and the rules for the agreement of parameters and return values. Function types and declarations are discussed in section 5.9.

9.1 FUNCTION DEFINITIONS

A function definition introduces a new function and provides the following information:

1. the type of the value returned by the function, if any
2. the type and number of the formal parameters
3. the visibility of the function outside the file in which it is defined
4. the code that is to be executed when the function is called

Do not confuse function *definitions* with function *declarations*. A function declaration provides access to a function that is defined elsewhere.

The syntax for a function definition is

function-definition ::= { *storage-class-specifier* }?
{ *type-specifier* }?
declarator
parameter-declaration-section
compound-statement

parameter-declaration-section ::= { *declaration* }*

Note that both the storage class specifier and the type specifier may be omitted from the function definition without ambiguity.

The only storage class specifiers that may appear in a function definition are `extern` and `static`. `extern` signifies that the function can be referenced from other files; that is, the function name is exported to the linker. `static` signifies that the function cannot be referenced from other files; that is, the name is not exported to the linker. If no storage class appears in a function definition, `extern` is assumed.

The storage class does not affect the visibility of the function within the file containing the definition. The function is always visible from the definition point to the end of the file. In particular, it is visible within the body of the function itself. (C allows any function to call itself recursively.)

References   declarators 4.5; `extern` storage class 4.3; function declarations 5.9; `static` storage class 4.3; type specifiers 4.4

9.2 FUNCTION TYPES

In a function definition, as in a declaration, the type specifier and the declarator together determine the "type" of a function. We will call them the *function specifier*. If no type specifier is present, `int` is assumed.

In a function definition, the declarator and type specifier must together specify type for the enclosed identifier of "function returning T," where T is any type (including `void`) except "array of . . ." or "function returning . . . ." In other words, functions may not return arrays or other functions. (However, they may return pointers to arrays or functions.) For example, the following syntactically legal function definition is nonsensical because the type of f is "pointer to function returning `int`":

```
int (*f) ()
{
    . . .
}
```

However, the following definition is legal, because the type of g is "function returning T" (where T is "pointer to array of `int`").

```
int (*g()) []
{
    ...
}
```

Another way of stating the restriction is that the definition must contain a function declarator, "*d*(. . .)," where *d* is the identifier that is the name of the function. If the function has parameters, they must be listed in the function declarator.

Consider the following examples of function specifiers:

`void f()`	f is a function with no parameters returning no result.
`int g(x, y)`	g is a function taking two parameters named x and y and returning a value of type `int`.
`int (*h(z)) []`	
	h is a function taking one parameter named z and returning a pointer to an array of integers.
`int (*(*d(w))[]) ()`	
	d is a function taking one parameter named w and returning a pointer to an array of pointers to functions returning integers. (Note that only the parameters of d are specified, not those of other functions mentioned in the declarator.)

References   declarators 4.5; function declarations 5.9; `static` storage class 4.3; `void` type 5.10

9.3 FORMAL PARAMETER DECLARATIONS

In function definitions, formal parameters are declared in two parts. As we have just seen, the names of the parameters are listed in the function declarator. In order to supply types for the parameters, the programmer declares each of the parameters (in any order) in the parameter declaration section. For example, to define a function that has three parameters—an integer, a double-precision floating-point number, and a pointer to an integer—the programmer can write:

```
void f(x, y, z)
   int x, *z;
   double y;
{
    ...
}
```

The parameter declaration section may contain declarations of the parameters, and perhaps declarations of types used in the parameter declarations.

The only storage class specifier that may be present in a parameter declaration is `register`, which is a hint to the compiler that the parameter will be used heavily and might better be stored in a register after the function has begun executing. The normal restrictions as to what types of parameters may be marked `register` apply (see section 4.3).

A parameter may be declared to be of any type except `void` or "function returning . . . ." Parameters of type "array of T" and (sometimes) "function returning T" may be declared, but these types are adjusted to be "pointer to T" and "pointer to function returning T," respectively. The mechanism is discussed in more detail in section 9.4.

It is permissible to include structure, union, or enumeration type definitions in the parameter declaration section, and to include `typedef` definitions. The scope of these definitions extends to the end of the function body. However, the usefulness of these definitions is marginal, and probably bad programming style. To illustrate this, consider the following function definition:

```
int process_record(r);
    struct { int a; int b; } *r;
{
    . . .
}
```

The inclusion of the `struct` definition as a side effect of the declaration for `r` is permissible but confusing, because no actual parameter could be declared to have that type. (The scope of the structure definition does not extend outside the function.) When we see in another file the code

```
extern struct { int first;
                int second; } *two_integers;
process_record(two_integers);
```

we can guess that the programmer is depending on:

1. the compiler's not checking that the types of the formal and actual parameters match (they don't match)
2. the programmer's being consistent about defining the same structured type in different places so that the the actual parameter's structure matches the formal parameter's structure (this consistency is not guaranteed because the compiler does not necessarily perform this type check)

Programmers who do things like this are living dangerously and invite ridicule from people who have to decipher their programs.

References   enumeration types 5.6; function declarator 4.5.4; `register` storage class 4.3; storage class specifiers 4.3; structure types 5.7; `typedef` 5.11; union types 5.8; `void` type 5.10

9.4 ADJUSTMENTS TO PARAMETER TYPES

C specifies that certain adjustments in the types of function arguments be made to simplify and regularize function arguments. The adjustments are made in two places: on the actual argument types at the point of the function call and on the formal argument types in function definitions.

The adjustments to the actual arguments are listed in section 6.14. Corresponding to these adjustments, adjustments are made to the types of a function's formal parameters as they appear in the parameter declaration section. In particular, if a formal parameter is declared to be of type `char`, `short`, or `float`, the compiler will expect an actual argument of type `int`, `int`, or `double` (respectively) to be passed to the function. For this reason, formal parameters declared to be of type `char`, `short`, or `float` are implicitly *promoted* to be of type `int`, `int`, and `double`, respectively. This permits many program libraries to be smaller than they would have to be if, for instance, multiple definitions of "square root" had to be provided for each of the argument types `short`, `int`, `float`, `double`, etc.

However, the compiler will ensure that the values of the parameters are appropriate to the declared type. That is, the function

```
void f(c)
  char c;
{
    int i;
    i = c;
    ...
}
```

is implemented as if it were written

```
void f(c)
    int c;
  {
    int i;
    i = (int) (char) c;
    ...
  }
```

(Not all compilers actually implement such explicit narrowing operations on parameters, just as some deficient compilers fail to implement narrowing casts in all cases. For maximum portability, programs should not depend critically on the truncation effects of such narrowing.)

A formal parameter declared to be of type "array of *T*" is treated as if it were declared to be of type "pointer to *T*." Because of the equivalence of pointers and arrays, this change is invisible to the programmer. For example, in the function

```
int sumarray(a, n)
  int a[], n;
{
    int sum=0, i;
    for (i = 0; i < n; i++)
        sum = sum + a[i];
    return sum;
}
```

the parameters a and n could have been declared as

```
int *a, n;
```

with no other change to the program. Although array names are not usually lvalues, a formal parameter declared to be an array is treated as an lvalue by many compilers.

Formal parameters of type "function returning . . ." are not permitted by the language. However, some compilers accept such parameters and implicitly convert them to type "pointer to function returning . . ." (sometimes also issuing a warning message). These compilers will also automatically dereference such a parameter when used in a function call. (In fact, they do this automatic dereferencing on any expression of type "pointer to function returning . . . ." For example:

```
extern (*h)();

void f(g)           /* Not a legal C program! */
  void g();
{
    g();            /* This works in some compilers. */
    (*g)();         /* So does this. */
    h();            /* So does this! */
    (*h)();         /* ...and, of course, this. */
}
```

We recommend adhering to the language specification and always declaring parameters to be pointers to functions.

References   array types 5.5; floating-point types 5.3; function argument conversions 6.14; function types 5.9; integer types 5.2; lvalue 7.1; pointer types 5.4

9.5 *PARAMETER-PASSING CONVENTIONS*

C provides only call-by-value parameter passing. This means that the values of the actual parameters are conceptually copied into a storage area local to the called function. It is possible to use a formal parameter name as the left side of an assignment, for instance, but in that case only the local copy of the parameter is altered.

If the programmer wants the called function to alter its actual parameters, the addresses of the parameters must be passed explicitly. For example, function `swap` below will not work correctly, because x and y are passed by value.

```
void swap(x, y)
/* swap: exchange the values of x and y */
/* Incorrect version! */
  int x, y;
{
    int temp;
    temp = x; x = y; y = temp;
}
...
    swap(a, b);   /* Fails to swap a and b. */
```

A correct implementation of the function requires that addresses of the arguments be passed:

```
void swap(x, y)
/* swap - exchange the values of *x and *y */
/* correct version */
  int *x, *y;
{
    int temp;
    temp = *x; *x = *y; *y = temp;
}
...
    swap(&a, &b);   /* Swaps contents of a and b. */
```

The local storage area for parameters is usually implemented on a push-down stack. However, the order of pushing parameters on the stack is not specified by the language, nor does the language prevent the compiler from passing parameters in registers. It is legal to apply the address operator '&' to a formal parameter name (unless it was declared with storage class `register`), thereby implying that the parameter in question would have to be in addressable storage when the address was taken. (Note that the address of a formal parameter is the address of the copy of the actual parameter, not the address of the actual parameter itself.)

References   address operator '&' 7.4.6; `register` storage class 4.3

9.6 AGREEMENT OF FORMAL AND ACTUAL PARAMETERS

Most modern programming languages such as Pascal and Ada check the agreement of formal and actual parameters to functions; that is, both the number of arguments and the types of the individual arguments must agree.   As in FORTRAN, this checking is not performed in C:

1. The syntax of declarations does not provide for a declaration of argument types to functions, and therefore no checking is possible when a function is supplied in another source file.
2. The lack of checking gives programmers some freedom in violating conventions on certain rare occasions, especially in implementing functions that take a variable number of arguments.

For example, in the function `hypotenuse` below, the call on `sqrt` does not generate a warning message, even though the actual parameter is of type `long` whereas the formal parameter is declared to have type `double`. `sqrt` will simply return a (probably) incorrect value.

```
double sqrt( x )
  double x;
{
    ...
}

long hypotenuse(x,y)
  long x,y;
{
    return (sqrt(x*x + y*y));
}
```

There is no portable way in C to write a function that accepts a variable number of arguments. Such functions can be written in C—`printf` and its variants are examples—but they are not portable. They depend on very specific knowledge of how parameters are passed on the stack, and they still need some way to determine the type and number of arguments. (For example, `printf` depends on the format string to indicate the number and types of the arguments.)

References   conversion of actual parameters 9.4; function argument conversions 6.14; `printf` 11.5.23

9.7 FUNCTION RETURN TYPES

A function may be defined to return a value of any type except "array of *T*" or "function returning *T*." These two cases must be handled by returning pointers to the array or function. The actual value, if any, returned by the function is specified by an expression in the `return` statement that causes the function to terminate. If control "falls out the bottom" of a function, it is as if

```
return;
```

had been executed.

The value returned by a function is not an lvalue (the return is "by value"), and therefore a function call cannot appear on the left side of an assignment operator. The language does not specify how the return value is to be transmitted to the calling program.

References   array types 5.5; function calls 7.3.6; function types 5.9; lvalue 7.1; pointer types 5.4

9.8 AGREEMENT OF ACTUAL AND DECLARED RETURN TYPE

A return statement with no expression,

```
return;
```

is always permitted, regardless of whether the function has a `void` or nonvoid return type. This rule is to provide backwards compatibility with compilers that do not implement `void`. When a function has a nonvoid return type, and a `return` statement with no arguments is executed, the value actually returned is unpredictable and it is therefore unwise to invoke the function in a context that requires a value. We recommend that this form of `return` be used *only* when the function is declared to have return type `void`.

If a function has a declared return type of `void`, it is an error to supply an expression in any `return` statement in the function. Although supplying a void return value, as in

```
void f()
{
    extern void g();
    ...
    return g();
}
```

would seem to be no more than confusing, many compilers will treat this as an error. It is also an error to call the function in a context that requires a value.

If the function has a declared return type T that is not `void`, then the type of any expression appearing in a `return` statement must be convertible to type T by assignment, and that conversion in fact happens on return. For instance, in a function with declared return type `int`, the statement

```
return 23.1;
```

is equivalent to

```
return (int) 23.1;
```

which is the same as

```
return 23;
```

With older compilers that do not implement `void`, it is the custom to omit the type specifier on those functions that return no useful value:

```
main()
{
    . . .
}
```

References   adjustments to formal parameters 9.4; lvalue 7.1; return statement 8.9; void type 5.10

10

Program Structure

In this chapter we will attempt to pull together a number of aspects of software engineering in C. We will do so by developing a complete implementation of a last-in first-out queue, or stack.

10.1 MODULARIZATION

We prefer to modularize programs by data types. That is, we think of a program as consisting of a number of *modules*, each of which implements a new, abstract data type by providing objects of the type and operations on the objects. These modules are sometimes called *type managers*, to emphasize that they have control over the internal representation of the types and the implementation of the operations on the types.

A stack can be viewed as such an abstract data type. An object of "stack type" can be imagined (under one implementation) as an array of values and a pointer into that array to mark the "top" of the stack. Operations on the stack include "create a new stack," "push a value onto the stack," "pop a value off the stack," and so forth.

When designing a new abstract data type, the programmer must answer many questions:

1. What functionality is required? What operations will be needed?
2. How often will the operations be invoked? What other performance criteria exist?

3. What implementations might be appropriate? Will the data structures have to be dynamically allocated, or will local or static allocation suffice? Is there an existing module that can be modified to meet the specifications of the new module?

4. How will the data type be used? What information must be exported to users?

5. How can the type be implemented securely and robustly? That is, how can users be prevented from corrupting the internal data structures of the type, and how can the type manager detect improper use of its operations?

6. What functional changes might be required in the future? Who will maintain the module? How does this affect the implementation?

7. What documentation will be needed?

This list could be extended further to include provisions for version control, internal development reviews, and so forth. However, this should be sufficient to indicate that a well-crafted module can involve much more than a few lines of code.

10.2 DESIGNING THE STACK MODULE

The first thing to do is to sketch out the functional properties of a stack. First, the operations:

- Allocate a new stack.
- Deallocate an old stack.
- Push a value onto the stack.
- Pop a value off the stack.

Experience with stacks has told us that two more operations are often useful:

- Return the top value from the stack without removing it.
- Find out how big the stack currently is and how far it can grow.

Given the operations, we must also ask about the values of the new type:

- What type of elements is the stack to hold?
- How big should the stack be?

Finally, we must worry about handling errors, such as overflow or underflow. After talking to the potential users of our stacks, we decide the following:

- The stacks will hold values of type int (although we suspect that the users will want a different element type later on).

- The stacks will be large and therefore should be dynamically allocated.

- Pushing and popping elements should be fast operations, and users can live with a fixed maximum size for each stack, although different stacks may have different maximums. Therefore, we decide that we can use an array implementation of stacks.

- The stacks will be used in a large product that is likely to have bugs while being completed. Therefore we will include some extra consistency checking that can be removed (for better performance) before the product is shipped.

10.3 DATA STRUCTURES

We'll begin by making some standard declarations and defining the data structures.

```
#include <stdio.h>
extern char *malloc();

typedef int stack_element_type;

typedef struct stack_struct {
        stack_element_type *base_of_stack;
        stack_element_type *end_of_stack;
        stack_element_type *next_free_element;
    } *stack_typo;
```

Stacks will be represented by type `stack_type`. No user of stacks needs to know how it is implemented, but in fact `stack_type` is a pointer to a structure containing three pointer components: `base_of_stack`, a pointer to the base of an array of elements; `end_of_stack`, a pointer to the first element beyond the end of the array; and `next_free_element`, a pointer to the array element that will receive the next pushed value (that is, the first array element following the top element of the stack). Note that we have also introduced the type `stack_element_type`; by changing the definition of this type we can have stacks that hold other kinds of elements.

The type `stack_type` is the "stack header"; the actual data will be held in an array that will also be dynamically allocated.

10.4 ROBUSTNESS

When the stack module is being developed, or when it is being used in a program that potentially has bugs, we'd like to perform some additional consistency checking on the stack data structure. Our strategy will be to use the preprocessor macro `stack_debugging` to control whether special consistency checks are compiled into the stack module. In particular, when `stack_debugging` is 1, a special function, `stack_check`, is defined. At run time, `stack_check` examines the contents of the stack data structure and verifies that the data structure is consistent. When `stack_debugging` is 0, `stack_check` is defined as a macro with no body, effectively eliminating the checks from the code. Here are the definitions for the debugging information:

```
#define stack_debugging 1

#if stack_debugging

/* interactive debugger (not included here) */
extern void debugger();

static void stack_check(stack)
   stack_type stack;
/*
    Check the internal consistency of the 'stack' data
    structure. If inconsistent, print a message and
    invoke a debugger. If consistent, just return.
*/
{
    if (stack == NULL) {
        printf("?Stack is NULL\n");
        debugger();
        return;
    }
    if (stack->base_of_stack == NULL) {
        printf("?Stack array is NULL\n");
        debugger();
        return;
    }
    if ( (stack->next_free_element <
                        stack->base_of_stack) ||
          (stack->next_free_element >
                        stack->end_of_stack)
        ) {
        printf("?Stack pointers are invalid.\n");
        debugger();
        return;
    }
    /* Stack is OK */
    return;
}
#else
/* If not debugging, then calls to stack_check
   will be quietly eliminated by the preprocessor.
 */
#define stack_check(stack)
#endif
```

Of course, we could have used other strategies for providing the consistency checks. A reasonable alternative to the above scheme would be to provide a run-time test to see if the data structures are to be checked. That is, we would always define the function `stack_check`, but would replace

```
#define stack_debugging 1
```

with

```
static int stack_debugging = 1;
```

and then replace all the calls on `stack_check` with

```
if (stack_debugging) stack_check(stack);
```

This scheme has the advantage of not requiring recompilation to turn checks on and off. Its disadvantage is that it involves the test of the variable `stack_debugging` on every operation. (This is probably not a significant overhead compared with the overhead of a function call.)

10.5 ALLOCATING AND DEALLOCATING STACKS

We now consider the creation and deletion of new stack objects. Here is the creation code:

```
stack_type stack_alloc(size)
  unsigned int size;
/* Create a new stack object with a maximum of "size"
   elements.  Return NULL if insufficient storage is
   available, or if "size" is not greater than zero.
*/
{
    stack_type stack;
    unsigned header_size =
                    sizeof(struct stack_struct);
    unsigned array_size =
                    size * sizeof(stack_element_type);

    if (size <= 0) return NULL;
    stack = (stack_type) malloc(header_size);
    if (stack == NULL) return NULL;
    stack->base_of_stack =
        (stack_element_type *) malloc(data_size);
    if (stack->base_of_stack == NULL) {
        /* Can't get the array, so free the header. */
        free(stack);
        return NULL;
    }
    stack->end_of_stack = stack->base_of_stack + size;
    stack->next_free_element = stack->base_of_stack;
    return stack;
}
```

Note how we check each call to `malloc` to be sure the requested storage was allocated.

The deallocation code is very simple, but it is an opportunity to make the type manager a bit more robust. It is always possible for the caller of `stack_free` to accidentally use the (deallocated) stack in a subsequent call on the type manager. So that this error may be caught quickly, `stack_free` zeros all the internal pointers before freeing the storage. If `stack_debugging` is 1, this helps to ensure that `stack_check` will fail if given a pointer to the old stack. However, even if `stack_debugging` is 0, the null pointers should cause the program to halt more quickly than it would if the pointers were just left dangling. Furthermore, the overhead of zeroing the pointers is small compared with the expected overhead of the storage allocator, so we don't worry about the extra code.

```
void stack_free(stack)
  stack_type stack;
/* Deallocate the given stack and return its
   storage to the heap.
 */
{
    stack_check(stack);
    /* Free the data array first. */
    free((char *) stack->base_of_stack);
    /* Clear the pointers so that "stack_check"
       is more likely to fail on a freed stack. */
    stack->base_of_stack     = NULL;
    stack->next_free_element = NULL;
    stack->end_of_stack      = NULL;
    /* Free the header. */
    free((char *) stack);
    return;
}
```

10.6 OPERATIONS

The operations on stacks are pretty simple. We have decided to handle overflow and underflow errors by having the type manager set an error flag through
a pointer provided by the caller. An alternative would be for the type manager
to export a variable that was used as a status indicator after each operation, or
use the standard variable errno that is used by the standard C library routines.
We think our scheme results in more readable programs, even though it involves a bit of overhead on calls. Notice also that we have used a type
boolean for the error flags to make clear our intended use.

```
typedef int boolean;

#define TRUE    1
#define FALSE   0
```

```
void stack_push(stack, data, overflow_ptr)
   stack_type stack;
   stack_element_type data;
   boolean *overflow_ptr;
/*
    Push "data" onto the stack.  If the stack is full,
    set "*overflow_ptr" to TRUE and don't do the push.
    Otherwise, set "*overflow_ptr" to FALSE.
*/
{
    stack_check(stack);
    if (stack->next_free_element
           >= stack->end_of_stack) {
        *overflow_ptr = TRUE;
    }
    else {
        *overflow_ptr = FALSE;
        *(stack->next_free_element++) = data;
    }
}

/* Dummy value of type "stack_element_type". */
static stack_element_type stack_element_novalue;
```

```
stack_element_type stack_pop(stack, underflow_ptr)
  stack_type stack;
  boolean *underflow_ptr;
/*
  If "stack" is empty, set "*underflow_ptr" to TRUE and
  return.  Otherwise, set "*underflow_ptr" to FALSE and
  remove and return the top stack element.
*/
{
    stack_check(stack);
    if (stack->next_free_element
            <= stack->base_of_stack) {
        *underflow_ptr = TRUE;
        return stack_element_novalue;
    }
    else {
        *underflow_ptr = FALSE;
        return *(--stack->next_free_element);
    }
}

stack_element_type stack_peek(stack, underflow_ptr)
    stack_type stack;
    boolean *underflow_ptr;
/*
   If "stack" is empty, set "*underflow_ptr" to TRUE
   and return. Otherwise set "*underflow_ptr" to FALSE,
   and return the top stack element.  (Do not remove
   it from the stack.)
*/
{
    stack_check(stack);
    if (stack->next_free_element
            <= stack->base_of_stack) {
        *underflow_ptr = TRUE;
        return stack_element_novalue;
    }
    else {
        *underflow_ptr = FALSE;
        return *(stack->next_free_element - 1);
    }
}
```

Notice in `stack_pop` and `stack_peek` the use of the static variable `stack_element_novalue` as a return value. We really don't want to return anything, because the stack has underflowed. However, we think just writing

```
return;
```

would be confusing, since the return value doesn't match the declared return type of the function. Writing

```
return 0;
```

would be better but depends on the fact that `stack_element_type` has a 0 value. By defining a variable containing "no return value," we maintain generality with any type `stack_element_type`.

Finally, there is a routine that returns the current and maximum sizes of a stack, and some boolean predicates to test whether the stack is empty or full. These predicates are macros for efficiency.

```
void stack_sizes(stack,
                 current_size_ptr,
                 allocated_size_ptr)
  stack_type stack;
  unsigned int *current_size_ptr, *allocated_size_ptr;
/*
    Set "*current_size_ptr" to the number of elements
    on the stack, and set "*allocated_size_ptr" to the
    number of elements the stack can hold.
*/
{
    stack_check(stack);
    *current_size_ptr =
       stack->next_free_element - stack->base_of_stack;
    *allocated_size_ptr =
       stack->end_of_stack - stack->base_of_stack;
    return;
}

#define stack_isempty(stack) \
         ((stack)->next_free_element == \
          (stack)->base_of_stack))

#define stack_isfull(stack) \
         ((stack)->next_free_element == \
          (stack)->end_of_stack))
```

10.7 PACKAGING THE MODULE

Now that the data structures and algorithms for the stack module are finished, we can give some thought to the best way to export the module's facilities to the user. We will have to provide declarations of the functions and macros implementing the operations, and we'll have to provide the type stack_type.

The custom in C is to collect these definitions in a *header file* that can be imported (with #include) by users of the module. The header file is also a good place to put some short documentation. Here is the header file for the stack module, which we have named stack.h:

```
/* stack.h      Definitions for stack-of-integers.

    Typical use:

        #include <stack.h>

        stack_type      stack;
        stack_element   data;
        unsigned int    current_size, maximum_size;
        boolean         overflow, underflow;

        stack = stack_alloc(100);
        if (stack==NULL) ...;

        stack_push(stack, data, &overflow);
        if (overflow) ...;

        data = stack_pop(stack, &underflow);
        if (underflow) ...;

        stack_sizes(stack,&current_size,&maximum_size);

        stack_free(stack);
*/

/* Short external names for operations. */

#define stack_alloc     stkall
#define stack_free      stkfre
#define stack_push      stkpsh
#define stack_pop       stkpop
#define stack_peek      stkpek
#define stack_sizes     stksiz
```

```
/* Type of elements in stack. */
typedef  int  stack_element_type;

/* Boolean error flags. */
typedef  int  boolean;

/* The stack type itself. */
typedef struct stack_struct {
          stack_element_type *base_of_stack;
          stack_element_type *end_of_stack;
          stack_element_type *next_free_element;
       } *stack_type;

/**** Operations *****/

extern stack_type stack_alloc();
/* Synopsis: (create a new stack with
             up to "size" elements)
   extern stack_type stack_alloc(size);
     stack_size_type size;
*/

extern void stack_free();
/* Synopsis: (deallocate "stack")
   extern void stack_free(stack);
     stack_type stack;
*/

extern void stack_push();
/* Synopsis: (push "data" onto "stack";
             set "*overflow_ptr" to TRUE
             if full and otherwise to FALSE)
   extern void stack_push(stack, data, overflow_ptr)
     stack_type stack;
     stack_element_type data;
     boolean *overflow_ptr;
*/
```

```
extern stack_element_type stack_pop();
/* Synopsis: (pop top element from "stack"; set
               "*underflow_ptr" to TRUE if empty
               and otherwise to FALSE)
    stack_element_type stack_pop(stack, underflow_ptr)
      stack_type stack;
      boolean *underflow_ptr;
*/

extern stack_element_type stack_peek();
/* Synopsis: (return, but don't pop, top element from
               "stack"; set "*underflow_ptr" to TRUE if
               empty and otherwise to FALSE)
    stack_element_type stack_peek(stack, underflow_ptr)
      stack_type stack;
      boolean *underflow_ptr;
*/

extern void stack_sizes();
/* Synopsis: (return current and maximum sizes
               of "stack")
    void stack_sizes(stack,
                     current_size_ptr,
                     allocated_size_ptr)
      stack_type stack;
      unsigned int *current_size_ptr,
      *allocated_size_ptr;
*/

/* Predicate: is stack empty? */
#define stack_isempty(stack) \
        ((stack)->next_free_element == \
         (stack)->base_of_stack))

/* Predicate: is stack full? */
#define stack_isfull(stack) \
        ((stack)->next_free_element == \
         (stack)->end_of_stack))
```

A couple of points should be mentioned here. First, because of the restrictions
on external names, we have defined macros that convert our names (and the
names that should be used by clients) to shorter names less likely to conflict in
the linker. (We have also been careful with the internal names, such as

stack_push; they all begin with the prefix stack_ to minimize conflicts.) Second, although our principal exported type is stack_type, we must also export stack_element_type and boolean, since we use those types in the definition of stack_type. Third, although we consider the implementation of stack_type to be "private" to our type manager, there is no way to actually hide the implementation from the user of the module. A caller could alter the components of the structure in arbitrary ways, thus corrupting the data. Finally, it is very helpful to include as much documentation in the header file as possible.

All the other code goes into the stack implementation module, stack.c, which should begin with the line

```
#include <stack.h>
```

since it will need the same type and macro definitions. To avoid duplication, the declarations for stack_element_type, stack_type, boolean, stack_isempty, and stack_isfull may be removed from stack.c since they are now supplied in stack.h.

11

The Run-time Library

Many facilities that are used in C programs are not a part of the C language as such but are parts of "standard libraries" that are written in C itself for use by other C programs. These facilities include:

- Operations on characters, such as converting from uppercase to lowercase.
- Operations on strings, such as copying and searching.
- Mathematical operations, such as trigonometric functions.
- Storage allocation procedures.
- Input and output operations.
- Communication with the host operating system.

Each of these facilities belongs to a particular library. The correct way to use a facility is to have, at the beginning of the user program, a preprocessor `#include` command to include the relevant library declarations; the facility may then be referred to by name within the user program. For example, in order to use the cosine function `cos` in a program, one should put the command

```
#include <math.h>
```

at the start of the program; one may then use `cos` in expressions.

The word *facility* has been used in order to evade the question of whether a facility is implemented as a function or a preprocessor macro. Most of the facilities are described below as if they were functions, but the implementor is free to provide a macro with equivalent behavior unless the facility is explicitly described as being a function. (Existing C implementations do in fact differ greatly in which facilities are implemented as macros and which as functions.) This freedom is granted to the implementor because in some cases significantly greater efficiency can be achieved if the use of macros is permitted. For example, the facility `isascii` can, in many implementations, be correctly implemented by this very simple macro:

```
#define isascii(x) ((unsigned)(x) <= 0177)
```

Such an implementation may result in much faster code than would be required by a call to a function. The implementor may use other implementation strategies as well, as long as the behavior of a facility conforms to its description when given appropriate arguments. To prevent confusion and subtle bugs, however, a facility implemented as a macro must nevertheless, unless its description explicitly states otherwise, evaluate every argument expression exactly once, just as if it were implemented as a function, to ensure that side effects are carried out in the expected manner, as if the argument expressions were function arguments.

Because implementations differ as to which facilities are functions and which are macros, the user should not provide function declarations for any library facility. Despite the fact that `isascii` is described as if it were a function, it might be a macro instead, and a user-supplied function declaration would be turned into garbage by preprocessor macro replacement. The *only* correct way to declare a library facility is to include the appropriate header file. Facilities are described here as if they were functions only as a convenient way of describing the types of the arguments and the type of the result.

When a facility is invoked and cannot complete an operation successfully, then it may do either or both of two things: return a special value indicating failure or store a nonzero error code into the external variable `errno`. The actions taken by various facilities are described explicitly below for each individual facility. Error codes and the external variable `errno` are described in section 11.6.

Many implementations of C provide other facilities in addition to the ones described here. A few do not provide all those described here. We have selected those that are in widespread use and not too dependent on the implementation.

For each functionlike facility, we give first the appropriate `#include` statement for obtaining its declaration, then a function declaration describing the types of the arguments and result (if any), and finally a prose description of its behavior.

11.1 CHARACTER PROCESSING

The facilities for handling characters are of two kinds: classification and conversion. Every character classification facility has a name beginning with "is" and returns a value of type int that is nonzero if the argument is in the specified class and zero if not. Every character conversion facility has a name beginning with "to" and returns a value of type int representing a character or EOF.

The value EOF (−1) is conventionally used as a value that is "not a real character." For example, fgetc (section 11.5.8) returns EOF when at end-of-file, because there is no "real character" to be read. It must be remembered, however, that the type char may be signed in some implementations, and so EOF is not necessarily distinguishable from a "real character" if nonstandard character values appear. (Standard character values are always nonnegative, even if the type char is signed.) All of the facilities described here operate properly on all values representable as type char or type unsigned char, and also on the value EOF, but are undefined for all other integer values, unless the individual description states otherwise.

The facilities isascii and toascii assume that the standard 128-character ASCII character set is used as the implementation's run-time character set, but the rest do not require this assumption and indeed serve to insulate code from the implementation's run-time character set.

A warning: Some implementations of C let the type char be signed and also support a type unsigned char, yet the character-handling facilities fail to operate properly on all values representable by type unsigned char. In some cases the facilities even fail to operate properly on all values representable by type char, but only handle "standard" character values and EOF.

All of the facilities described here are declared by the library header file string.h.

11.1.1 isalnum

```
#include <ctype.h>
int isalnum(c)
  char c;
```

isalnum returns a nonzero value if c is the code for an alphanumeric character; that is, one of the following:

```
0 1 2 3 4 5 6 7 8 9
A B C D E F G H I J K L M N O P Q R S T U V W X Y Z
a b c d e f g h i j k l m n o p q r s t u v w x y z
```

Otherwise the returned value is zero.

11.1.2 `isalpha`

```
#include <ctype.h>
int isalpha(c)
  char c;
```

`isalpha` returns a nonzero value if `c` is the code for an alphabetic character; that is, one of the following:

```
A B C D E F G H I J K L M N O P Q R S T U V W X Y Z
a b c d e f g h i j k l m n o p q r s t u v w x y z
```

Otherwise the returned value is zero.

11.1.3 `isascii`

```
#include <ctype.h>
int isascii(c)
  char c;
```

Unlike most of of the character classification functions, `isascii` operates properly on any value of type `int`. The value is nonzero if `c` is nonnegative and less than `0200` (the size of the standard 128-character ASCII character set) and otherwise is zero.

11.1.4 `iscntrl`

```
#include <ctype.h>
int iscntrl(c)
  char c;
```

`iscntrl` returns a nonzero value if `c` is the code for a "control character"; that is, any character that is not a printing character. If the standard 128-character ASCII character set is in use, the control characters are those with codes `000` through `037`, and also code `0177`. See `isprint` (section 11.1.11).

11.1.5 `iscsym`

```
#include <ctype.h>
int iscsym(c)
  char c;
```

iscsym returns a nonzero value if c is the code for a character that may appear in an identifier acceptable to the C compiler that compiled the program. This will include at least these characters:

```
0 1 2 3 4 5 6 7 8 9 _
A B C D E F G H I J K L M N O P Q R S T U V W X Y Z
a b c d e f g h i j k l m n o p q r s t u v w x y z
```

and other characters may be included as well, depending on the implementation. Otherwise the returned value is zero.

11.1.6 iscsymf

```
#include <ctype.h>
int iscsymf(c)
  char c;
```

iscsymf returns a nonzero value if c is the code for a character that may appear as the first character of an identifier acceptable to the C compiler that compiled the program. This will include at least these characters:

```
_
A B C D E F G H I J K L M N O P Q R S T U V W X Y Z
a b c d e f g h i j k l m n o p q r s t u v w x y z
```

and other characters may be included as well, depending on the implementation. Otherwise the returned value is zero.

11.1.7 isdigit

```
#include <ctype.h>
int isdigit(c)
  char c;
```

isdigit returns a nonzero value if c is the code for a decimal digit; that is, one of the following:

```
0 1 2 3 4 5 6 7 8 9
```

Otherwise the returned value is zero.

11.1.8 isgraph

```
#include <ctype.h>
int isgraph(c)
    char c;
```

isgraph returns a nonzero value if c is the code for a "graphic character"; that is, any printing character other than space. Otherwise zero is returned. If the standard 128-character ASCII character set is in use, the graphic characters are those with codes 041 through 0176; that is, the following (but not space):

```
! " # $ % & ' ( ) * + , - . /
0 1 2 3 4 5 6 7 8 9 : ; < = > ?
@ A B C D E F G H I J K L M N O
P Q R S T U V W X Y Z [ \ ] ^ _
` a b c d e f g h i j k l m n o
p q r s t u v w x y z { | } ~
```

11.1.9 islower

```
#include <ctype.h>
int islower(c)
    char c;
```

islower returns a nonzero value if c is the code for a lowercase alphabetic character; that is, one of the following:

```
a b c d e f g h i j k l m n o p q r s t u v w x y z
```

Otherwise the returned value is zero.

11.1.10 isodigit

```
#include <ctype.h>
int isodigit(c)
    char c;
```

isodigit returns a nonzero value if c is the code for an octal digit; that is, one of the following:

```
0  1  2  3  4  5  6  7
```

Otherwise the returned value is zero.

11.1.11 isprint

```
#include <ctype.h>
int isprint(c)
   char c;
```

isprint returns a nonzero value if c is the code for a "printing character";
that is, any character that is not a control character. Otherwise zero is returned.
If the standard 128-character ASCII character set is in use, the printing characters are those with codes 040 through 0176; that is, space plus the following:

```
!  "  #  $  %  &  '  (  )  *  +  ,  -  .  /
0  1  2  3  4  5  6  7  8  9  :  ;  <  =  >  ?
@  A  B  C  D  E  F  G  H  I  J  K  L  M  N  O
P  Q  R  S  T  U  V  W  X  Y  Z  [  \  ]  ^  _
`  a  b  c  d  e  f  g  h  i  j  k  l  m  n  o
p  q  r  s  t  u  v  w  x  y  z  {  |  }  ~
```

11.1.12 ispunct

```
#include <ctype.h>
int ispunct(c)
   char c;
```

ispunct returns a nonzero value if c is the code for a "printing character";
that is, any character that is not a control character and not alphanumeric.
Otherwise zero is returned. If the standard 128-character ASCII character set is
in use, the punctuation characters are space plus the following:

```
!  "  #  $  %  &  '  (  )  *  +  ,  -  .  /  :  ;  <  =  >  ?
@  [  \  ]  ^  _  `  {  |  }  ~
```

11.1.13 isspace

```
#include <ctype.h>
int isspace(c)
   char c;
```

isspace returns a nonzero value if c is the code for a whitespace character. Otherwise zero is returned. If the standard 128-character ASCII character set is in use, the printing characters are those with codes 011 (horizontal tab), 012 (newline), 013 (vertical tab), 014 (form feed), 015 (carriage return), and 040 (space).

Some implementations of C provide not this exact function but a variant called iswhite.

11.1.14 isupper

```
#include <ctype.h>
int isupper(c)
    char c;
```

isupper returns a nonzero value if c is the code for an uppercase alphabetic character; that is, one of the following:

A B C D E F G H I J K L M N O P Q R S T U V W X Y Z

Otherwise the returned value is zero.

11.1.15 isxdigit

```
#include <ctype.h>
int isxdigit(c)
    char c;
```

isxdigit returns a nonzero value if c is the code for a hexadecimal digit; that is, one of the following:

```
0  1  2  3  4  5  6  7  8  9
A  B  C  D  E  F
a  b  c  d  e  f
```

Otherwise the returned value is zero.

11.1.16 toascii

```
#include <ctype.h>
int toascii(c)
    char c;
```

toascii accepts any integer value and reduces it to the range of valid ASCII characters (codes 0 through 0177) by discarding all but the low seven bits of the value. If the argument is already a valid ASCII code, then the result is equal to the argument.

11.1.17 toint

```
#include <ctype.h>
int toint(c)
  char c;
```

toint returns the "weight" of a hexadecimal digit: 0 for the argument '0', 1 for '1', ..., 9 for '9', 10 for either 'A' or 'a', ..., and 15 for either 'F' or 'f'. toint returns −1 if the argument is not a hexadecimal digit character.

11.1.18 tolower

```
#include <ctype.h>
int tolower(c)
  char c;
```

If c is an uppercase letter, then tolower returns the corresponding lowercase letter; otherwise c is returned unchanged.

See also _tolower (section 11.1.20), which is much faster if the programmer can guarantee that c is in fact an uppercase letter.

11.1.19 toupper

```
#include <ctype.h>
int toupper(c)
  char c;
```

If c is a lowercase letter, then toupper returns the corresponding uppercase letter; otherwise c is returned unchanged.

See also _toupper (section 11.1.21), which is much faster if the programmer can guarantee that c is in fact a lowercase letter.

11.1.20 _tolower

```
#include <ctype.h>
int _tolower(c)
   char c;
```

If c is an uppercase letter, then `_tolower` returns the corresponding lowercase letter. The result of `_tolower` is undefined for all other arguments.

See also `tolower` (section 11.1.18), which is slower but produces a defined result for any character or EOF.

11.1.21 _toupper

```
#include <ctype.h>
int _toupper(c)
   char c;
```

If c is a lowercase letter, then `_toupper` returns the corresponding uppercase letter. The result of `_toupper` is undefined for all other arguments.

See also `toupper` (section 11.1.19), which is slower but produces a defined result for any character or EOF.

11.2 STRING PROCESSING

By convention, strings in C are of variable length and are terminated by a null character (that is, `'\0'`). The compiler automatically supplies an extra null character after all string constants, but it is up to the programmer to make sure that strings created in string variables (that is, character arrays) end with a null character.

All the characters in a string, not counting the terminating null character, are together called the *contents* of the string. An empty string contains no characters and is represented by a pointer to a null character. Note that this is *not* the same as a null character pointer (NULL), which is a pointer that points to no character at all. When we speak of a "pointer to the first character of a string," we mean a pointer to the terminating null character if the string is empty and to the first character of the contents if the string is not empty.

All of the string-handling facilities described here assume that strings are terminated by a null character. When characters are transferred to a destination string, no test is made for overflow of the destination. It is up to the programmer to make sure that the destination area in memory is large enough to contain the result string, including the terminating null character.

All of the facilities described here are declared by the library header file `string.h`.

11.2.1 strcat

```
#include <string.h>
char *strcat(s1, s2)
  char *s1, *s2;
```

strcat appends the contents of the string s2 to the end of the string s1. A pointer to the first character of s1 is returned. The null character that terminates s1 (and perhaps other characters following it in memory) is overwritten with characters from s2 and a new terminating null character. Characters are copied from s2 until a null character is encountered in s2.

The results are unpredictable if the two string arguments overlap in memory. In particular, it does not necessarily work to supply the same string as both arguments in an attempt to double its length.

See also strncat (section 11.2.7), which appends a limited number of characters.

11.2.2 strchr

```
#include <string.h>
char *strchr(s, c)
  char *s, c;
```

strchr searches the null-terminated string s for the first occurrence of the character c. If the character c is found in the string, a pointer to the first occurrence is returned. If the character is not found, a null character pointer (NULL) is returned. The terminating null character is considered to be a part of s for the purposes of this search, so searching for a null character will return a pointer to the null character, not a null pointer.

In some implementations of C this function is called index.

See also strrchr (section 11.2.12), which returns a pointer to the *last* occurrence of a character.

11.2.3 strcmp

```
#include <string.h>
int strcmp(s1, s2)
  char *s1, *s2;
```

strcmp lexicographically compares the contents of the null-terminated string s1 with the contents of the null-terminated string s2. It returns a value of type

int that is less than zero if s1 is less than s2; equal to zero if s1 is equal to
s2; and greater than zero if s1 is greater than s2.

Two strings are equal if their contents are identical. String s1 is lexicographically less than string s2 under either of two circumstances:

1. The contents of the strings are equal up to some character position, and at
   that first differing character position the character from s1 is less than the
   character from s2.
2. The string s1 is shorter than the string s2, and the contents of s1 are
   identical to those of s2 up to length of s1.

See also strncmp (section 11.2.8), which compares a limited number of
characters.

11.2.4 strcpy

```
#include <string.h>
char *strcpy(s1, s2)
  char *s1, *s2;
```

strcpy copies the contents of the string s2 to the string s1, overwriting the
old contents of s1. The entire contents of s2 are copied, plus the terminating
null, even if s2 is longer than s1. A pointer to the first character of s1 is
returned.

The results are unpredictable if the two string arguments overlap in
memory.

See also strncpy (section 11.2.9), which copies a specified number of
characters.

11.2.5 strcspn

```
#include <string.h>
int strcspn(s, set)
  char *s, *set;
```

strcspn searches the null-terminated s for the first occurrence of a character
that is included in the null-terminated string set, skipping over characters that
are not in set. The second argument is regarded as a set of characters; the
order of the characters, or whether there are duplications, does not matter. The
value returned is the length of the longest initial segment of s that consists of
characters *not* found in set. If no character of s appears in set, then the total
length of s (not counting the terminating null character) is returned; note that

this will occur if `set` is an empty string.

In some implementations of C this function is called `instr`.

See also `strspn` (section 11.2.15), which searches for a character that is *not* in a set, skipping over characters that *are* in the set.

11.2.6 strlen

```
#include <string.h>
int strlen( string )
  char *string;
```

`strlen` returns the number of characters in `s` preceding the terminating null. The length of an empty string is zero.

In some implementations of C this function is called `lenstr`.

11.2.7 strncat

```
#include <string.h>
char *strncat(s1, s2, n)
  char *s1, *s2;
  int n;
```

`strncat` appends up to n characters from the contents of null-terminated `s2` to the end of null-terminated `s1`. A pointer to `s1` is returned. The null character that terminates `s1` (and perhaps other characters following it in memory) is overwritten with characters from `s2` and a new terminating null character; the memory area beginning with `s1` is thus assumed to be large enough to hold both strings.

Characters are copied from `s2`. If the null character that terminates `s2` is encountered before n characters have been copied, then the null character is copied, but no more characters after that are copied. If no null character appears among the first n characters of `s2`, then the net effect is that the first n characters are copied and then a null character is supplied to terminate the destination string; that is, $n+1$ characters in all are written, the first replacing the null character that formerly terminated `s1`.

If the value of n is zero or negative, then this function makes no net change to the contents of memory.

The results are unpredictable if the two string arguments overlap in memory.

See also `strcat` (section 11.2.1), which appends an unlimited number of characters.

11.2.8 `strncmp`

```
#include <string.h>
int strncmp(s1, s2, n)
  char *s1, *s2;
  int n;
```

`strncmp` lexicographically compares up to n characters of the null-terminated string s1 with up to n characters of the null-terminated string s2. It returns a value of type `int` that is less than zero if s1 is less than s2; equal to zero if s1 is equal to s2; and greater than zero if s1 is greater than s2. In comparing the strings, the entire string is used if it contains fewer than n characters, and otherwise only the first n characters are considered; the characters of the string so considered are called the `restricted contents`.

The two strings are considered equal if their restricted contents are identical. String s1 is lexicographically less than string s2 under either of two circumstances:

1. The restricted contents of the strings are equal up to some character position, and at that first differing character position the character from s1 is less than the character from s2.
2. The string s1 is shorter than the string s2, and the restricted contents of s1 are identical to those of s2 up to length of s1.

If the value of n is zero or negative, then the restricted contents of each string are empty; in this case the two strings are considered to be equal, and zero is returned.

See also `strcmp` (section 11.2.3), which compares an unlimited number of characters.

11.2.9 `strncpy`

```
#include <string.h>
char *strncpy(s1, s2, n)
  char *s1, *s2;
  int n;
```

`strncpy` copies exactly n characters to s1. It copies up to n characters from s2. If there are fewer than n characters in s2 before the terminating null character, then null characters are written into s1 as padding until exactly n characters have been written. If there are n or more characters in s2, then only n characters are copied, and so only a truncated copy of s2 is transferred to s1. It follows that the copy in s1 is terminated with a null by strncpy only if the length of s2 (not counting the terminating null) is less than n.

If the value of n is zero or negative, then this function makes no net change to the contents of memory.

The results are unpredictable if the two string arguments overlap in memory.

See also strcpy (section 11.2.9), which copies an unlimited number of characters.

11.2.10 strpbrk

```
#include <string.h>
char *strpbrk(s, set)
  char *s, *set;
```

strpbrk searches the null-terminated string s for the first occurrence of one of the characters included in the null-terminated string set, skipping over characters that are not in set. The second argument is regarded as a set of characters; the order of the characters, or whether there are duplications, does not matter. If such a character is found within s, then a pointer to that character is returned. If no character within s occurs in set, then a null character pointer (NULL) is returned.

See also strrpbrk (section 11.2.13), which searches for the *last* character that is in a set.

11.2.11 strpos

```
#include <string.h>
int strpos(s, c)
  char *s, c;
```

strpos searches the null-terminated string s for the first occurrence of the character c. If the character c is found in the string, the position of the first occurrence is returned (where the first character of s is considered to be at position 0). If the character is not found, the value −1 is returned. The terminating null character is considered to be a part of s for the purposes of this search, so searching for a null character will return the position of the terminating null character (which is equal to the length of the string), not the value −1.

Some implementations of C provide not this exact function but a variant called scnstr.

See also strrpos (section 11.2.14), which returns the position of the *last* occurrence of a character.

11.2.12 `strrchr`

```
#include <string.h>
char *strrchr(s, c)
  char *s, c;
```

`strrchr` searches the null-terminated string s for the last occurrence of the character c. If the character c is found in the string, a pointer to the last occurrence is returned. If the character is not found, a null character pointer (NULL) is returned. The terminating null character is considered to be a part of the string for the purposes of this search, but nevertheless also terminates the string, so searching for a null character will return a pointer to the (first!) null character, not a null pointer.

In some implementations of C this function is called `rindex`.

See also `strchr` (section 11.2.2), which returns a pointer to the *first* occurrence of a character.

11.2.13 `strrpbrk`

```
#include <string.h>
char *strrpbrk(s, set)
  char *s, *set;
```

`strrpbrk` searches the null-terminated string s for occurrences of characters included in the null-terminated string `set`. The second argument is regarded as a set of characters; the order of the characters, or whether there are duplications, does not matter. If such a character is found within s, then a pointer to the *last* such character within s is returned. If no character within s occurs in `set`, then a null character pointer (NULL) is returned.

See also `strpbrk` (section 11.2.10), which searches for the *first* character that is in a set.

11.2.14 `strrpos`

```
#include <string.h>
int strrpos( s, c )
  char *s, c;
```

`strrpos` searches the null-terminated string s for the character c. If the character c is found in the string, the position of the *last* occurrence is returned (where the first character of s is considered to be at position 0). If the character is not found, the value −1 is returned. The terminating null character is considered to be a part of s for the purposes of this search, so searching for a null character will return the position of the terminating null character (which is equal to the length of the string), not the value −1.

See also `strpos` (section 11.2.11), which returns the position of the *first* occurrence of a character.

11.2.15 strspn

```
#include <string.h>
int strspn(s, set)
  char *s, *set;
```

`strspn` searches the null-terminated s for the first occurrence of a character that is not included in the null-terminated string `set`, skipping over characters that are in `set`. The second argument is regarded as a set of characters; the order of the characters, or whether there are duplications, does not matter. The value returned is the length of the longest initial segment of s that consists of characters found in `set`. If every character of s appears in `set`, then the total length of s (not counting the terminating null character) is returned. If `set` is an empty string, then the first character of s will not be found in it, and so zero will be returned.

In some implementations of C this function is called `notstr`.

See also `strcspn` (section 11.2.5), which searches for a character that *is* in a set, skipping over characters that are *not* in the set.

11.3 MATHEMATICAL FUNCTIONS

Some of the facilities described in this section are declared by the library header file `math.h`. Others (`abs`, for example) are predeclared in the C compiler, and so their use does not require inclusion of a library header file.

All of the operations on floating-point numbers are defined only for arguments of type `double`, because of the rule that all actual function arguments of type `float` are converted to type `double` before the call is performed.

11.3.1 abs

```
#include <math.h>
int abs(x)
  int x;
```

`abs` returns the absolute value of its argument. The argument and the result are both of type `int`. More precisely, if the argument is nonnegative, then the argument itself is returned; but if the argument is negative, then the result of negating the argument (as if by the unary '−' operator) is returned.

The value of `abs` is undefined for any negative argument for which the unary '−' operator is also undefined. For example, if the implementation uses a two's-complement representation for integers, the absolute value of the smallest representable negative signed integer will be undefined.

Note that `abs` cannot be used to take the absolute value of a `long int`; its argument must be of type `int`.

See also `fabs` (section 11.3.10), which returns the absolute value of a floating-point number, and `labs` (section 11.3.14), which returns the absolute value of a `long int`.

11.3.2 `acos`

```
#include <math.h>
double acos(x)
    double x;
```

`acos` computes a floating-point approximation to the trigonometric arc cosine function of the argument value. The argument and the result are both of type `double`. The result is in radians and lies (approximately) between 0 and π.

If the argument is less than −1.0 or greater than 1.0, then the value 0 is returned, and the error code EDOM is stored into the external variable `errno`.

11.3.3 `asin`

```
#include <math.h>
double asin(x)
    double x;
```

`asin` computes a floating-point approximation to the trigonometric arc sine function of the argument value. The argument and the result are both of type `double`. The result is in radians and lies (approximately) between $-\pi/2$ and $\pi/2$.

If the argument is less than −1.0 or greater than 1.0, then the value 0 is returned, and the error code EDOM is stored into the external variable `errno`.

11.3.4 `atan`

```
#include <math.h>
double atan(x)
  double x;
```

`atan` computes a floating-point approximation to the trigonometric arc tangent function of the argument value. The argument and the result are both of type `double`. The result is in radians and lies (approximately) between $-\pi/2$ and $\pi/2$.

In some implementations of C this function is called `arctan`.

11.3.5 `atan2`

```
#include <math.h>
double atan2(y, x)
  double y, x;
```

`atan2` computes a floating-point approximation to the trigonometric arc tangent function of the value `y/x`. The result is computed in such a way as to take the signs of the two arguments into account to determine quadrant information. Viewed in terms of a Cartesian coordinate system, the result is the angle between the positive x-axis and a line drawn from the origin through the point (x, y).

The argument and the result are both of type `double`. The result is in radians and lies (approximately) between $-\pi$ and π. It is permissible for `x` to be zero; the result is then (approximately) $\pi/2$ or $-\pi/2$, depending on whether `y` is positive or negative.

If both `x` and `y` are zero, then the value 0 is returned and the error code `EDOM` is stored into the external variable `errno`.

In some implementations of C, `atan2` returns a value other than zero (such as $\pi/2$) when both arguments are zero.

11.3.6 `ceil`

```
#include <math.h>
double ceil(x)
  double x;
```

`ceil` rounds its argument up to an integer; that is, it returns the smallest (that is, farthest from positive infinity) floating-point number not less than x whose value is an exact mathematical integer. If the value of the argument is already a mathematical integer, then the result equals the argument.

The argument and the result are both of type `double`.

See also `floor` (section 11.3.11), which rounds its argument down toward negative infinity.

11.3.7 cos

```
#include <math.h>
double cos(x)
  double x;
```

cos computes a floating-point approximation to the trigonometric cosine function of the argument value, where the argument is taken to be in radians. The argument and the result are both of type double.

No error checks are performed, but the programmer should be aware that the results may be meaningless for arguments whose absolute value is very large, because the cosine function is periodic and the precision of the floating-point representation is limited.

11.3.8 cosh

```
#include <math.h>
double cosh(x)
  double x;
```

cosh computes a floating-point approximation to the hyperbolic cosine function of the argument value. The argument and the result are both of type double.

If the argument is so great in absolute value that the correct result value is too large to be represented, then the largest representable positive floating-point number is returned and the error code ERANGE is stored into the external variable errno.

11.3.9 exp

```
#include <math.h>
double exp(x)
  double x;
```

exp computes a floating-point approximation to the exponential function; that is, *e* raised to the power x, where *e* is the base of the natural logarithms. The argument and the result are both of type double.

If the argument is so large that the correct result value is too large to be represented, then the largest representable positive floating-point number is returned and the error code ERANGE is stored into the external variable errno.

11.3.10 fabs

```
#include <math.h>
double fabs(x)
    double x;
```

fabs returns the absolute value of its argument. The argument and the result are both of type double. More precisely, if the argument is nonnegative, then the argument itself is returned; but if the argument is negative, then the result of negating the argument (as if by the unary '−' operator) is returned.

The value of fabs is undefined for any negative argument for which the unary '−' operator is also undefined.

See also abs (section 11.3.1), which returns the absolute value of an integer.

11.3.11 floor

```
#include <math.h>
double floor(x)
    double x;
```

floor rounds its argument down to an integer. It returns the largest (that is, farthest from negative infinity) floating-point number not greater than x whose value is an exact mathematical integer. If the value of the argument is already a mathematical integer, then the result equals the argument.

The argument and the result are both of type double.

See also ceil (section 11.3.6), which rounds its argument up toward positive infinity.

11.3.12 fmod

```
#include <math.h>
double fmod(x, y)
    double x, y;
```

fmod returns a floating-point number approximating a mathematical value f such that f has the same sign as x, the absolute value of f is less than the absolute value of y, and there exists an integer k such that k*y+f equals x.

The two arguments and the result are all of type double.

The name fmod is a misnomer, because the value it computes is properly called a *remainder*. (The result of a true modulus operation would have the same sign as y, not the same sign as x. This makes a difference only when one of the arguments is negative and the other is not.) Note that the C binary operator '%' is colloquially, in the same confusing way, sometimes referred to as the "remainder" operator and sometimes as the "mod" operator. The official definition of the '%' operator is (intentionally) vague on this point: it might be a remainder operator in one implementation and a mod operator in another. All that matters is that '%' bears a certain relationship to the division operator '/', whose definition for negative arguments is itself (intentionally) vague.

fmod should not be confused with modf (section 11.3.18), a function that extracts the fractional and integer parts of a floating-point number.

11.3.13 frexp

```
double frexp(x, nptr)
  double x;
  int *nptr;
```

frexp splits a floating-point number into a fraction f and an exponent n, such that the absolute value of f is less than 1.0 but not less than 0.5 and such that f times *radix* raised to the power n is equal to x, where *radix* is the radix used by the floating-point representation (typically 2). The fraction f is returned, and as a side effect the exponent n is stored into the place pointed to by nptr.

The first argument and the result are both of type double; the second argument is a pointer to an integer.

The inverse of this operation is provided by the facility ldexp (section 11.3.15).

11.3.14 labs

```
#include <math.h>
long int labs(x)
  long int x;
```

labs returns the absolute value of its argument. The argument and the result are both of type long int. More precisely, if the argument is nonnegative, then the argument itself is returned; but if the argument is negative, then the result of negating the argument (as if by the unary '−' operator) is returned.

The value of labs is undefined for any negative argument for which the unary '−' operator is also undefined. For example, if the implementation uses a two's-complement representation for integers, the absolute value of the smallest representable negative long signed integer will be undefined.

See also abs (section 11.3.1), which returns the absolute value of an int, and fabs (section 11.3.10), which returns the absolute value of a floating-point number.

11.3.15 ldexp

```
double ldexp(x, n)
    double x;
    int n;
```

ldexp computes the value x times *radix* raised to the power n, where *radix* is the radix used by the floating-point representation (typically 2).

The first argument and the result are both of type double; the second argument is of type int.

An inverse to this operation is provided by the facility frexp (section 11.3.13), which splits a floating-point number into a fraction and an exponent.

11.3.16 log

```
#include <math.h>
double log(x)
    double x;
```

log computes a floating-point approximation to the natural logarithm function. The argument and the result are both of type double.

If the argument is nonpositive, then the negative of the largest representable positive floating-point number is returned and the error code EDOM is stored into the external variable errno.

In some implementations of C this function is called ln.

11.3.17 log10

```
#include <math.h>
double log10(x)
    double x;
```

log10 computes a floating-point approximation to the base-10 logarithm function. The argument and the result are both of type double.

If the argument is nonpositive, then the negative of the largest representable positive floating-point number is returned and the error code EDOM is stored into the external variable errno.

11.3.18 modf

```
double modf(x, nptr)
    double x;
    int *nptr;
```

modf splits a floating-point number into a fractional part f and an integer part n, such that the absolute value of f is less than 1.0 and such that f plus n is equal to x. The fractional part f is returned, and as a side effect the integer part n is stored into the place pointed to by nptr.

The first argument and the result are both of type double; the second argument is a pointer to an integer.

The name modf is a misnomer, because the value it computes is properly called a *remainder*. (See the description of fmod for further discussion of the distinction between "remainder" and "mod" operations.)

modf should not be confused with fmod (section 11.3.12), a function that computes the remainder from evenly dividing one floating-point number by another. The two facilities are related in an interesting way: When x is positive, the value returned by modf(x, nptr) is equal to the value returned by fmod(x, 1.0).

11.3.19 pow

```
#include <math.h>
double pow(x, y)
  double x, y;
```

pow computes a floating-point approximation to the power function; that is, *x* raised to the power y. The arguments and the result are all of type double.

Certain special cases deserve explicit mention. When x is nonzero and y is zero, the result is (approximately) 1.0. When x is zero and y is positive, the result is zero. When x is negative and the value of y is an integer (but not so large that the integer is not represented precisely), then pow(x, y) is computed as pow(-x, y) if y is even and as -pow(-x, y) if y is odd.

If the arguments are such that the correct result value is too large to be represented, then the largest representable positive floating-point number is returned and the error code ERANGE is stored into the external variable errno.

If x is negative and y is not an exact integer, or if x is zero and y is nonpositive, then the negative of the largest representable positive floating-point number is returned and the error code EDOM is stored into the external variable errno.

11.3.20 rand

```
int rand()
```

Successive calls to rand return values in the range 0 to the largest representable positive value of type int (inclusive) that are the successive results of a pseudorandom-number generator.

See srand (section 11.3.24) for a discussion of how the pseudorandom-number generator may be initialized.

11.3.21 sin

```
#include <math.h>
double sin(x)
    double x;
```

sin computes a floating-point approximation to the trigonometric sine function of the argument value, where the argument is taken to be in radians. The argument and the result are both of type double.

No error checks are performed, but the programmer should be aware that the results may be meaningless for arguments whose absolute value is very large, because the sine function is periodic and the precision of the floating-point representation is limited.

11.3.22 sinh

```
#include <math.h>
double sinh(x)
    double x;
```

sinh computes a floating-point approximation to the hyperbolic sine function of the argument value. The argument and the result are both of type double.

If the argument is positive and too large, then the largest representable positive floating-point number is returned. If the argument is negative and too large, then the negative of the largest representable positive floating-point number is returned. In either case, the error code ERANGE is stored into the external variable errno.

In some implementations of C, sinh returns the largest representable positive floating-point number rather than its negative for large negative arguments.

11.3.23 sqrt

```
#include <math.h>
double sqrt(x)
    double x;
```

sqrt computes a floating-point approximation to the square root of the argument. The argument and the result are both of type double.

If the argument is negative, then 0.0 is returned and the error code EDOM is stored into the external variable errno.

11.3.24 srand

```
srand(seed)
  unsigned seed;
```

srand may be used to initialize the pseudorandom-number generator that is used to generate successive values for call to rand (section 11.3.20).

After a call to srand, successive calls to rand will produce a certain series of pseudorandom numbers. If srand is called again with the same argument, then after that point successive calls to rand will produce the same series of pseudorandom numbers. If srand is called again with a different argument, then after that point successive calls to rand will produce a new series (probably quite different) of pseudorandom numbers.

Successive calls made to rand before srand is ever called in a user program will produce the same series of pseudorandom numbers that would be produced after srand is called with argument 1.

11.3.25 tan

```
#include <math.h>
double tan(x)
  double x;
```

tan computes a floating-point approximation to the trigonometric tangent function of the argument value, where the argument is taken to be in radians. The argument and the result are both of type double.

If the argument is so close to an odd multiple of $\pi/2$ that the correct result value is too large to be represented, then the largest representable positive floating-point number is returned and the error code ERANGE is stored into the external variable errno.

The programmer should be aware that the results may be meaningless for arguments whose absolute value is very large, because the tangent function is periodic and the precision of the floating-point representation is limited. However, tan performs no check for very large arguments.

11.3.26 tanh

```
#include <math.h>
double tanh(x)
  double x;
```

tanh computes a floating-point approximation to the hyperbolic tangent function of the argument value. The argument and the result are both of type double.

11.4 STORAGE ALLOCATION

The storage allocation facilities provide a simple form of heap memory management that allows a program to repeatedly request allocation of a "fresh" region of memory and perhaps later to deallocate such a region when it is no longer needed. Explicitly deallocated regions are recycled by the storage manager for satisfaction of further allocation requests.

When a region of memory is allocated in response to a request, a pointer to the region is returned to the caller. This pointer will be of type "pointer to character" but is guaranteed to be properly aligned for any data type. The caller may then use a cast operator to convert this pointer to another pointer type.

If an implementation of C provides the `brk` and `sbrk` facilities for setting the UNIX "break address," then the implementation usually forbids any program that uses `brk` or `sbrk` to use any of the facilities described in this section, because using one may interfere with the operation of the other.

The facilities described in this section are predeclared in the C compiler, and so their use does not require inclusion of a library header file.

11.4.1 `calloc`

```
char *calloc(elt_count, elt_size)
  unsigned elt_count, elt_size;
```

`calloc` allocates a region of memory large enough to hold an array of `elt_count` elements, each of size `elt_size`. The region of memory is cleared (all bits are set to zero). A pointer to the first element of the region is returned. Typically, the caller will immediately cast the result pointer to an appropriate pointer type (a pointer to the array element type):

```
{
    unsigned sample_limit;
    double *samples;
    . . .
    samples = (double *) calloc(sample_limit,
                  sizeof(double));
    . . .
}
```

Note that the second argument to `calloc` often may be conveniently computed by using the `sizeof` operator.

If it is impossible for some reason to perform the requested allocation, `calloc` returns a null pointer (`NULL`).

See also `clalloc` (section 11.4.3), which takes arguments of type `unsigned long int`, and `malloc`, which does not clear the allocated region.

11.4.2 cfree

```
cfree(ptr)
  char *ptr;
```

cfree allows the programmer to deallocate a region of memory previously allocated by calloc (or clalloc). The argument to cfree must be a pointer equivalent (except for possible intermediate type casting) to a pointer previously returned by calloc that has not already been given to cfree. Once a region of memory has been explicitly freed, it should not be used for any other purpose; the storage manager may recycle the memory region and use it to satisfy later requests made through malloc, calloc, or realloc. The programmer should assume that giving a region of memory to cfree causes the entire contents of the memory region to be destroyed and replaced by garbage information.

In some implementations cfree is identical to free (section 11.4.4), and memory regions allocated by calloc and malloc may be freed indiscriminately by free or cfree with no ill effects. For maximum portability, however, it is best to use cfree only to deallocate memory allocated by calloc, and free only to deallocate memory allocated by malloc.

11.4.3 clalloc

```
char *clalloc(elt_count, elt_size)
  unsigned long elt_count, elt_size;
```

clalloc allocates a region of memory large enough to hold an array of elt_count elements, each of size elt_size. The region of memory is cleared (all bits are set to zero). A pointer to the first element of the region is returned.

clalloc is just like calloc, except that its arguments are of type unsigned long int rather than unsigned int. (In some implementations it is possible to allocate arrays so large that numbers of type unsigned int are not large enough to specify them.)

If it is impossible for some reason to perform the requested allocation, clalloc returns a null pointer (NULL).

See calloc (section 11.4.1), which takes arguments of type unsigned int, and malloc, which does not clear the allocated region.

11.4.4 free

```
free(ptr)
  char *ptr;
```

free allows the programmer to deallocate a region of memory previously allocated by malloc (or mlalloc, realloc, or relalloc). The argument to free must be a pointer equivalent (except for possible intermediate type casting) to a pointer previously returned by malloc that has not already been given to free. Once a region of memory has been explicitly freed, it should not be used for any other purpose; the storage manager may recycle the memory region and use it to satisfy later requests made through malloc, calloc, or realloc. The programmer should assume that giving a region of memory to free causes the entire contents of the memory region to be destroyed and replaced by garbage information.

See also cfree (section 11.4.2), which should be used to deallocate regions of memory allocated by calloc.

11.4.5 malloc

```
char *malloc(size)
  unsigned size;
```

malloc allocates a region of memory large enough to hold an object whose size (as measured by the sizeof operator) is size. The region of memory is not specially initialized in any way; the caller must assume that it contains garbage information. A pointer to the first element of the region is returned. Typically, the caller will immediately cast the result pointer to an appropriate pointer type:

```
/* A linked list of (x, y, z) points in
   three-dimensional space.
 */
typedef struct list {
    struct list *next;
    double x, y, z;
} POINT_LIST;

/* Add a new point (x, y, z) to the list
   that is pointed to by pp.
 */
void addpoint(pp, x, y, z)
  POINT_LIST **pp;
  double x, y, z;
{
    POINT_LIST *sp;
    /* Allocate a new POINT_LIST object. */
    sp = (POINT_LIST *) malloc(sizeof(POINT_LIST));
    /* Install the specified coordinate data. */
    sp->x = x;
    sp->y = y;
    sp->z = z;
    /* Link it into the list at the front. */
    sp->next = *pp;
    *pp = sp;
}
```

As shown in the example, the argument to malloc is often computed by using the sizeof operator.

If it is impossible for some reason to perform the requested allocation, malloc returns a null pointer (NULL).

See also mlalloc (section 11.4.6), which takes arguments of type unsigned long int, and calloc, which explicitly clears the allocated region.

11.4.6 mlalloc

```
char *mlalloc(size)
  unsigned long size;
```

mlalloc allocates a region of memory large enough to hold an object whose size (as measured by the sizeof operator) is size. The region of memory is not specially initialized in any way; the caller must assume that it contains garbage information. A pointer to the first element of the region is returned.

mlalloc is just like malloc, except that its arguments are of type unsigned long int rather than unsigned int. (In some implementations it is possible to allocate memory regions so large that numbers of type unsigned int are not large enough to specify them.)

If it is impossible for some reason to perform the requested allocation, mlalloc returns a null pointer (NULL).

See malloc (section 11.4.5), which takes arguments of type unsigned int, and calloc, which explicitly clears the allocated region.

11.4.7 realloc

```
char *realloc(ptr, size)
  char *ptr;
  unsigned size;
```

realloc takes a pointer to a previously allocated memory region and changes its size while preserving its contents. If necessary, the contents are copied to a new memory region. A pointer to the (possibly new) memory region is returned. If the new size is smaller than the old size, then some of the old contents at the end of the old region will be discarded. If the new size is larger than the old size, then all of the old contents are preserved and new space is added at the end; the new space is not specially initialized in any way, and the caller must assume that it contains garbage information.

If realloc returns a pointer that is different from its first argument, then the region of memory pointed to by the argument was deallocated and should not be used.

Typically, the caller will immediately cast the result pointer to an appropriate pointer type. Here is a typical use of realloc:

```
{
    unsigned sample_limit,sample_count,sample_increment;
    double *samples;
     . . .
    /* If the samples array is full, reallocate it. */
    if (sample_count == sample_limit) {
        /* Increase the limit by a suitable amount. */
        sample_limit += sample_increment;
        /* Reallocate the array, preserving the old
            contents. */
        samples = (double *)
                    realloc((char *) samples,
                            sample_limit *
                                sizeof(double));
    }
    /* Add new sample to the array. */
    samples[sample_count++] = new_sample;
     . . .
}
```

If it is impossible for some reason to perform the requested reallocation, `realloc` returns a null pointer (NULL).

11.4.8 `relalloc`

```
char *relalloc(ptr,size)
    char *ptr;
    unsigned long size;
```

`relalloc` takes a pointer to a previously allocated memory region and changes its size while preserving its contents. If necessary, the contents are copied to a new memory region. A pointer to the (possibly new) memory region is returned.

`relalloc` is just like `realloc` (section 11.4.7), except that its arguments are of type `unsigned long int` rather than `unsigned int`. (In some implementations it is possible to allocate memory regions so large that numbers of type `unsigned int` are not large enough to specify them.)

If it is impossible for some reason to perform the requested allocation, `relalloc` returns a null pointer (NULL).

11.5 STANDARD I/O

11.5.1 EOF

```
#include <stdio.h>
#define EOF (-1)
```

The value EOF is conventionally used as a value that is "not a real character."
For example, fgetc (section 11.5.8) returns EOF when at end-of-file, because
there is no "real character" to be read. It must be remembered, however, that
the type char may be signed in some implementations, and so EOF is not
necessarily distinguishable from a "real character" if nonstandard character
values appear. (Standard character values are always nonnegative, however,
even if the type char is signed.) When the value EOF is read, it is best to use
the feof facility (section 11.5.5) to determine whether end-of-file has indeed
been encountered.

11.5.2 FILE

```
#include <stdio.h>
/* FILE is a data type. */
```

The data type FILE is used to hold information about a file, or more generally,
a *stream*. A stream can be a file or some other source or consumer of data,
including a terminal. Normally the programmer does not allocate FILE objects
but obtains pointers to FILE objects (*file pointers*) that have been allocated by
the standard I/O system through facilties such as fopen (section 11.5.10). A
file pointer may be used as an argument to most of the I/O facilities.

Among the information included in a FILE object is the current *position*
within the file. The position determines the place in the file at which the next
input or output operation will occur. This position can be retrieved by the
ftell function and can be set by the fseek and rewind functions.

Do not confuse a file pointer with a *file descriptor*, which is an integer used
in low-level UNIX I/O routines. (It is actually an index into an internal table.)
None of the functions described in this chapter operate on, or produce, file
descriptors.

11.5.3 clearerr

```
#include <stdio.h>
void clearerr(stream)
  FILE *stream;
```

clearerr resets any error indication on the specified stream. See `ferror`
(section 11.5.6), which is used to test the error indicator for a stream. After
`clearerr` has been used to reset an error indication, `ferror` will report that
no error has occurred for that stream unless and until another error occurs.

11.5.4 fclose

```
#include <stdio.h>
int fclose(stream)
  FILE *stream;
```

The function `fclose` takes a stream, which should be open for input or output. The stream is closed in an appropriate and orderly fashion, including any
necessary emptying and freeing of internal data buffers.

If any error is detected, `fclose` returns EOF; otherwise, it returns 0.

See `fopen` for information on opening a stream.

11.5.5 feof

```
#include <stdio.h>
int feof(stream)
  FILE *stream;
```

`feof` takes an input stream. If end-of-file has been detected while reading
from the input stream, then a nonzero value is returned; otherwise, zero is
returned.

11.5.6 ferror

```
#include <stdio.h>
int ferror(stream)
  FILE *stream;
```

`ferror` takes a stream as its argument. If an error has occurred while reading
from or writing to the stream, then `ferror` returns a nonzero value; otherwise, zero is returned.

Using `ferror` to test a stream does not reset the error indicator for the
stream. Once an error has occurred for a given stream, repeated calls to
`ferror` will continue to report an error unless `clearerr` is used to explicitly
reset the error indication. Closing the stream, as with `fclose`, will also reset
the error indication.

11.5.7 fflush

```
#include <stdio.h>
int fflush(stream)
  FILE *stream;
```

The function fflush takes a stream, which should be open for output. If the stream is buffered, then any internally buffered data is written to the destination device in order to empty the buffer. The stream remains open.

If any error is detected, fflush returns EOF; otherwise, it returns 0.

11.5.8 fgetc

```
#include <stdio.h>
int fgetc(stream)
  FILE *stream;
```

fgetc takes a stream, which must be open for input. It reads the next character from the stream and returns it as a value of type int. Successive calls to fgetc will return successive characters from the input stream.

If an error occurs or the stream is at end-of-file, fgetc returns EOF. The feof facility should be used in this case to determine whether end-of-file has really been reached.

fgetc is a true function; getc (section 11.5.20) is a macro equivalent to fgetc except that the argument expression must not have any side effects.

11.5.9 fgets

```
#include <stdio.h>
char *fgets(s, n, stream)
  char *s;
  int n;
  FILE *stream;
```

The function fgets takes three arguments: a string s, a count n, and a stream, which must be open for input. Characters are read from the specified stream until end-of-file is reached, until a newline is seen, or until the number of characters read is not less than n.

The argument s is assumed to point to the beginning of an array. The characters read are stored into successive locations of the array, and then an extra terminating null character is appended to the stored characters.

If the input is terminated because a newline was seen, the newline character is stored in the array just before the terminating null character. In this fgets differs from gets; if the input for gets is terminated by a newline, gets does not store the newline character before the terminating null character.

If end-of-file is encountered immediately, before any characters at all have been read from the stream, then no characters are stored into the string s (not even a null character), and a null pointer is returned. If an error occurs during the input operation, then a null pointer is returned and the array s may be unaltered, partially altered, or filled with invalid data. If the input operation is successful, then s is returned.

11.5.10 `fopen`

```
#include <stdio.h>
FILE *fopen(pathname, type)
    char *pathname, *type;
```

The function `fopen` takes a pathname and a type; each is specified as a character string. The pathname is used in an implementation-dependent manner to identify or create a file. (A *pathname* is sometimes called a *file name*; however, the pathname often includes a directory path to the file.)

A stream is associated with the file in a manner indicated by the type argument. A pointer of type `FILE *` is returned; this pointer can be used to identify the stream for other input/output operations. If any error is detected, however, `fopen` stores an error code into `errno` and returns a null pointer.

The following values are permitted for the type specification:

`"r"`   Open an existing file for reading. Return an input stream.

`"w"`   Create a new file, or truncate an existing one, for writing. Return an output stream.

`"a"`   Create a new file, or append to an existing one, for writing. Return an output stream.

`"r+"`   Open an existing file for update (both reading and writing), starting at the beginning of the file. Return an input/output stream.

`"w+"`   Create a new file, or truncate an existing one, for update (both reading and writing). Return an input/output stream.

`"a+"`   Create a new file, or append to an existing one, for update (both reading and writing). Return an input/output stream.

When a file is opened for update ('+' is present in the type string), the resulting stream may be used for both input and output. However, an output operation may not be followed by an input operation without an intervening call to `fseek` or `rewind`, and an input operation may not be followed by an output operation without an intervening call to `fseek` or `rewind` or an input operation that encounters end-of-file.

11.5.11 fprintf

```
#include <stdio.h>
int fprintf(stream, format, argument1, argument2, ...)
  FILE *stream;
  char *format;
```

fprintf performs output formatting, sending the output to the stream specified as the first argument. The second argument is a format control string. Additional arguments may be required, depending on the contents of the control string. A series of output characters is generated as directed by the control string; these characters are sent to specified stream.

The function fprintf is like printf in its operation; the only difference is that fprintf permits the output stream to be specified explicitly, while printf always sends the output to the standard output stream stdout. See printf (section 11.5.23) for a discussion of the formatting operations.

11.5.12 fputc

```
#include <stdio.h>
int fputc(c, stream)
  char c;
  FILE *stream;
```

fputc takes a character and a stream, which must be open for output. It writes the character to the stream and also returns the character as a value of type int. Successive calls to fputc will write the given characters successively to the output stream.

If an error occurs, fputc returns EOF instead of the character that was to have been written.

If the output stream is unbuffered, then each character will be sent to the destination immediately, but if the output stream is buffered, then characters are saved up in memory and sent to the destination in blocks.

fputc is a true function; putc (section 11.5.24) is a macro equivalent to fputc except that the actual argument expressions to putc must not have any side effects.

11.5.13 fputs

```
#include <stdio.h>
int fputs(s, stream)
  char *s;
  FILE *stream;
```

fputs takes a null-terminated string and a stream, which must be open for output. It writes all the characters of the string, not including the terminating null character, to the stream. The effect is as if fputc were used to write out successive characters of the string.

If an error occurs, fputs returns EOF. Otherwise, *fputs* returns a value other than EOF. (A typical implementation of fputs actually does use fputc to write out the characters of the string, and returns whatever value is returned by the last call to fputc. Unfortunately, if the string is empty, no call is made to fputc and that implementation of fputs will return an unpredictable result. This is an implementation error, but the programmer would do well to beware of this boundary case.)

If the output stream is unbuffered, then the characters will be sent to the destination immediately, but if the output stream is buffered, then characters are saved up in memory and sent to the destination in blocks.

Note that fputs, unlike puts, does not supply an extra newline character after writing out the contents of the string; fputs writes exactly the contents of the given string and nothing more.

11.5.14 fread

```
#include <stdio.h>
int fread(ptr, size_of_ptr, count, stream)
  char *ptr;
  unsigned size_of_ptr;
  int count;
  FILE *stream;
```

The function fread reads a block of binary data into a specified buffer. The first argument is a pointer that points to the first item in the buffer. The second argument must be the size of the items; if the first argument is specified as p, then the second argument should be computed by the expression sizeof(*p). The third argument is the maximum number of items to be read. The fourth argument must be a stream that is open for input.

Input proceeds until end-of-file is encountered, an error condition occurs, or the number of items read is not less than the specified maximum number. If the specified maximum is less than 1, then no input is done and the buffer area is not modified.

The stream is left positioned after the data actually read. If an error occurs during the input operation, the resulting stream position is unpredictable. Positions may be read and set using the functions fseek, ftell, and rewind.

The actual number of items read is returned by fread. Note that if the specified maximum is greater than 0 but fread returns 0, then either an immediate end-of-file or an error may have occurred. The two situations may be distinguished by use of the function ferror or feof.

11.5.15 freopen

```
#include <stdio.h>
FILE *freopen(pathname, type, stream)
  char *pathname, *type;
  FILE *stream;
```

The function freopen takes a pathname, a type, and a stream; the first two arguments are specified as character strings in the same manner as for the function fopen.

The operation of freopen is much like a call to fclose followed by a call to fopen that recycles the stream instead of throwing it away and then creating a new one. First the stream is closed. Then the pathname is used in an implementation-dependent manner to identify or create a file. The stream is associated with the file in a manner indicated by the type argument. If the entire operation is successful, then the third argument is returned; this pointer can be used to identify the stream for other input/output operations. If any error is detected, however, then freopen stores an error code into errno and returns a null pointer. Note that the original stream is always closed, regardless of whether the reopening is successful.

One of the main uses of freopen is to reassociate one of the standard input/output streams stdin, stdout, and stderr with some other file.

11.5.16 fscanf

```
#include <stdio.h>
int fscanf(stream, format, pointer1, pointer2, ...)
  FILE *stream;
  char *format;
```

fscanf performs parsing of formatted input text, reading characters from the stream specified as the first argument. The second argument is a format control string. Additional arguments may be required, depending on the contents of the control string. Each argument after the control string must be a pointer; converted values read from the input stream are stored into the locations pointed to by the pointers.

The function fscanf is like scanf in its operation; the only difference is that fscanf permits the input stream to be specified explicitly, while scanf always takes its input from the standard input stream stdin. See scanf (section 11.5.28) for a discussion of the formatting operations.

11.5.17 fseek

```
#include <stdio.h>
int fseek(stream, offset, type)
  FILE *stream;
  long offset;
  int type;
```

The function `fseek` allows random access within a file. The first argument must be a stream that is open for input or output.

The third argument must have the value 0, 1, or 2. If it is 0, then the position of the stream is set equal to the second argument. Values returned by the function `ftell` are suitable for use as the second argument. (The call `fseek(stream,0L,0)` will rewind the stream to the beginning.)

If the third argument is 1, then the position of the stream is set equal to the current position plus the signed offset.

If the third argument 2, then the position of the stream is set to the end of the file plus the signed offset. This functionality is often used to extend a file with "empty space."

If the operation succeeds, then `fseek` returns 0; otherwise, `fseek` returns a nonzero value. Any effects of a call to `ungetc` are undone by a call to `fseek`. The programmer should be warned that not all implementations of `fseek` treat calls of types 1 and 2 consistently.

11.5.18 `ftell`

```
#include <stdio.h>
long ftell(stream)
  FILE *stream;
```

The function `ftell` takes a stream that is open for input or output and returns the position in the stream in the form of a value suitable for the second argument to `fseek`. Using `fseek` on a saved result of `ftell` will result in resetting the position of the stream to the place in the file at which `ftell` had been called.

11.5.19 `fwrite`

```
#include <stdio.h>
int fwrite(ptr, size_of_ptr, count, stream)
  char *ptr;
  unsigned size_of_ptr;
  int count;
  FILE *stream;
```

The function `fwrite` writes a block of binary data from a specified buffer. The first argument is a pointer that points to the first item in the buffer. The second argument must be the size of the items; if the first argument is specified as p, then the second argument should be computed by the expression sizeof(*p). The third argument is the maximum number of items to be written. The fourth argument must be a stream that is open for output.

Output proceeds until an error condition occurs or the number of items written is equal to specified maximum number. If the specified maximum is less than 1, then no output is done.

The position in the stream is advanced by the amount of data actually read. If an error occurs during the output operation, the resulting position is unpredictable. Positions may be read and set using the functions fseek, ftell, and rewind.

The actual number of items read is returned by fwrite. If an error occurs, fwrite return zero. The buffer area is not modified by fwrite in any way.

11.5.20 getc

```
#include <stdio.h>
int getc(stream)
   FILE *stream;
```

getc takes a stream, which must be open for input. It reads the next character from the stream and returns it as a value of type int. Successive calls to getc will return successive characters from the input stream.

If an error occurs or the stream is at end-of-file, getc returns EOF. The feof facility should be used in this case to determine whether end-of-file has really been reached.

getc is usually implemented as a macro. The argument expression should not have any side effects, because it may be evaluated more than once. The fgetc facility (section 11.5.8) is a true function equivalent in operation to getc.

See also getchar, which reads a character from the standard input stream stdin.

11.5.21 getchar

```
#include <stdio.h>
int getchar()
```

getchar reads the next character from the standard input stream stdin and returns it as a value of type int. Successive calls to getchar will return successive characters from the standard input stream.

If an error occurs or the stream is at end-of-file, getchar returns EOF. The feof facility should be used in this case to determine whether end-of-file has really been reached.

getchar is usually implemented as a macro. Note that a call to getchar requires an empty argument list following the name.

See also getc, which reads a character from a user-specified input stream. The call getchar() is precisely equivalent in effect to the call getc(stdin).

11.5.22 gets

```
#include <stdio.h>
char *gets(s)
    char *s;
```

The function gets takes one argument: a character pointer s. Characters are read from the standard input stream stdin until end-of-file is reached or until a newline is seen.

The argument s is assumed to point to the beginning of an array of characters. The characters read are stored into successive locations of the array, and then an extra terminating null character is appended to the stored characters.

If the input is terminated because a newline was seen, the newline character is absorbed from the input stream but is *not* stored in the array. In this gets differs from fgets; if the input for fgets is terminated by a newline, fgets does store the newline character before the terminating null character.

If end-of-file is encountered immediately, before any characters at all have been read from the stream, then no characters are stored into the string s (not even a null character), and a null pointer is returned.

If an error occurs during the input operation, then a null pointer is returned and the array s may be unaltered, partially altered, or filled with invalid data. If the input operation is successful, then s is returned.

The use of gets can be dangerous because it is always possible for the input length to exceed the storage available in the character array.

11.5.23 printf

```
#include <stdio.h>
int printf(format, argument1, argument2, ...)
    char *format;
```

printf performs output formatting, sending the output to the standard output stream stdout. The first argument is a format control string. Additional arguments may be required, depending on the contents of the control string. A series of output characters is generated as directed by the control string; these characters are sent to the standard output stream.

The functions fprintf and sprintf are related to printf; fprintf allows the output stream to be specified by an argument, whereas sprintf causes the output characters to be stored into a string.

The value returned by `printf` is EOF if an error occurred during the output operation; otherwise, the result is some value other than EOF. In some implementations `printf` returns the number of characters sent to the output stream if no error occurs; we recommend this convention for new implementations. However, not all existing implementations provide this specific return value.

The control string is simply text to be copied verbatim, except that the string may contain *conversion specifications*. A conversion specification may call for the processing of some number of additional arguments, resulting in a formatted conversion operation that generates output characters not explicitly contained in the control string. There should be exactly the right number of arguments, each of exactly the right type, to satisfy the conversion specifications in the control string; otherwise, the results are unpredictable. If any conversion specification is malformed then the effects are unpredictable.

The sequence of characters output for a conversion specification may be conceptually divided into three elements: the *converted value* proper, which reflects the value of the converted argument; the *prefix*, which, if present, is typically a sign or a space; and the *padding*, which is a sequence of spaces or zero digits added if necessary to increase the width of the output sequence to a specified minimum. The prefix always precedes the converted value. Depending on the conversion specification, the padding may precede the prefix, separate the prefix from the converted value, or follow the converted value.

A conversion specification begins with a percent sign '%'. Following the percent sign, the following conversion specification elements should appear in the following order:

1. Zero or more optional *flag characters*, which modify the meaning of the main conversion operation.

–	Left-justify within the field width rather than right-justify.
0	Use '0' for the pad character rather than space.
+	Always produce a sign, either '+' or '–'.
space	Always produce either the sign '–' or a space.
'#'	Use a variant of the main conversion operation.

   The effects of the flag characters are described in more detail below.

2. An optional *minimum field width*, expressed as an decimal integer constant; that is, as a nonempty sequence of decimal digits. The sequence of digits should not begin with a zero digit (which can be confused with a flag). The field width may also be specified by an asterisk '*', in which case an argument is consumed; the argument must be of type `int`, and its value specifies the minimum field width. If the converted value results in fewer

characters than the specified field width then pad characters (spaces or zeros) are used to pad the value to the specified width. If the converted value results in more characters than the specified field width, the field is expanded to accomodate it.

3. An optional *precision* specification, expressed as a period '.' followed by an optional decimal integer. If the period appears but the integer is missing, the integer is assumed to be zero, which usually has a different effect from omitting the entire precision specification. The precision may also be specified by an asterisk '*' following the period, in which case an argument is consumed; the argument must be of type int, and its value specifies the precision. The result of specifying a negative precision is unpredictable. The precision specification is used to control the number of digits to be printed for a numeric conversion, and is described in detail in conjunction with the main conversion operations.

4. An optional *long size* specification, expressed as the character '1' (lowercase letter L), which in conjunction with the conversion operations 'd', 'o', 'u', 'x', and 'X' indicates that the argument is long.

5. A required *conversion operation*, expressed as a single character: 'c', 'd', 'e', 'E', 'f', 'g', 'G', 'o', 's', 'u', 'x', 'X', or '%'.

If either the field width or the precision is specified with an asterisk, then the argument consumed by the asterisk precedes any arguments consumed by the main conversion operation. If both the field width and the precision are specified with asterisks, then the field-width argument precedes the precision argument. The general rule is that situations in conversion specifications that consume arguments are paired with arguments in the obvious strict left-to-right order.

The flag characters and their meanings are as follows:

–   If a minus-sign flag is present, then the converted value will be left-justified within the field; that is, any padding will be placed to the right of the converted value. If no minus sign is present, then the converted value will be right-justified within the field; that is, any padding will be placed to the left of the converted value. This flag is relevant only when an explicit minimum field width is specified and the converted value is smaller than that minimum width.

0   If a zero-digit flag is present, then '0' will be used as the pad character if padding is to be placed to the left of the converted value. If no zero-digit flag is present then space will be used as the pad character. (Space is always used as the pad character if padding is to be placed to the right of the converted value; that is, if the '–' flag character is present.) The '0' flag is relevant only when an explicit minimum field width is specified and the converted value is smaller than that

minimum width. (In the original description of C this option was described as a leading zero digit on the field width specifiation rather than as a flag character. This point of view is confusing, because everywhere else in C a leading zero causes an integer to be treated as octal rather than as decimal, but that is not the case in a field width specification. In any case, most implementations of C process the leading '0' as if it were a flag character. For maximum portability, the programmer should specify the '0' flag last if more than one flag is specified.)

+   If a plus-sign flag is present, then the result of a signed conversion will always begin with a sign; that is, an explicit '+' will precede a converted positive value. (Negative values are always preceded by '−' regardless of whether a plus-sign flag is specified.) This flag is relevant only for the conversion operations 'd', 'e', 'E', 'f', 'g', and 'G'.

space   If a space flag is present and the first character in the converted value resulting from a signed conversion is not a sign ('+' or '−'), then a space will be added before the converted value. The adding of this space on the left is independent of any padding that may be placed to the left or right under control of the minus-sign flag character. If both the space and plus-sign flags appear in a single conversion specification, the space flag is effectively ignored because the plus-sign flag ensures that that the converted value will always begin with a sign. This flag is relevant only for the conversion operations 'd', 'e', 'E', 'f', 'g', and 'G'.

If a number-sign flag is present, then an alternate form of the main conversion operation is used. This flag is relevant only for the conversion operations 'e', 'E', 'f', 'g', 'G', 'o', 'x', and 'X'. The modifications implied by the number-sign flag are described in conjunction with the relevant main conversion operations.

The conversion operations are very complicated. Brief descriptions of each operation are given here first, for convenient reference; detailed explanations then follow.

d   Signed decimal conversion from type `int` or `long`.

u   Unsigned decimal conversion from type `unsigned` or `unsigned long`.

o   Unsigned octal conversion from type `unsigned` or `unsigned long`.

x, X   Unsigned hexadecimal conversion from type `unsigned` or `unsigned long`. The x operation uses `0123456789abcdef` as digits, whereas the X operation uses `0123456789ABCDEF`.

c   The argument is printed as a character.

s   The argument is printed as a string.

f   Signed decimal floating-point conversion is performed. The output is in the form `[-]ddd.dddd`, loosely speaking. The precision specifies the number of digits to be printed after the decimal point.

e, E   Signed decimal floating-point conversion is performed. The output is in the form `[-]d.ddddde+dd` or `[-]d.dddddE+dd`, loosely speaking. One digit appears before the decimal point; the precision specifies the number of digits to be printed after the decimal point.

g, G   Signed decimal floating-point conversion is performed. Loosely speaking, if the value to be printed is not too large or too small, then f format is used; otherwise, e or E format is used. The general idea is to use whichever format will require less space. The precision specifies the number of significant digits to be printed.

%   A single percent sign is printed.

Detailed explanations of how each conversion operation is performed follow. Each operation computes and prints a prefix and a converted value, in that order. Either the prefix or the converted value may be empty. Additional padding may be printed before or after the prefix/value pair.

The padding is handled in the same way for each conversion operator. If the prefix and converted value together are shorter than the minimum field width, then enough padding is added to increase the width to the specified minimum. If the '−' flag is present, then space is the pad character, and the padding follows the converted value. If the '−' flag is not present but the '0' flag is present, then '0' is the pad character, and the padding is placed between the prefix and the converted value. If neither the '−' flag nor the '0' flag is present, then space is the pad character, and the padding precedes the prefix.

Here are the detailed explanations of how the individual conversion operators compute a prefix and converted value.

d   Signed decimal conversion is performed. One argument is consumed, which should be of type int (or type long int if the '1' (long size) specification is present).

The converted value consists of a sequence of decimal digits that represents the absolute value of the argument. This sequence is as short as possible but not shorter than the specified precision. The converted value will have leading zeros if necessary to satisfy the precision specification; these leading zeros are independent of any padding, which might also introduce leading zeros (see below). If the precision is 1, then the converted value will not have a leading '0' unless the argument is 0, in which case a single '0' is output. If the precision is 0 and the argument is 0, then the converted value is empty (the null string). If no precision is specified, then a precision of 1 is assumed.

The prefix is computed as follows. If the argument is negative, the prefix is a minus sign. If the argument is nonnegative and the '+' flag is specified, then the prefix is a plus sign. If the argument is nonnegative, the space flag is specified, and the '+' flag is not specified, then the prefix is a space. Otherwise, the prefix is empty.

The '#' flag is not relevant to the 'd' conversion operation.

u   Unsigned decimal conversion is performed. One argument is consumed, which should be of type `unsigned` (or type `unsigned long` if the '1' (long size) specification is present).

The converted value consists of a sequence of decimal digits that represents the value of the argument. This sequence is as short as possible but not shorter than the specified precision. The converted value will have leading zeros if necessary to satisfy the precision specification; these leading zeros are independent of any padding, which might also introduce leading zeros (see below). If the precision is 1, then the converted value will not have a leading '0' unless the argument is 0, in which case a single '0' is output. If the precision is 0 and the argument is 0, then the converted value is empty (the null string). If no precision is specified, then a precision of 1 is assumed.

The prefix is always empty.

The '+', space, and '#' flags are not relevant to the u conversion operation.

o   Unsigned octal conversion is performed. One argument is consumed, which should be of type `unsigned` (or type `unsigned long` if the '1' (long size) specification is present).

The converted value consists of a sequence of decimal digits that represents the value of the argument. This sequence is as short as possible but not shorter than the specified precision. The converted value will have leading zeros if necessary to satisfy the precision specification; these leading zeros are independent of any padding, which might also introduce leading zeros (see below). If the precision is 1, then the converted value will not have a leading '0' unless the argument is 0, in which case a single '0' is output. If the precision is 0 and the argument is 0, then the converted value is empty (the null string). If no precision is specified, then a precision of 1 is assumed.

If the '#' flag is present, then the prefix is 0. If the '#' flag is not present, then the prefix is empty.

The '+' and space flags are not relevant to the o conversion operation.

x, X   Unsigned hexadecimal conversion is performed. One argument is consumed, which should be of type `unsigned` (or type `unsigned long` if the '`l`' (long size) specification is present).

The converted value consists of a sequence of decimal digits that represents the value of the argument. This sequence is as short as possible but not shorter than the specified precision. The x operation uses `0123456789abcdef` as digits, whereas the X operation uses `0123456789ABCDEF`. The converted value will have leading zeros if necessary to satisfy the precision specification; these leading zeros are independent of any padding, which might also introduce leading zeros (see below). If the precision is 1, then the converted value will not have a leading '0' unless the argument is 0, in which case a single '0' is output. If the precision is 0 and the argument is 0, then the converted value is empty (the null string). If no precision is specified, then a precision of 1 is assumed.

If the '`#`' flag is present, then the prefix is `0x` (for the x operation) or `0X` (for the X operation). If the '`#`' flag is not present, then the prefix is empty.

The '`+`' and space flags are not relevant to the x conversion operation.

c   The argument is printed as a character. One argument is consumed, which should be of type `int` or `unsigned`. The value of this integer argument must be a valid encoding of some character; if it is not a valid character code, then the results are unpredictable. The converted value is the single character specified by the argument.

The prefix is always empty.

The '`+`', space, and '`#`' flags, the precision specification, and the '`l`' (long size) specification are not relevant to the c conversion operation.

s   The argument is printed as a string. One argument is consumed, which should be of type "pointer to `char`." If no precision specification is given, then the converted value is the sequence of characters in the string argument up to but not including the terminating null character. If a precision specification p is given, then the converted value is the first p characters of the string, or up to but not including the terminating null character, whichever is shorter.

The prefix is always empty.

The '`+`', space, and '`#`' flags and the '`l`' (long size) specification are not relevant to the s conversion operation.

f   Signed decimal floating-point conversion is performed. One argument is consumed, which should be of type `double`. (Note that if an argument of type `float` is given, it is converted to type `double` by the usual function argument conversions before `printf` ever sees it, so it does work to use '`%f`' to print a number of type `float`.)

The converted value consists of a sequence of decimal digits, possibly with an embedded decimal point, that represents the approximate absolute value of the argument. At least one digit appears before the decimal point, but no more than are necessary to represent the value (that is, no extraneous leading zeros are produced). The precision specifies the number of digits to appear after the decimal point. If the precision is 0, then no digits appear after the decimal point; moreover, the decimal point itself also does not appear unless the '`#`' flag is present. If no precision is specified, then a precision of 6 is assumed.

If the floating-point value cannot be represented exactly in the number of digits produced, then the converted value should be the result of rounding the exact floating-point value to the number of decimal places produced. (However, some implementations do not perform correct rounding in all cases.)

The prefix is computed as follows. If the argument is negative, the prefix is a minus sign. If the argument is nonnegative and the '`+`' flag is specified, then the prefix is a plus sign. If the argument is nonnegative, the space flag is specified, and the '`+`' flag is not specified, then the prefix is a space. Otherwise, the prefix is empty.

The '`l`' (long size) specification is not relevant to the f conversion operation.

e, E   Signed decimal floating-point conversion is performed. One argument is consumed, which should be of type `double`. (An argument of type `float` is permitted, as for the f conversion.)

The converted value consists of a decimal digit, then possibly a decimal point and more decimal digits, then the letter e (for the e operation) or E (for the e operation), then a plus sign or minus sign, then finally at least two more decimal digits. The part before the letter e or E represents a value between 1 (inclusive) and 10 (exclusive). The part after the letter e or E represents an exponent value as a signed decimal integer. The value of the first part, multiplied by 10 raised to the value of the second part, is approximately equal to the absolute value of the argument.

Exactly one digit appears before the decimal point. The precision specifies the number of digits to appear after the decimal point; the total number of digits printed before the letter e or E is therefore one greater than the specified precision. (Compare this to the g and G conversion operations, where if e format is used the number of digits printed is exactly equal to the precision.) If the precision is 0, then no digits appear after the decimal point; moreover, the decimal point itself also does not appear unless the '#' flag is present. If no precision is specified, then a precision of 6 is assumed.

The exponent is printed always with a sign and always with at least two decimal digits. If more than two digits are needed to represent the exponent, then as few as are necessary are printed.

If the floating-point value cannot be represented exactly in the number of digits produced, then the converted value should be the result of rounding the exact floating-point value to the number of decimal places produced. (However, some implementations do not perform correct rounding in all cases.)

The prefix is computed as follows. If the argument is negative, the prefix is a minus sign. If the argument is nonnegative and the '+' flag is specified, then the prefix is a plus sign. If the argument is nonnegative, the space flag is specified, and the '+' flag is not specified, then the prefix is a space. Otherwise, the prefix is empty.

The '1' (long size) specification is not relevant to the e conversion operation.

g, G   Signed decimal floating-point conversion is performed. One argument is consumed, which should be of type `double`. (An argument of type `float` is permitted, as for the f, e, and E conversions.) Only the g conversion operator is discussed below; the G operation is identical except that wherever g uses e conversion, G uses E conversion.

If the specified precision is less than 1, then a precision of 1 is used. If no precision is specified, then a precision of 6 is assumed.

The conversion process may be explained as follows. Let p be the precision to be used for the g conversion operation. Produce a converted value as if for e conversion operator, using a precision for the e conversion equal to $p-1$ and assuming the '#' flag to be present (regardless of whether it is present in the g conversion specification). Let the exponent value (the part of the converted value after the letter e) be called n. If n is greater than p or less than -3, then the converted value from the e conversion is used as the converted value for the g conversion. (Some implementations use a lower bound of -4 instead of -3.) If, however, n is between -3 and p (inclusive), then a new converted value is produced by using f conversion with a precision equal to $p-n$ and assuming the '#' flag to be present (regardless of whether it is present in the g conversion specification).

If the '#' flag is not present in the g conversion specification, the converted value is then modified by stripping off trailing zeros in the following manner. If the converted value resulted from e conversion, then call the character just before the letter e the "last fraction character"; if the converted value resulted from f conversion, then call the last character in the converted value the "last fraction character." Then the rule is that if the last fraction character is '0' then that character is discarded and the stripping process is repeated; if the last fraction character is '.' then that character is discarded and the stripping process is terminated; otherwise, no character is discarded and the stripping process is terminated. The effect is to discard zero digits that do not contribute significantly to the value, and then to discard the decimal point if no digits immediately follow it. Note that only g conversion performs this process of discarding trailing zeros; f and e conversions never do this.

The prefix is computed as follows. If the argument is negative, the prefix is a minus sign. If the argument is nonnegative and the '+' flag is specified, then the prefix is a plus sign. If the argument is nonnegative, the space flag is specified, and the '+' flag is not specified, then the prefix is a space. Otherwise, the prefix is empty.

The 'l' (long size) specification is not relevant to the g conversion operation.

%   A single percent sign is printed. Because a percent sign is used to indicate the beginning of a conversion specification, it is necessary to write two of them in order to have one printed.

No arguments are consumed. The converted value is the single character '%'.

The prefix is always empty.

Note that padding is performed for this conversion operation just as for any other conversion operation; for example, the conversion specification %05% will print 0000%; that is, a percent sign right-justified with '0' padding in a field of width 5.

The '+', space, and '#' flags, the precision specification, and the 'l' (long size) specification are not relevant to the % conversion operation.

Tables 11-1 and 11-2 give some examples of how the various conversion operations work and how the various flags affect them. For example, the third row of Table 11-1 was generated by this call to printf:

```
printf("%6s|%5d|%#5o|%#5x|%#7.2f|%#10.2e|%#10.4g|\n",
       "%#", 45, 45, 45, 12.678, 12.678, 12.678);
```

The other rows were generated by similar calls differing only in which combina-

```
Value        45      45      45   12.678        12.678        12.678
Operation 5d      5o      5x      7.2f       10.2e         10.4g
Flags
      %|    45|    55|    2d|   12.68|  1.27e+01|       12.68|
     %0|00045|00055|0002d|0012.68|001.27e+01|0000012.68|
     %#|    45|  055| 0x2d|   12.68|  1.27e+01|       12.68|
    %#0|00045|00055|0x02d|0012.68|001.27e+01|0000012.68|
      % |    45|    55|    2d|   12.68|  1.27e+01|       12.68|
     % 0| 0045|00055|0002d| 012.68| 01.27e+01| 000012.68|
     % #|    45|  055| 0x2d|   12.68|  1.27e+01|       12.68|
    % #0| 0045|00055|0x02d| 012.68| 01.27e+01| 000012.68|
     %+|   +45|    55|    2d|  +12.68| +1.27e+01|      +12.68|
    %+0|+0045|00055|0002d|+012.68|+01.27e+01|+000012.68|
    %+#|   +45|  055| 0x2d|  +12.68| +1.27e+01|      +12.68|
   %+#0|+0045|00055|0x02d|+012.68|+01.27e+01|+000012.68|
    %+ |   +45|    55|    2d|  +12.68| +1.27e+01|      +12.68|
   %+ 0|+0045|00055|0002d|+012.68|+01.27e+01|+000012.68|
   %+ #|   +45|  055| 0x2d|  +12.68| +1.27e+01|      +12.68|
  %+ #0|+0045|00055|0x02d|+012.68|+01.27e+01|+000012.68|
     %-|45    |55    |2d    |12.68   |1.27e+01   |12.68      |
    %-0|45    |55    |2d    |12.68   |1.27e+01   |12.68      |
    %-#|45    |055   |0x2d  |12.68   |1.27e+01   |12.68      |
   %-#0|45    |055   |0x2d  |12.68   |1.27e+01   |12.68      |
    %- | 45   |55    |2d    | 12.68  | 1.27e+01  | 12.68     |
   %- 0| 45   |55    |2d    | 12.68  | 1.27e+01  | 12.68     |
   %- #| 45   |055   |0x2d  | 12.68  | 1.27e+01  | 12.68     |
  %- #0| 45   |055   |0x2d  | 12.68  | 1.27e+01  | 12.68     |
   %-+|+45   |55    |2d    |+12.68  |+1.27e+01  |+12.68     |
  %-+0|+45   |55    |2d    |+12.68  |+1.27e+01  |+12.68     |
  %-+#|+45   |055   |0x2d  |+12.68  |+1.27e+01  |+12.68     |
 %-+#0|+45   |055   |0x2d  |+12.68  |+1.27e+01  |+12.68     |
  %-+ |+45   |55    |2d    |+12.68  |+1.27e+01  |+12.68     |
 %-+ 0|+45   |55    |2d    |+12.68  |+1.27e+01  |+12.68     |
 %-+ #|+45   |055   |0x2d  |+12.68  |+1.27e+01  |+12.68     |
 %-+ #0|+45  |055   |0x2d  |+12.68  |+1.27e+01  |+12.68     |
```

This table demonstrates the effects of the flag characters on various conversion operations. Across the top of the table are shown the value printed for each column (45 for the first three columns, and 12.678 for the last three) and the conversion operation, plus width and precision, used to print it. Down the left side are shown all possible combinations of the five flag characters.

Table 11-1: Examples of Output Formatting (Part 1)

```
Value    "zap"    '*'   none  -3.4567        -3.4567        -3.4567
Operation 5s      5c    5%    7.2f           10.2e          10.4g
Flags
      % |  zap|     *|     %|    -3.46| -3.46E+00|        -3.457|
     %0|00zap|0000*|0000%|-003.46|-03.46E+00|-00003.457|
     %#|  zap|     *|     %|    -3.46| -3.46E+00|        -3.457|
    %#0|00zap|0000*|0000%|-003.46|-03.46E+00|-00003.457|
     % |  zap|     *|     %|    -3.46| -3.46E+00|        -3.457|
    % 0|00zap|0000*|0000%|-003.46|-03.46E+00|-00003.457|
    % #|  zap|     *|     %|    -3.46| -3.46E+00|        -3.457|
   % #0|00zap|0000*|0000%|-003.46|-03.46E+00|-00003.457|
    %+|  zap|     *|     %|    -3.46| -3.46E+00|        -3.457|
   %+0|00zap|0000*|0000%|-003.46|-03.46E+00|-00003.457|
   %+#|  zap|     *|     %|    -3.46| -3.46E+00|        -3.457|
  %+#0|00zap|0000*|0000%|-003.46|-03.46E+00|-00003.457|
   %+ |  zap|     *|     %|    -3.46| -3.46E+00|        -3.457|
  %+ 0|00zap|0000*|0000%|-003.46|-03.46E+00|-00003.457|
  %+ #|  zap|     *|     %|    -3.46| -3.46E+00|        -3.457|
 %+ #0|00zap|0000*|0000%|-003.46|-03.46E+00|-00003.457|
    %-|zap  |*    |%    |-3.46  |-3.46E+00 |-3.457   |
    %-0|zap  |*    |%    |-3.46  |-3.46E+00 |-3.457   |
    %-#|zap  |*    |%    |-3.46  |-3.46E+00 |-3.457   |
   %-#0|zap  |*    |%    |-3.46  |-3.46E+00 |-3.457   |
    %- |zap  |*    |%    |-3.46  |-3.46E+00 |-3.457   |
   %- 0|zap  |*    |%    |-3.46  |-3.46E+00 |-3.457   |
   %- #|zap  |*    |%    |-3.46  |-3.46E+00 |-3.457   |
  %- #0|zap  |*    |%    |-3.46  |-3.46E+00 |-3.457   |
   %-+|zap  |*    |%    |-3.46  |-3.46E+00 |-3.457   |
  %-+0|zap  |*    |%    |-3.46  |-3.46E+00 |-3.457   |
  %-+#|zap  |*    |%    |-3.46  |-3.46E+00 |-3.457   |
 %-+#0|zap  |*    |%    |-3.46  |-3.46E+00 |-3.457   |
  %-+ |zap  |*    |%    |-3.46  |-3.46E+00 |-3.457   |
 %-+ 0|zap  |*    |%    |-3.46  |-3.46E+00 |-3.457   |
 %-+ #|zap  |*    |%    |-3.46  |-3.46E+00 |-3.457   |
%-+ #0|zap  |*    |%    |-3.46  |-3.46E+00 |-3.457   |
```

This table demonstrates the effects of the flag characters on various conversion operations. Across the top of the table are shown the value printed for each column (the string "zap" for the first column; the character '*' for the second; none for the third, which uses the '%' conversion operation; and and -3.4567 for the last three) and the conversion operation, plus width and precision, used to print it. Down the left side are shown all possible combinations of the five flag characters.

Table 11-2:   Examples of Output Formatting (Part 2)

tion of flags was used. The third row of Table 11-2 was generated by this call to
`printf`:

```
printf("%6s|%#5s|%#5c|%#5%|%#7.2f|%#10.2e|%#10.4g|\n",
       "%#", "zap", '*', -3.4567, -3.4567, -3.4567);
```

The examples in these tables by no means illustrate all of the interesting effects
that can be obtained with `printf`.

11.5.24 `putc`

```
#include <stdio.h>
int putc(c, stream)
  char c;
  FILE *stream;
```

`putc` takes a character and a stream, which must be open for output. It writes
the character to the stream and also returns the character as a value of type
`int`. Successive calls to `putc` will write the given characters successively to
the output stream.

If an error occurs, `putc` returns EOF instead of the character that was to
have been written.

If the output stream is unbuffered, then each character will be sent to the
destination immediately, but if the output stream is buffered, then characters
are saved up in memory and sent to the destination in blocks.

`putc` is usually implemented as a macro. The argument expression must
not have any side effects, because it may be evaluated more than once. The
`fputc` facility (section 11.5.12) is a true function equivalent in operation to
`putc`.

See also `putchar`, which writes a character to the standard output stream
`stdout`.

11.5.25 `putchar`

```
#include <stdio.h>
int putchar(c)
  char c;
```

`putchar` takes a character and writes it to the standard output stream `stdout`
and also returns the character as a value of type `int`. Successive calls to
`putchar` will write the given characters successively to the standard output
stream.

If an error occurs, `putchar` returns EOF instead of the character that was
to have been written.

If the output stream is unbuffered, then each character will be sent to the destination immediately, but if the output stream is buffered, then characters are saved up in memory and sent to the destination in blocks.

putchar is guaranteed to be implemented as a macro.

See also putc, which writes a character to a user-specified output stream. The call putchar(c) is precisely equivalent in effect to the call putc(c, stdout).

11.5.26 puts

```
#include <stdio.h>
int puts(s)
   char *s;
```

puts takes a null-terminated string and writes all the characters of the string, not including the terminating null character, to the standard output stream stdout; it then writes an additional newline character to the standard output stream. If the string itself contains a newline before the terminating null character, then two newlines will be written: one from the string, plus the extra one that is always added on by puts. The effect is as if putc were used to write out successive characters of the string and then a newline character.

If an error occurs, puts returns EOF. Otherwise, puts returns a value other than EOF. (A typical implementation of puts actually does use putc to write out the characters of the string, and returns whatever value is returned by the last call to putc; that is, the call used to emit the extra newline.)

If the output stream is unbuffered, then the characters will be sent to the destination immediately, but if the output stream is buffered, then characters are saved up in memory and sent to the destination in blocks.

To write a string to an arbitrary output stream, fputs may be used. Note that fputs, unlike puts, does not supply an extra newline character after writing out the contents of the string; fputs writes exactly the contents of the given string and nothing more.

11.5.27 rewind

```
#include <stdio.h>
void rewind(stream)
   FILE *stream;
```

The function rewind resets a stream to its beginning. The first argument must be a stream that is open for input or output. The position in the stream is reset to the beginning of the file. No value is returned by rewind.

The function fseek may be used to perform more general setting operations on the position. rewind is equivalent to fseek(stream,0L,0).

11.5.28 scanf

```
#include <stdio.h>
int scanf(format, pointer1, pointer2, ...)
  char *format;
```

scanf performs parsing of formatted input text, reading characters from the standard input stream stdin. The first argument is a format control string. Additional arguments may be required, depending on the contents of the control string. Each argument after the control string must be a pointer; converted values read from the input stream are stored into the locations pointed to by the pointers. The storing by scanf of a value into a location is called an *assignment*; successive assignments use successive pointer arguments.

The functions fscanf and sscanf are related to scanf; fscanf allows the input stream to be specified by an argument, whereas sscanf causes the input characters to be taken from a specified string.

The input operation may terminate prematurely because the input stream reaches end-of-file or because there is a conflict between the control string and a character read from the input stream. The value returned by scanf is the number of successful assignments performed before termination of the operation for either reason. If the input reaches end-of-file before any conflict or assignment is performed, then scanf returns EOF.

The control string is a picture of the expected form of the input. One may think of scanf as performing a simple matching operation between the control string and the input stream. The contents of the control string may be divided into three categories:

1. Whitespace characters. A whitespace character in the control string causes whitespace characters to be read and discarded. The first input character encountered that is not a whitespace character remains as the next character to be read from the input stream. Note that if several consecutive whitespace characters appear in the control string, the effect is the same as if only one had appeared. Thus any sequence of consecutive whitespace characters in the control string will match any sequence of consecutive whitespace characters, possibly of different length, from the input stream.

2. Conversion specifications. A conversion specification begins with a percent sign '%'; the remainder of the syntax for conversion specifications is described in detail below. The number of characters read from the input stream depends on the conversion operation. As a rule of thumb, a conversion operation processes characters until either (a) end-of-file is reached, or (b) a whitespace character or other inappropriate character is encountered, or (c) the number of characters read for the conversion operation equals the explicitly specified maximum field width. A conversion operation may cause an assignment to a location indicated by the next

pointer argument to be used.

3. Other characters. Any character other than a whitespace character or a percent sign must match the next character of the input stream. If it does not match, a conflict has occurred; the scanf operation is terminated, and the conflicting input character remains in the input stream to be read by the next input operation on that stream.

There should be exactly the right number of pointer arguments, each of exactly the right type, to satisfy the conversion specifications in the control string; otherwise, the results are unpredictable. If any conversion specification is malformed then the effects are unpredictable.

A conversion specification begins with a percent sign '%'. Following the percent sign, the following conversion specification elements should appear in the following order:

1. An optional *assignment suppression flag*, written as an asterisk '*'. If this is present for a conversion operation that normally performs an assignment, then characters are read and processed from the input stream in the usual way for that operation, but no assignment is performed and no pointer argument is consumed.

2. An optional *maximum field width*, expressed as an unsigned decimal integer; that is, as a nonempty sequence of decimal digits. This width must not be zero; it must be a positive number.

3. An optional *size specification*, expressed as the character h, meaning short, or as the character '1' (lowercase letter L), meaning long. The letter 'h' may be used with the 'd', 'u', 'o', or 'x' operation to indicate assignment to a location of type short or unsigned short. The letter '1' may be used with the 'd', 'u', 'o', or 'x' operation to indicate assignment to a location of type long or unsigned long. The letter '1' may be used with the 'e', 'f', or 'g' operation to indicate assignment to a location of type double rather than type float.

4. A required *conversion operation*, expressed (with one exception) as a single character: 'c', 'd', 'e', 'E', 'f', 'g', 'G', 'o', 's', 'u', 'x', 'X', '%', or '['. The exception is the '[' operation, which causes all following characters up to and including the next ']' to be part of the conversion specification.

The conversions specifications for scanf are similar in syntax and meaning to those for printf. In a few cases it is possible to use the same format control string for both scanf and printf. However, there are certain differences. The '[' conversion operation is peculiar to scanf. On the other hand, scanf does not admit any precision specification of the kind accepted by printf, nor any of the flag characters '−', '+', space, '0', and # that are accepted by printf. For printf, an explicitly specified field width is a minimum; for scanf, it is a maximum. Whereas printf allows a field width to be specified by a computed argument, indicated by using an asterisk for the field width, `scanf` uses the asterisk for another purpose, namely assignment suppression; this is perhaps the most glaring inconsistency of all. It is best to regard the control string syntaxes for `printf` and `scanf` as being only vaguely similar; do not use the documentation for one as a guide to the other.

The conversion operations are very complicated. Brief descriptions of each operation are given here first, for convenient reference; detailed explanations then follow.

d   Signed decimal conversion is performed. A value of type `int`, `short`, or `long` is assigned, depending on the size specification.

u   Unsigned decimal conversion is performed. A value of type `unsigned`, `unsigned short`, or `unsigned long` is assigned, depending on the size specification.

o   Unsigned octal conversion is performed. A value of type `unsigned`, `unsigned short`, or `unsigned long` is assigned, depending on the size specification.

x, X   Unsigned hexadecimal conversion is performed. A value of type `unsigned`, `unsigned short`, or `unsigned long` is assigned, depending on the size specification. The x and X operations are completely identical; either will accept all of the characters `0123456789abcdefABCDEF` as valid hexadecimal digits. A prefix `0x` or `0X` may appear in the input but is not required.

c   One or more characters are read and assigned, as many as specified by the field width. No terminating null character is appended.

s   A whitespace-delimited string is read and assigned and an extra terminating null character is appended.

f, e, E, g, G
               Signed decimal floating-point conversion is performed. A value of type `float` or `double` is assigned, depending on the size specification. These operations are all identical.

%   A single percent sign is expected in the input. No pointer argument is consumed.

[Input characters are scanned over and assigned. The characters following the '[' in the control string up to and including the next ']' indicate what characters may be scanned over. The scanned characters are stored as a string, and an extra terminating null character is appended.

Detailed explanations of how each conversion operation is performed follow.

d   Signed decimal conversion is performed. One pointer argument is consumed; it must be of type `int` _ 'if no size specification is present), type `short` * (if an 'h' size specification is present), or type `long` * (if an 'l' size specification is present).

First, any leading whitespace characters are skipped; they are not counted toward the maximum field width. An optional sign ('+' or '-') may be present, followed by some number of decimal digits (possibly none). Characters are read until end-of-file is reached, until a nondigit character is seen (in which case that character remains unread), or (if a field width was specified) until the maximum number of characters has been read. The characters read are then interpreted as a signed decimal number and converted to a signed integer value. If no digits are read, the value is zero. If the value expressed by the input is too large to be represented as a signed integer of the appropriate size, then an unpredictable value results.

The value is assigned to the location indicated by the next pointer argument unless the assignment suppression flag '*' is present in the conversion specification.

u   Unsigned decimal conversion is performed. One pointer argument is consumed; it must be of type `unsigned` * (if no size specification is present), type `unsigned short` * (if an 'h' size specification is present), or type `unsigned long` * (if an 'l' size specification is present).

First, any leading whitespace characters are skipped; they are not counted toward the maximum field width. Then decimal digits (possibly none) are read. Characters are read until end-of-file is reached, until a nondigit character is seen (in which case that character remains unread), or (if a field width was specified) until the maximum number of characters has been read. The characters read are then interpreted as a decimal number and converted to an unsigned integer value. If no digits are read, the value is zero. If the value expressed by the input is too large to be represented as an unsigned integer of the appropriate size, then an unpredictable value results.

The value is assigned to the location indicated by the next pointer argument unless the assignment suppression flag '*' is present in the conversion specification.

o   Unsigned octal conversion is performed. One pointer argument is consumed; it must be of type `unsigned` * (if no size specification is present), type `unsigned short` * (if an 'h' size specification is present), or type `unsigned long` * (if an 'l' size specification is present).

First, any leading whitespace characters are skipped; they are not counted toward the maximum field width. Then octal digits (possibly none) are read. Characters are read until end-of-file is reached, until a nondigit character is seen (in which case that character remains unread), or (if a field width was specified) until the maximum number of characters has been read. If the digit '8' or '9' is seen in the input, the result is unpredictable.

The characters read are interpreted as an octal number (regardless of whether there was a leading '0' in the input) and converted to an unsigned integer value. If no digits are read, the value is zero. If the value expressed by the input is too large to be represented as an unsigned integer of the appropriate size, then an unpredictable value results.

The value is assigned to the location indicated by the next pointer argument unless the assignment suppression flag '*' is present in the conversion specification.

x, X   Unsigned hexadecimal conversion is performed. One pointer argument is consumed; it must be of type `unsigned *` (if no size specification is present), type `unsigned short *` (if an 'h' size specification is present), or type `unsigned long *` (if an 'l' size specification is present).

First, any leading whitespace characters are skipped; they are not counted toward the maximum field width. If the next character is '0' and the one after that is 'x' or 'X' then they are counted toward the maximum field width but are otherwise ignored. Then hexadecimal digits (possibly none) are read. Characters are read until end-of-file is reached, until a character not in the set `0123456789abcdefABCDEF` is seen (in which case that character remains unread), or (if a field width was specified) until the maximum number of characters has been read.

The characters read are interpreted as a hexadecimal number (regardless of whether there was a leading '0x' or `0X` in the input) and converted to an unsigned integer value. If no digits are read, the value is zero. If the value expressed by the input is too large to be represented as an unsigned integer of the appropriate size, then an unpredictable value results.

The value is assigned to the location indicated by the next pointer argument unless the assignment suppression flag '*' is present in the conversion specification.

The x and X operations are completely identical; either will accept all of the characters `0123456789abcdefABCDEF` as valid hexadecimal digits. Compare these to the x and X conversion operations for `printf`.

c   One or more characters are read. One pointer argument is consumed; it must be of type `char *`.

The c conversion operation does *not* skip over initial whitespace characters.

If no field width is specified, then exactly one character is read (unless the input stream is at end-of-file, in which case the conversion operation fails). The character value is assigned to the location indicated by the next pointer argument unless the assignment suppression flag '*' is present in the conversion specification.

If a field width is specified, then the pointer argument is assumed to point to the beginning of an array, and the field width specifies the number of characters to be read; the conversion operation fails if end-of-file is encountered before that many characters have been read. The characters read are stored into successive locations of the array unless the assignment suppression flag '*' is present in the conversion specification. No extra terminating null is appended to the characters that are read.

Size specification is not relevant to the c conversion operation.

s   A string is read. One pointer argument is consumed; it must be of type char *.

First, any leading whitespace characters are skipped; they are not counted toward the maximum field width. Characters are read until end-of-file is reached, until a whitespace character is seen (in which case that character remains unread), or (if a field width was specified) until the maximum number of characters has been read. If end-of-file is encountered before any non-whitespace character is seen, the conversion operation is considered to have failed.

The pointer argument is assumed to point to the beginning of an array of characters. The characters read are stored into successive locations of the array unless the assignment suppression flag '*' is present in the conversion specification. If assignment is not suppressed then an extra terminating null is appended to the stored characters.

Size specification is not relevant to the s conversion operation.

The s conversion operation can be dangerous if no maximum field width is specified because it is always possible for the input length to exceed the storage available in the character array.

The s operation with an explicit field width differs from the c operation with an explicit field width. The c operation does not skip over whitespace characters, and will read exactly as many characters as were specified unless end-of-file is encountered; the s operation skips over initial whitespace characters, will be terminated by a whitespace character after reading in some number of characters that are not whitespace, and will append a null character to the stored characters.

f, e, E, g, G

Signed decimal floating-point conversion is performed. One pointer argument is consumed; it must be of type `float *` (if no size specification is present), or type `double *` (if an 'l' size specification is present).

First, any leading whitespace characters are skipped; they are not counted toward the maximum field width. The expected input format consists of an optional sign, zero or more decimal digits, an optional decimal point, zero or more decimal digits, and then possibly the letter 'e' or E, which is present may be followed by an optional sign and then zero or more decimal digits.

The characters read are interpreted as a floating-point number representation and converted to a floating-point number of the specified size. If no digits are read, or at least no digits are read before the letter 'e' or 'E' is seen, then the value is zero. If no digits are seen after the letter 'e' or 'E' then the exponent part of the decimal representation is assumed to be zero. If the value expressed by the input is too large or too small to be represented as a floating-point number of the appropriate size, then an unpredictable value results. If the value expressed by the input is not too large or too small but nevertheless cannot be represented exactly as a floating-point number of the appropriate size, then some form of rounding or truncation occurs.

The value is assigned to the location indicated by the next pointer argument unless the assignment suppression flag '*' is present in the conversion specification.

The f, e, E, g, and G conversion operations are completely identical; any one of them will accept any style of floating-point representation, with or without an exponent part.

%

A single percent sign is expected in the input. Because a percent sign is used to indicate the beginning of a conversion specification, it is necessary to write two of them in order to have one matched. No pointer argument is consumed. The assignment suppression flag, field width, and size specification are not relevant to the % conversion operation.

[

A string is read. One pointer argument is consumed; it must be of type `char *`.

The '[' conversion operation does *not* skip over initial whitespace characters. The conversion specification indicates explicitly exactly what characters may be read as a part of the input field.

The '[' must be followed in the control string by more characters, terminated by ']'. All the characters up to and including the ']' are part of the conversion specification. If the character immediately following the '[' is the circumflex '^', it has a special meaning as a negation flag; all other characters between the '[' and ']', including '^' if it does not immediately follow the initial '[', are treated alike. The characters in the control string between the initial '[' and the terminating ']', other than the negation flag if it is present, are regarded as a set in the mathematical sense. Note that '[' may be in the set, but ']' cannot be. Moreover, '^' can be in the set only if a negation flag is present or if some other character precedes the '^'; it is impossible to have a set consisting only of '^' without a negation flag.

Characters are read until end-of-file is reached, until a terminating character is seen (in which case that character remains unread), or (if a field width was specified) until the maximum number of characters has been read. If a negation flag is not present, then a character is a terminating character if it is *not* in the set; if a negation flag is present, then a character is a terminating character if it *is* in the set. Looking at the other side of the coin, if no negation flag is present then only characters in the set are read, but if a negation flag is present then only characters not in the set are read.

The pointer argument is assumed to point to the beginning of an array of characters. The characters read are stored into successive locations of the array unless the assignment suppression flag '*' is present in the conversion specification. If assignment is not suppressed then an extra terminating null is appended to the stored characters.

Size specification is not relevant to the '[' conversion operation.

Like the 's' conversion, the '[' conversion operation can be dangerous if no maximum field width is specified because it is always possible for the input length to exceed the storage available in the character array.

Note that none of the conversion operations normally skips over trailing whitespace characters as a matter of course. Trailing whitespace characters (such as the newline that terminates a line of input) will remain unread unless explicitly matched in the control string. However, doing this may be tricky because a whitespace character in the control string will attempt to match many whitespace character in the input, resulting in an attempt to read beyond a newline character, for example.

It is not possible to directly determine whether matches of literal character in the control string succeed or fail. It is also not possible to directly determine whether conversion operations involving suppressed assignment succeed or fail. The value returned by scanf reflects only the number of successful assignments performed.

11.5.29 `sprintf`

```
#include <stdio.h>
int sprintf(s, format, argument1, argument2, ...)
  char *s, *format;
```

`sprintf` performs output formatting, writing the output characters to the string specified as the first argument. After the output operation is performed, an extra terminating null character is written. The second argument is a format control string. Additional arguments may be required, depending on the contents of the control string.

The function `sprintf` is like `printf` in its operation; the only difference is that `sprintf` stores the output characters into a string, while `printf` always sends the output to the standard output stream `stdout`. See `printf` for a discussion of the formatting operations.

It is the programmer's responsibility to ensure that the destination string area is large enough to contain the output generated by the formatting operation.

11.5.30 `sscanf`

```
#include <stdio.h>
int sscanf(s, format, pointer1, pointer2, ...)
  char *s, *format;
```

`sscanf` performs parsing of formatted input text, reading characters from the string specified as the first argument. The second argument is a format control string. Additional arguments may be required, depending on the contents of the control string. Each argument after the control string must be a pointer; converted values read from the input stream are stored into the locations pointed to by the pointers.

The function `sscanf` is like `scanf` in its operation; the only difference is that `sscanf` takes input characters from a string, while `scanf` always takes its input from the standard input stream `stdin`. Encountering a terminating null character in the input string is considered equivalent in effect to encountering end-of-file. See `scanf` for a discussion of the formatting operations.

11.5.31 `stderr`

```
#include <stdio.h>
extern FILE *stderr;
```

Normally, when a C program begins execution, the external variable `stderr` will contain a stream that has been opened for output. It is intended that any error messages produced by the program be written to this "standard error" stream. In an interactive environment, this stream will typically be associated with the user's terminal.

11.5.32 stdin

```
#include <stdio.h>
extern FILE *stdin;
```

Normally, when a C program begins execution, the external variable stdin will contain a stream that has been opened for input. It is intended that normal input produced by the program be read from this "standard input" stream. In an interactive environment, this stream will typically be associated with input from the user's terminal.

11.5.33 stdout

```
#include <stdio.h>
extern FILE *stdout;
```

Normally, when a C program begins execution, the external variable stdout will contain a stream that has been opened for output. It is intended that normal output produced by the program be written to this "standard output" stream. In an interactive environment, this stream will typically be associated with output to the user's terminal.

11.5.34 ungetc

```
#include <stdio.h>
int ungetc(c, stream)
  char c;
  FILE *stream;
```

The character c is pushed back onto the specified stream, which must be open for input. That character will be returned by the next call to getc on that stream.

It may be that the character cannot be pushed back. On the other hand, some streams may allow more than one character to be pushed back. One character of pushback is guaranteed provided the stream is buffered and at least one character has been read from the stream since then last fseek, fopen, or freopen operation on the stream.

If the character can be pushed back, then ungetc returns c; otherwise, ungetc returns EOF. An attempt to push the value EOF back onto the stream as a character has no effect on the stream and returns EOF.

A call to `fseek` or `freopen` erases all memory of pushed-back characters from the stream.

The function `ungetc` is useful for implementing input-scanning operations such as `scanf`. A program can "peek ahead" at the next input character by reading it and then putting it back if it is unsuitable.

11.6 ERROR CODES

```
#include <errno.h>
extern int errno;
#define ERANGE ...
```

When a library facility is invoked and cannot complete an operation successfully, then it may do either or both of two things: return a special value indicating failure, or store a nonzero error code into the external variable `errno`.

The error codes may differ from one implementation to another, especially those for failures of I/O operations.

These error codes for the mathematical functions are standard:

EDOM   An argument was not in the domain accepted by a mathematical function. An example of this is giving a negative argument to the `log` function.

ERANGE   The result of a mathematical function is out of range; the function has a well-defined mathematical result but cannot be represented because of the limitations of the implementation's floating-point format. An example of this is trying to use the `pow` function to raise a large number to a very large power.

A

The ASCII Character Set

The ASCII character set is the one most commonly used by C implementations. In the table below, each column gives an ASCII character and its octal, decimal, and hexadecimal value.

Oct	Dec	Hex	Character	Oct	Dec	Hex	Character
00	0	0x0	`'\0'`	040	32	0x20	`' '` (space)
01	1	0x1	`'\001'`	041	33	0x21	`'!'`
02	2	0x2	`'\002'`	042	34	0x22	`'"'`
03	3	0x3	`'\003'`	043	35	0x23	`'#'`
04	4	0x4	`'\004'`	044	36	0x24	`'$'`
05	5	0x5	`'\005'`	045	37	0x25	`'%'`
06	6	0x6	`'\006'`	046	38	0x26	`'&'`
07	7	0x7	`'\007'`	047	39	0x27	`'\''`
010	8	0x8	`'\b'`	050	40	0x28	`'('`
011	9	0x9	`'\i'`	051	41	0x29	`')'`
012	10	0xA	`'\n'`	052	42	0x2A	`'*'`
013	11	0xB	`'\v'`	053	43	0x2B	`'+'`
014	12	0xC	`'\f'`	054	44	0x2C	`','`
015	13	0xD	`'\r'`	055	45	0x2D	`'-'`
016	14	0xE	`'\016'`	056	46	0x2E	`'.'`
017	15	0xF	`'\017'`	057	47	0x2F	`'/'`
020	16	0x10	`'\020'`	060	48	0x30	`'0'`
021	17	0x11	`'\021'`	061	49	0x31	`'1'`
022	18	0x12	`'\022'`	062	50	0x32	`'2'`
023	19	0x13	`'\023'`	063	51	0x33	`'3'`
024	20	0x14	`'\024'`	064	52	0x34	`'4'`
025	21	0x15	`'\025'`	065	53	0x35	`'5'`
026	22	0x16	`'\026'`	066	54	0x36	`'6'`
027	23	0x17	`'\027'`	067	55	0x37	`'7'`
030	24	0x18	`'\030'`	070	56	0x38	`'8'`
031	25	0x19	`'\031'`	071	57	0x39	`'9'`
032	26	0x1A	`'\032'`	072	58	0x3A	`':'`
033	27	0x1B	`'\033'`	073	59	0x3B	`';'`
034	28	0x1C	`'\034'`	074	60	0x3C	`'<'`
035	29	0x1D	`'\035'`	075	61	0x3D	`'='`
036	30	0x1E	`'\036'`	076	62	0x3E	`'>'`
037	31	0x1F	`'\037'`	077	63	0x3F	`'?'`

Oct	Dec	Hex	Character	Oct	Dec	Hex	Character
0100	64	0x40	'@'	0140	96	0x60	'`'
0101	65	0x41	'A'	0141	97	0x61	'a'
0102	66	0x42	'B'	0142	98	0x62	'b'
0103	67	0x43	'C'	0143	99	0x63	'c'
0104	68	0x44	'D'	0144	100	0x64	'd'
0105	69	0x45	'E'	0145	101	0x65	'e'
0106	70	0x46	'F'	0146	102	0x66	'f'
0107	71	0x47	'G'	0147	103	0x67	'g'
0110	72	0x48	'H'	0150	104	0x68	'h'
0111	73	0x49	'I'	0151	105	0x69	'i'
0112	74	0x4A	'J'	0152	106	0x6A	'j'
0113	75	0x4B	'K'	0153	107	0x6B	'k'
0114	76	0x4C	'L'	0154	108	0x6C	'l'
0115	77	0x4D	'M'	0155	109	0x6D	'm'
0116	78	0x4E	'N'	0156	110	0x6E	'n'
0117	79	0x4F	'O'	0157	111	0x6F	'o'
0120	80	0x50	'P'	0160	112	0x70	'p'
0121	81	0x51	'Q'	0161	113	0x71	'q'
0122	82	0x52	'R'	0162	114	0x72	'r'
0123	83	0x53	'S'	0163	115	0x73	's'
0124	84	0x54	'T'	0164	116	0x74	't'
0125	85	0x55	'U'	0165	117	0x75	'u'
0126	86	0x56	'V'	0166	118	0x76	'v'
0127	87	0x57	'W'	0167	119	0x77	'w'
0130	88	0x58	'X'	0170	120	0x78	'x'
0131	89	0x59	'Y'	0171	121	0x79	'y'
0132	90	0x5A	'Z'	0172	122	0x7A	'z'
0133	91	0x5B	'['	0173	123	0x7B	'{'
0134	92	0x5C	'\'	0174	124	0x7C	'|'
0135	93	0x5D	']'	0175	125	0x7D	'}'
0136	94	0x5E	'^'	0176	126	0x7E	'~'
0137	95	0x5F	'_'	0177	127	0x7F	'\177'

B

Syntax of the C Language

This appendix contains a complete copy of the C syntax as it is presented in the text. A more rigorous, LALR(1) grammar for C appears in appendix C.

B.1 *LEXICAL*

identifier ::= *first-character* { *following-character* }*

first-character ::= *letter* | *underscore*

following-character ::= *letter* | *underscore* | *digit*

letter ::= 'A' | 'B' | 'C' | 'D' | 'E' | 'F' | 'G' | 'H' | 'I'
     | 'J' | 'K' | 'L' | 'M' | 'N' | 'O' | 'P' | 'Q' | 'R'
     | 'S' | 'T' | 'U' | 'V' | 'W' | 'X' | 'Y' | 'Z'
     | 'a' | 'b' | 'c' | 'd' | 'e' | 'f' | 'g' | 'h' | 'i'
     | 'j' | 'k' | 'l' | 'm' | 'n' | 'o' | 'p' | 'q' | 'r'
     | 's' | 't' | 'u' | 'v' | 'w' | 'x' | 'y' | 'z'

underscore ::= '_'

digit ::= '0' | '1' | '2' | '3' | '4' | '5' | '6' | '7' | '8' | '9'

constant ::= *integer-constant*
            | *floating-point-constant*
            | *character-constant*
            | *string-constant*

integer-constant ::= *decimal-constant*
       | *octal-constant*
       | *hexadecimal-constant*

decimal-constant ::=
    nonzero-digit { *digit* }* { *long-marker* }?

octal-constant ::=
    '0' { *octal-digit* }* { *long-marker* }?

hexadecimal-constant ::=
    hex-marker { *hex-digit* }+ { *long-marker* }?

digit ::= '0' | '1' | '2' | '3' | '4' | '5' | '6' | '7' | '8' | '9'

nonzero-digit ::= '1' | '2' | '3' | '4' | '5' | '6' | '7' | '8' | '9'

octal-digit ::= '0' | '1' | '2' | '3' | '4' | '5' | '6' | '7'

hex-digit ::=
    '0' | '1' | '2' | '3' | '4' | '5' | '6' | '7' | '8' | '9'
  | 'a' | 'b' | 'c' | 'd' | 'e' | 'f'
  | 'A' | 'B' | 'C' | 'D' | 'E' | 'F'

long-marker ::= 'l' | 'L'

hex-marker ::= '0x' | '0X'

floating-constant ::= *digit-sequence* *exponent*
          | *dotted-digits* { *exponent* }?

exponent ::= ('e' | 'E') { '+' | '−' }? *digit-sequence*

dotted-digits ::= *digit-sequence* '.'
        | *digit-sequence* '.' *digit-sequence*
        | '.' *digit-sequence*

digit-sequence ::= { *digit* }+

character-constant ::= ' ' ' *character* ' ' '

string-constant ::= ' " ' { *character* }* ' " '

character ::= *printing-character* | *escape-character*

escape-character ::= '\' *escape-code*

escape-code ::= *character-escape-code* | *numeric-escape-code*

character-escape-code ::=
    'n' | 't' | 'b' | 'r' | 'f' | 'v' | '\' | ''' | '"'

numeric-escape-code ::=
    octal-digit { *octal-digit* { *octal-digit* }? }?

B.2 PREPROCESSOR

'#' define *identifier sequence-of-tokens*

'#' define *identifier* '(' { *identifier* # ',' }+ ')' *sequence-of-tokens*

'#' undef *identifier*

'#' include '"' *filename* '"'

'#' include '<' *filename* '>'

'#' if *constant-expression*

'#' elif *constant-expression*

'#' else

'#' endif

'#' ifdef *identifier*

'#' ifndef *identifier*

defined *identifier*

defined '(' *identifier* ')'

'#' line *integer-constant* '"' *filename* '"'

'#' line *integer-constant*

'#' *integer-constant filename*

B.3 DECLARATIONS

program ::= { *top-level-declaration* }*

top-level-declaration ::= *function-definition*
        | *declaration*

function-definition ::= { *storage-class-specifier* }?
        { *type-specifier* }?
        declarator
        { *parameter-declaration* }*
        compound-statement

compound-statement ::=
     '{' { *inner-declaration* }* { *statement* }* '}'

parameter-declaration ::= *declaration*

inner-declaration ::= *declaration*

declaration ::= { *storage class-specifier* }?
        type-specifier
        { *possibly-initialized-declarator* # ',' }* ';'

possibly-initialized-declarator ::=
     declarator { '=' *initializer* }?

storage-class-specifier ::= auto
               | extern
               | register
               | static
               | typedef

type-specifier ::= *enumeration-type-specifier*
        | *floating-point-type-specifier*
        | *integer-type-specifier*
        | *structure-type-specifier*
        | *typedef-name*
        | *union-type-specifier*
        | *void-type-specifier*

declarator ::= *simple-declarator*
        | '(' *declarator* ')'
        | *function-declarator*
        | *array-declarator*
        | *pointer-declarator*

simple-declarator ::= *identifier*

pointer-declarator ::= '*' *declarator*

array-declarator ::= *declarator* '[' { *constant-expression* }? ']'

constant-expression ::= *expression*

function-declarator ::= *declarator* '(' { *parameter-list* }? ')'

parameter-list ::= { *identifier* # ',' }+

initializer ::= *expression*
        | '{' { *initializer* # ',' }+ { ',' }? '}'

B.4 TYPES

integer-type-specifier ::= *signed-type-specifier*
        | *unsigned-type-specifier*
        | *character-type-specifier*

signed-type-specifier ::= short { int }?
        | int
        | long { int }?

unsigned-type-specifier ::= `unsigned short` { `int` }?
                  | `unsigned` { `int` }?
                  | `unsigned long` { `int` }?

character-type-specifier ::= { `unsigned` }? `char`

floating-type-specifier ::= `float`
                | `long float`
                | `double`

enumeration-type-specifier ::= *enumeration-type-definition*
                   | *enumeration-type-reference*

enumeration-type-definition ::= `enum` { *enumeration-tag* }?
                 '{' *enumeration-definition-list* '}'

enumeration-type-reference ::= `enum` *enumeration-tag*

enumeration-tag ::= *identifier*

enumeration-definition-list ::= { *enumeration-constant-definition* # ',' } +

enumeration-constant-definition ::= *enumeration-constant* { '=' *expression* }?

¹⁄numeration-constant ::= *identifier*

structure-type-specifier ::= *structure-type-definition*
               | *structure-type-reference*

structure-type-definition ::= `struct` { *structure-tag* }? '{' *field list* '}'

structure-type-reference ::= `struct` *structure-tag*

structure-tag ::= *identifier*

component-declaration-list ::= { *component-declaration* ';' } +

component-declaration ::= *type-specifier component-declarator-list* ';'

component-declarator-list ::= { *component-declarator* # ',' } +

component-declarator ::= *simple-component*
                | *bit field*

simple-component ::= *declarator*

bit-field ::= { *declarator* }? ':' *width*

width ::= *expression*

union-type-specifier ::= *union-type-definition*
              | *union-type-reference*

union-type-definition ::= union { *union-tag* }?
           '{' *component-declaration-list* '}'

union-type-reference ::= union *union-tag*

union-tag ::= *identifier*

void-type-specifier ::= void

typedef-name ::= *identifier*

type-name ::= *type-specifier abstract-declarator*

abstract-declarator ::= *empty-abstract-declarator*
            | *nonempty abstract-declarator*

empty-abstract-declarator ::=

nonempty-abstract-declarator ::= '(' *nonempty-abstract-declarator* ')'
           | *abstract-declarator* '(' ')'
           | *abstract-declarator* '[' { *expression* }? ']'
           | '*' *abstract-declarator*

B.5 EXPRESSIONS

expression ::= *comma-expression*
          | *no-comma-expression*

no-comma-expression ::= *assignment-expression*
       | *conditional-expression*
       | *logical-expression*
       | *binary-expression*
       | *unary-expression*
       | *primary-expression*

primary-expression ::= *name*
       | *literal*
       | *parenthesized-expression*
       | *subscript-expression*
       | *component-selection-expression*
       | *function-call*

parenthesized-expression ::= ' (' *expression* ') '

subscript-expression ::= *primary-expression* ' [' *expression* '] '

component-selection-expression ::= *direct-component-selection*
       | *indirect-component-selection*

direct-component-selection ::= *primary-expression* ' . ' *name*

indirect-component-selection ::= *primary-expression* ' -> ' *name*

function-call ::= *primary-expression*
      ' (' { *no-comma-expression* # ' , ' }* ') '

unary-expression ::= *cast-expression*
       | *sizeof-expression*
       | *prefix-expression*
       | *postfix-expression*

prefix-expression ::= *unary-minus-expression*
       | *logical-negation-expression*
       | *bitwise-negation-expression*
       | *address-expression*
       | *indirection-expression*
       | *preincrement-expression*
       | *predecrement-expression*

postfix-expression ::= *postincrement-expression*
        | *postdecrement-expression*

cast-expression ::= '(' *type-name* ')' *prefix-expression*

sizeof-expression ::= sizeof '(' *type-name* ')'
        | sizeof *prefix-expression*

unary-minus-expression ::= '−' *unary-expression*

logical-negation-expression ::= '!' *unary-expression*

bitwise-negation-expression ::= '∼' *unary-expression*

address-expression ::= '&' *unary-expression*

indirection-expression ::= '∗' *unary-expression*

preincrement-expression ::= '++' *unary-expression*

postincrement-expression ::= *primary-expression* '++'

predecrement-expression ::= '−−' *unary-expression*

postdecrement-expression ::= *primary-expression* '−−'

binary-expression ::= *bitwise-or-expression*
        | *bitwise-xor-expression*
        | *bitwise-and-expression*
        | *equality-expression*
        | *inequality-expression*
        | *shift-expression*
        | *additive-expression*
        | *multiplicative-expression*

multiplicative-expression ::= *multiplication*
        | *division*
        | *remainder*

multiplication ::= *expression* '∗' *expression*

division ::= *expression* '/' *expression*

remainder ::= *expression* '%' *expression*

additive-expression ::= *addition-expression*
      | *subtraction-expression*

addition-expression ::= *expression* '+' *expression*

subtraction-expression ::= *expression* '−' *expression*

shift-expression ::= *left-shift-expression*
     | *right-shift-expression*

left-shift-expression ::= *expression* '<<' *expression*

right-shift-expression ::= *expression* '>>' *expression*

inequality-expression ::= *expression inequality-operator expression*

inequality-operator ::= '<' | '<=' | '>' | '>='

equality-expression ::= *expression equality-operator expression*

equality-operator ::= '==' | '!='

bitwise-and-expression ::= *expression* '&' *expression*

bitwise-xor-expression ::= *expression* '^' *expression*

bitwise-or-expression ::= *expression* '|' *expression*

logical-operator-expression ::= *logical-or-expression*
       | *logical-and-expression*

logical-and-expression ::= *expression* '&&' *expression*

logical-or-expression ::= *exprecsion* '||' *expression*

conditional-expression ::= *expression* '?' *expression* ':' *expression*

assignment-expression ::= *expression assignment-operator expression*

assignment-operator ::= '=' | '+=' | '−=' | '*=' | '/=' | '%='
                            | '<<=' | '>>=' | '&=' | '^=' | '|='

comma-expression ::= *expression* ',' *expression*

B.6 STATEMENTS

statement ::= *expression-statement*
          | *labeled-statement*
          | *compound-statement*
          | *conditional-statement*
          | *iterative-statement*
          | *switch-statement*
          | *break-statement*
          | *continue-statement*
          | *return-statement*
          | *goto-statement*
          | *null-statement*

conditional-statement ::= *if-statement*
                        | *if-else-statement*

iterative-statement ::= *do-statement*
                      | *while-statement*
                      | *for-statement*

expression-statement ::= *expression* ';'

labeled-statement ::= *label* ':' *statement*

label ::= *named-label*
        | *case-label*
        | *default-label*

compound-statement ::= '{' { *declaration* }* { *statement* }* '}'

conditional-statement ::= *if-statement* | *if-else-statement*

if-statement ::= if '(' *expression* ')' *statement*

if-else-statement ::= if '(' *expression* ')' *statement* else *statement*

iterative-statement ::= *while-statement*
                   | *do-statement*
                   | *for-statement*

while-statement ::= `while` '`(`' *expression* '`)`' *statement*

do-statement ::= `do` *statement* `while` '`(`' *expression* '`)`' '`;`'

for-statement ::= `for` *for-expressions* *statement*

for-expressions ::= '`(`' { *expression* }? '`;`'
                 { *expression* }? '`;`'
                 { *expression* }? '`)`'

switch-statement ::= `switch` '`(`' *expression* '`)`' *statement*

case-label ::= `case` *constant-expression*

default-label ::= `default`

break-statement ::= `break` '`;`'

continue-statement ::= `continue` '`;`'

return-statement ::= `return` { *expression* }? '`;`'

goto-statement ::= `goto` *identifier* '`;`'

named-label ::= *identifier*

null-statement ::= '`;`'

B.7 FUNCTIONS

function-definition ::= { *storage-class-specifier* }?
                       { *type-specifier* }?
                       declarator
                       parameter-declaration-section
                       compound-statement

parameter-declaration-section ::= { *declaration* }*

C

LALR(1) Grammar for C

This appendix contains an LALR(1) grammar for the C language, excluding the preprocessor. LALR(1) grammars are important because there are specialized tools called *parser generators* that can constuct good parsers from LALR(1) grammars. The grammar in this appendix is derived from the input to such a generator.

C.1 TERMINAL SYMBOLS

The following tokens, recognized by the compiler's lexical analysis phase, are considered to be terminal symbols by the parser. Notice two things about these symbols:

1. There are two terminal symbols that are lexically identical: `<typedef name>` and `<identifier>`. This resolves a grammatical ambiguity but requires the lexer to obtain semantic information about `typedef` names.
2. Compound assignment operators such as '+=' are assumed to be single tokens. If they are written as separate tokens ('+ =', for instance) the lexer can combine them into a single token.

```
<identifier>     <typedef_name>     <dec_int>     <hex_int>
<oct_int>  <float>  <string>  <char>
```

```
void  auto  static  extern  register  typedef  char  float
double  int  short  long  unsigned  struct  union  enum  if
else  while  do  for  switch  break  continue  return  goto
case  default  sizeof
```

```
;   }   ,   {   :   =   (   )   ]   *   [   .   ->   ++   --   &   -   !   ~
/   %   +   <<   >>   <   <=   >=   >   ==   !=   ^   |   &&   ||   ?   +=
-=   *=   /=   %=   >>=   <<=   &=   ^=   |=
```

C.2 PRODUCTIONS

The syntactic productions are listed below, expressed in a modified BNF notation:

1. Nonterminals are written as a sequences of letters, digits, and underscores surrounded by '<' and '>'.

2. Productions with several alternatives, such as

   ```
   A ::= B | C
   ```

   are written as the multiple productions

   ```
   A ::= B
   A ::= C
   ```

3. Names of the form <0001> are nonterminal symbols with no special properties; the names were generated automatically by a software tool that constructs LALR(1) parsers.

In some ways the grammar here is less restrictive than the one used in the text. For instance, declarations may begin with any combination of type and storage class specifiers, and compound statements may have statements and declarations intermixed. We have chosen to detect some grammatical errors during semantic analysis so that better error diagnostics can be generated.

In other ways, this grammar is more precise. Expression precedence and associativity is explicit in this grammar, and the "dangling else" ambiguity is resolved by the addition of "balanced" and "unbalanced" statement productions (<bal_stmt> and <unbal_stmt>). A statement is "unbalanced" if it ends with an if statement that has no else clause.

```
<goal> ::= <program>

<0001> ::=
<0001> ::= <0001> <top_level_declaration>

<program> ::= <0001>

<top_level_declaration> ::= <top_level_data_declaration>
<top_level_declaration> ::= <top_level_function_declaration>

<top_level_data_declaration> ::= <opt_decl_specifier> ;
<top_level_data_declaration> ::= <opt_decl_specifier>
                                 <list_init_dcltr> ;

<0002> ::=
<0002> ::= <0002> <parameter_declaration>

<top_level_function_declaration> ::= <opt_decl_specifier>
                                     <dcltr>
                                     <0002>
                                     <compound_stmt>

<local_data_declaration> ::= <decl_specifier> ;
<local_data_declaration> ::= <decl_specifier>
                             <list_init_dcltr> ;

<parameter_declaration> ::= <decl_specifier> ;
<parameter_declaration> ::= <decl_specifier> <list_dcltr> ;

<typename_declaration> ::= <decl_specifier> <abs_dcltr>

<0003> ::=
<0003> ::= <0003> <struct_declaration>

<list_struct_declaration> ::= <0003>

<0004> ::= <formal_declaration>
<0004> ::= <0004> , <formal_declaration>

<formals_declaration> ::=
<formals_declaration> ::= <0004>

<formal_declaration> ::= <opt_decl_specifier> <dcltr>

<opt_decl_specifier> ::=
<opt_decl_specifier> ::= <decl_specifier>

<0005> ::= <tc_specifier>
<0005> ::= <0005> <tc_specifier>

<decl_specifier> ::= <0005>
```

```
<tc_specifier> ::= <std_class>
<tc_specifier> ::= <type_specifier>

<std_class> ::= auto
<std_class> ::= static
<std_class> ::= extern
<std_class> ::= register
<std_class> ::= typedef

<type_specifier> ::= <typedef_name>
<type_specifier> ::= <std_type>
<type_specifier> ::= <struct_specifier>
<type_specifier> ::= <enum_specifier>

<std_type> ::= char
<std_type> ::= float
<std_type> ::= double
<std_type> ::= int
<std_type> ::= short
<std_type> ::= long
<std_type> ::= unsigned
<std_type> ::= void

<struct_specifier> ::= <struct_type> <struct_name>
<struct_specifier> ::= <union_type> <union_name>
<struct_specifier> ::= <struct_type>
                      { <list_struct_declaration> }
<struct_specifier> ::= <struct_type> <str_tag_dcltr>
                      { <list_struct_declaration> }
<struct_specifier> ::= <union_ctype>
                      { <list_struct_declaration> }
<struct_specifier> ::= <union_ctype> <un_tag_dcltr>
                      { <list_struct_declaration> }

<struct_ctype> ::= struct

<union_ctype> ::= union

<struct_declaration> ::= <decl_specifier> <list_struct_dcltr> ;

<struct_dcltr> ::= <dcltr>
<struct_dcltr> ::= : <exp>
<struct_dcltr> ::= <dcltr> : <exp>

<0006> ::= <enum_dcltr>
<0006> ::= <0006> , <enum_dcltr>

<0007> ::= { <0006> }
<0007> ::= { <0006> , }
```

```
<enum_specifier> ::= <enum_ctype> <enum_name>
<enum_specifier> ::= <enum_ctype> <0007>
<enum_specifier> ::= <enum_ctype> <en_tag_dcltr> <0007>

<enum_ctype> ::= enum

<enum_dcltr> ::= <name_dcltr>
<enum_dcltr> ::= <name_dcltr> = <exp>

<name_dcltr> ::= <identifier>

<str_tag_dcltr> ::= <identifier>

<un_tag_dcltr> ::= <identifier>

<en_tag_dcltr> ::= <identifier>

<key_dcltr> ::= <identifier>

<p1_dcltr> ::= <name_dcltr>
<p1_dcltr> ::= ( <dcltr> )

<p2_dcltr> ::= <p1_dcltr>
<p2_dcltr> ::= <p2_dcltr> ( <formals_declaration> )
<p2_dcltr> ::= <p2_dcltr> [ ]
<p2_dcltr> ::= <p2_dcltr> [ <list_exp> ]

<0008> ::= <key_dcltr>
<0008> ::= <0008> , <key_dcltr>

<p3_dcltr> ::= <p2_dcltr>
<p3_dcltr> ::= * <p3_dcltr>

<dcltr> ::= <p3_dcltr>

<init_dcltr> ::= <dcltr>
<init_dcltr> ::= <dcltr> = <init_exp>

<0009> ::= <init_exp>
<0009> ::= <0009> , <init_exp>

<init_exp> ::= <exp>
<init_exp> ::= { <0009> }
<init_exp> ::= { <0009> , }

<p1_abs_dcltr> ::= ( <p3_abs_dcltr> )
```

```
<p2_abs_dcltr> ::= <p1_abs_dcltr>
<p2_abs_dcltr> ::= <p2_abs_dcltr> ( )
<p2_abs_dcltr> ::= ( )
<p2_abs_dcltr> ::= <p2_abs_dcltr> [ ]
<p2_abs_dcltr> ::= <p2_abs_dcltr> [ <list_exp> ]
<p2_abs_dcltr> ::= <e_abs_dcltr> [ ]
<p2_abs_dcltr> ::= <e_abs_dcltr> [ <list_exp> ]

<p3_abs_dcltr> ::= <p2_abs_dcltr>
<p3_abs_dcltr> ::= * <p3_abs_dcltr>
<p3_abs_dcltr> ::= * <e_abs_dcltr>

<e_abs_dcltr> ::=

<abs_dcltr> ::= <p3_abs_dcltr>
<abs_dcltr> ::= <e_abs_dcltr>

<0010> ::= <init_dcltr>
<0010> ::= <0010> , <init_dcltr>

<list_init_dcltr> ::= <0010>

<0011> ::= <struct_dcltr>
<0011> ::= <0011> , <struct_dcltr>

<list_struct_dcltr> ::= <0011>

<0012> ::= <dcltr>
<0012> ::= <0012> , <dcltr>

<list_dcltr> ::= <0012>

<0013> ::=
<0013> ::= <0013> <decl or stmt>

<compound_stmt> ::= { <0013> }

<decl or stmt> ::= <local_data_declaration>
<decl or stmt> ::= <stmt>

<basic_stmt> ::= <e_stmt>
<basic_stmt> ::= <compound_stmt>
<basic_stmt> ::= <do_stmt>
<basic_stmt> ::= <break_stmt>
<basic_stmt> ::= <continue_stmt>
<basic_stmt> ::= <return_stmt>
<basic_stmt> ::= <goto_stmt>
<basic_stmt> ::= <null_stmt>
```

```
<bal_stmt> ::= <basic_stmt>
<bal_stmt> ::= <bal_while_stmt>
<bal_stmt> ::= <bal_for_stmt>
<bal_stmt> ::= <bal_ifelse_stmt>
<bal_stmt> ::= <bal_switch_stmt>
<bal_stmt> ::= <label> <bal_stmt>

<unbal_stmt> ::= <unbal_while_stmt>
<unbal_stmt> ::= <unbal_for_stmt>
<unbal_stmt> ::= <unbal_if_stmt>
<unbal_stmt> ::= <unbal_ifelse_stmt>
<unbal_stmt> ::= <unbal_switch_stmt>
<unbal_stmt> ::= <label> <unbal_stmt>

<bal_ifelse_stmt> ::= if ( <list_exp> ) <bal_stmt>
                      else <bal_stmt>

<unbal_ifelse_stmt> ::= if ( <list_exp> ) <bal_stmt>
                        else <unbal_stmt>

<unbal_if_stmt> ::= if ( <list_exp> ) <stmt>

<stmt> ::= <bal_stmt>
<stmt> ::= <unbal_stmt>

<e_stmt> ::= <list_exp> ;

<bal_while_stmt> ::= while ( <list_exp> ) <bal_stmt>

<unbal_while_stmt> ::= while ( <list_exp> ) <unbal_stmt>

<do_stmt> ::= do <stmt> while ( <list_exp> ) ;

<0014> ::= ; ) <bal_stmt>
<0014> ::= ; <list_exp> ) <bal_stmt>

<0015> ::= ; <0014>
<0015> ::= ; <list_exp> <0014>

<bal_for_stmt> ::= for ( <0015>
<bal_for_stmt> ::= for ( <list_exp> <0015>

<0016> ::= ; ) <unbal_stmt>
<0016> ::= ; <list_exp> ) <unbal_stmt>

<0017> ::= ; <0016>
<0017> ::= ; <list_exp> <0016>

<unbal_for_stmt> ::= for ( <0017>
<unbal_for_stmt> ::= for ( <list_exp> <0017>

<bal_switch_stmt> ::= switch ( <list_exp> ) <bal_stmt>
```

```
<unbal_switch_stmt> ::= switch ( <list_exp> ) <unbal_stmt>

<break_stmt> ::= break ;

<continue_stmt> ::= continue ;

<return_stmt> ::= return ;
<return_stmt> ::= return <list_exp> ;

<goto_stmt> ::= goto <label_name> ;

<null_stmt> ::= ;

<label> ::= <name_label>
<label> ::= <case_label>
<label> ::= <default_label>

<name_label> ::= <identifier> :

<case_label> ::= case <exp> :

<default_label> ::= default :

<literal> ::= <dec_int>
<literal> ::= <oct_int>
<literal> ::= <hex_int>
<literal> ::= <float>
<literal> ::= <char>
<literal> ::= <string>

<id_name> ::= <identifier>

<struct_name> ::= <identifier>

<union_name> ::= <identifier>

<enum_name> ::= <identifier>

<label_name> ::= <identifier>

<field_name> ::= <identifier>

<paren_exp> ::= ( <list_exp> )

<primary_p1_exp> ::= <id_name>
<primary_p1_exp> ::= <literal>
<primary_p1_exp> ::= <paren_exp>
<primary_p1_exp> ::= sizeof ( <typename_declaration> )
```

```
<primary_p2_exp> ::= <primary_p1_exp>
<primary_p2_exp> ::= <primary_p2_exp> [ <list_exp> ]
<primary_p2_exp> ::= <primary_p2_exp> ( )
<primary_p2_exp> ::= <primary_p2_exp> ( <list_exp> )
<primary_p2_exp> ::= <primary_p2_exp> . <field_name>
<primary_p2_exp> ::= <primary_p2_exp> -> <field_name>

<primary_exp> ::= <primary_p2_exp>

<postfix_exp> ::= <primary_exp>
<postfix_exp> ::= <postfix_exp> <postfix_op>

<postfix_op> ::= ++
<postfix_op> ::= --

<prefix_exp> ::= <postfix_exp>
<prefix_exp> ::= sizeof <prefix_exp>
<prefix_exp> ::= <prefix_op> <cast_exp>
<prefix_exp> ::= * <cast_exp>
<prefix_exp> ::= & <cast_exp>
<prefix_exp> ::= <negate_op> <cast_exp>

<prefix_op> ::= ++
<prefix_op> ::= --

<negate_op> ::= -
<negate_op> ::= !
<negate_op> ::= ~

<cast_exp> ::= <prefix_exp>
<cast_exp> ::= ( <typename declaration> ) <cast_exp>

<unary_oper_exp> ::= <cast_exp>

<mult_oper_exp> ::= <unary_oper_exp>
<mult_oper_exp> ::= <mult_oper_exp> <mult_op> <unary_oper_exp>

<mult_op> ::= *
<mult_op> ::= /
<mult_op> ::= %

<add_oper_exp> ::= <mult_oper_exp>
<add_oper_exp> ::= <add_oper_exp> <add_op> <mult_oper_exp>

<add_op> ::= +
<add_op> ::= -

<shift_oper_exp> ::= <add_oper_exp>
<shift_oper_exp> ::= <shift_oper_exp> <shift_op> <add_oper_exp>

<shift_op> ::= <<
<shift_op> ::= >>
```

```
<rel_oper_exp> ::= <shift_oper_exp>
<rel_oper_exp> ::= <rel_oper_exp> <rel_op> <shift_oper_exp>

<rel_op> ::= <
<rel_op> ::= <=
<rel_op> ::= >=
<rel_op> ::= >

<equ_oper_exp> ::= <rel_oper_exp>
<equ_oper_exp> ::= <equ_oper_exp> <equ_op> <rel_oper_exp>

<equ_op> ::= ==
<equ_op> ::= !=

<bitand_oper_exp> ::= <equ_oper_exp>
<bitand_oper_exp> ::= <bitand_oper_exp> & <equ_oper_exp>

<bitxor_oper_exp> ::= <bitand_oper_exp>
<bitxor_oper_exp> ::= <bitxor_oper_exp> ^ <bitand_oper_exp>

<bitor_oper_exp> ::= <bitxor_oper_exp>
<bitor_oper_exp> ::= <bitor_oper_exp> | <bitxor_oper_exp>

<and_oper_exp> ::= <bitor_oper_exp>
<and_oper_exp> ::= <and_oper_exp> && <bitor_oper_exp>

<or_oper_exp> ::= <and_oper_exp>
<or_oper_exp> ::= <or_oper_exp> || <and_oper_exp>

<cond_exp> ::= <or_oper_exp>
<cond_exp> ::= <or_oper_exp> ? <list_exp> : <cond_exp>

<assign_exp> ::= <cond_exp>
<assign_exp> ::= <cond_exp> <asgn_op> <exp>

<asgn_op> ::= =
<asgn_op> ::= +=
<asgn_op> ::= -=
<asgn_op> ::= *=
<asgn_op> ::= /=
<asgn_op> ::= %=
<asgn_op> ::= >>=
<asgn_op> ::= <<=
<asgn_op> ::= &=
<asgn_op> ::= ^=
<asgn_op> ::= |=

<exp> ::= <assign_exp>

<list_exp> ::= <exp>
<list_exp> ::= <list_exp> , <exp>
```

Index